11/25/70

To Nort!

Hope you enjoy
the results of our
intense research.

Mother and Dad

Happy Birthday

S0-BAC-215

HOW DID IT BEGIN?

By the same author

THE STAR OF DAVID (1955, 1956, 1965)
THE ETERNAL FLAME (1958)

How Did It Begin?

*Customs & Superstitions
and their Romantic Origins*

R. BRASCH

DAVID McKAY COMPANY, INC.

NEW YORK, N.Y.

HOW DID IT BEGIN?

COPYRIGHT © 1965 BY LONGMANS, GREEN AND CO., LTD. AUSTRALIA

All rights reserved, including the right to reproduce
this book, or parts thereof, in any form, except for
the inclusion of brief quotations in a review.

FIFTH PRINTING, MARCH 1967

LIBRARY OF CONGRESS CATALOG CARD NUMBER: 66-15971

MANUFACTURED IN THE UNITED STATES OF AMERICA

To the memory of Gerald de Vahl Davis —
a great scholar, leader and friend.

ACKNOWLEDGEMENTS

First and foremost I should like to thank my wife to whom, as always, I owe an enormous debt of gratitude. She participated in the creation of this book in every phase. She not only typed the manuscript but shared with me in the excitement of research. Her untiring work, sound judgment and many valuable suggestions were a constant source of encouragement and inspiration. This book explains the origin of the helpmate. Certainly, my wife exemplified the true meaning of the term.

I wish to thank the Australian Broadcasting Commission, People Magazine, Sydney Morning Herald and Brisbane Courier Mail for their kind permission to reproduce my broadcasts and features.

I am especially grateful to Mr. O. G. Olsen for all his kindness and friendship. The courtesy and assistance of the staff of both the Mitchell and Public Libraries of N.S.W. were greatly appreciated. Individual acknowledgement is given to the many sources, including the representatives of various countries, who so kindly supplied illustrations.

ACKNOWLEDGMENTS

contents

fOREWORÒ

To explore the origin of our customs and superstitions is a great adventure and its reward a goldmine of fascinating information. Everyone wants to know how it all began. We are anxious to discover the reason why we do certain things and why we express our attitudes, feelings and convictions in definite prescribed ways.

Blue for boys and pink for girls, black cats that augur good luck or portend misfortune, the little slit in the lapel, the throwing of confetti at weddings and fish on Friday — they all have found their place in our pattern of life, manner of dressing and religious tradition not just accidentally. Though we may now take them for granted, there is nothing in life that has not its initial significant meaning and purpose.

The story of our customs is not always easy to trace. Frequently they go back into the obscurity of the most distant past. Many of them owe their existence not merely to one single desire, need or fear, but are the result of a combination of factors and thus present a mosaic which, in many cases, consists of pagan beliefs, primitive superstition and modern reinterpretations.

Layers of legend are woven around historical facts and early, but now obsolete, practical considerations. And again, most misleadingly, many present-day explanations are manifestly false and mere rationalizations. Often several possible roots offer themselves.

The study of the origin of our customs is thus significant for many reasons. By exploring and explaining them, some most interesting facts about the complex history of man and the curious working of the human mind are revealed. Moreover, to know the purpose of our habits and actions inevitably enriches our appreciation of their value. In the case of superstitions, however, the very act of digging up their roots helps us to kill them and thus to rid ourselves from fears that otherwise would go on haunting us even in our so-called enlightened age.

This book is the result of many years of research all over the world. Its object is twofold: to serve as a handy source of information as well as to help the reader in his search for a meaning in the things we do and say (often so thoughtlessly) from birth to death, at play and work, within and without the realm of religion.

R.B.

HOW DID IT BEGIN?

the ORIGIN
of superstitions

SUPERSTITIONS have been with man from his earliest days and even in the scientific age of today the most enlightened of us are often tempted to keep them, as there might be "something in them". For superstitions are not always as irrational and illogical as may be imagined. They have a reason, a background, and a practical explanation.

From earliest times men assumed the existence of powers which could influence their lives for better or worse. To placate the anger of these forces or to buy their good will became (to some people) almost an obsession neurosis, which has been responsible for many habits and customs that are meticulously observed even nowadays.

The fact is that, at some time or other, everybody, no matter what his education or place in life, is a slave to superstition. Mostly, however, we do not realize it. We cleverly rationalize the meaning of superstitions and refer to them as beautiful customs. No doubt they belong to the social life of both the civilized and the savage. To trace their origins is a rewarding adventure, prompting us whether to be or not to be—superstitious.

SPILLING SALT

From the beginning of civilization salt was important in daily diet and was considered a holy substance. No sacrifice, whether according to Biblical rite or pagan tradition, could be offered without the addition of salt. Its presence at every table was held to be a necessity and a meal without it thought to be profane. Salt is still used today in the baptismal ritual of the Catholic Church.

Even our everyday speech testifies to the importance of salt. We speak of people "not being worth their salt". The word *salary*, meaning "pertaining to salt", is derived from the fact that in the Roman Empire soldiers were paid either with lumps of salt or an allowance to buy salt.

Salt purifies. Hence it became a symbol of incorruptibility. That is why the Greek philosopher Pythagoras saw in it an emblem of justice which had to belong to every table. It was to remind all those participating in the meal of this essential virtue. To upset the salt was seen already then as a forewarning of an injustice.

Salt is a preservative. This made it a symbol of lasting friendship, as well as of immortality. Therefore Arabs to this day put salt in front of a stranger to assure him of their good will, and in many countries salt was put into the coffin as a reminder of the soul's survival. When the Bible wished to stress God's everlasting bond with man, it spoke, likewise, of "the covenant of salt". In Scotland, brewers used to throw a handful of salt on top of the mash, believing that its purifying character would ward off witches.

It was a combination of these various traditions and factors that from Roman days to our time made the spilling of salt an omen of ill luck which could be averted only if the offender threw a pinch of it with his right hand over his left shoulder.

An explanation frequently given, though confusing cause and effect, relates to the famous painting of the Last Supper by Leonardo da Vinci. On his canvas the salt, facing Judas, is depicted as being upset. The scene captured the moment when, according to the Gospels, Jesus startled His Apostles with the announcement that one of them would betray Him. Their faces vividly show consternation and grief. But Judas, to appear as innocent as the rest, whilst clasping in his right hand the bag with the 30 pieces of silver, raises his left hand as if in a gesture of horror. By that very movement he upset the salt. The fact that this Passover meal immediately preceded the betrayal of Jesus made people assume that there was a causal connection between the spilling of salt and Jesus's crucifixion. However, there is no confirmation of any such occurrence. It is obvious that da Vinci merely made use of the much older superstition to dramatize further his picture.

THE UNLUCKY NUMBER 13

The superstition of the unlucky 13 is widely spread all over the world. In France you can never live in a house of that number. It just does not exist. After No. 12 follows No. 12½ and then immediately No. 14. Italian lotteries never use the number either. Even in factual and business-like America, many skyscrapers "skip" the 13th floor. Most airlines omit the seats of that number on their planes. Some people in France used even to commercialize this superstition by offering their services as 14th paid guest at parties that otherwise would count only 13. Not a few sailors have refused to leave port on the 13th day of the month.

That 13 is unlucky, and especially so at table, is a superstition which also goes back to pre-Christian days. Fear of the figure 13 is found in Norse mythology. It stems from the fable about a banquet held in Valhalla, to which 12 gods had been invited. But Loki, the spirit of strife and evil, gate-crashed, making the number 13 and as a result Balder, the favourite of the gods, was killed.

At Christ's Last Supper there were, apart from Jesus Himself, His 12 Apostles and, therefore, a company of 13 altogether. As this supper preceded Christ's crucifixion, it certainly was taken as an omen of misfortune and death.

There is a less superstitious and more rational explanation which says that statistical surveys showed insurance companies that of any group of 13 one person would die within less than 12 months.

KNOCKING ON WOOD

Fear often haunts man, not least in moments of happiness. He is afraid that some jealous agency, real or imagined, may try to deprive him of his good fortune. To talk of personal good luck became almost a challenge of fate, and that in turn gave rise to

many precautionary measures, some belonging to the psycho-
pathology of everyday life. One of these is the custom of touching wood.

The usual explanation associates it with the cross of Christ.
Churches all over the world treasure pieces of wood which, they
believe, once were part of the real cross. To touch them would
assure sustained happiness. Touching any kind of wood, in
memory of the cross, was an obvious further development of
the custom.

Another interpretation, still in the realm of religion, recalls the
ancient days when a church offered sanctuary. Once a pursued
person reached the holy precinct and touched the church's
wooden door, nothing could happen to him. He was under the
protection of the cross. No one would have dared to apprehend
him there as that would have been tantamount to sacrilege.

Yet a further explanation dates back to the more distant past,
when people lived in wooden huts. Those who were prosperous
were afraid of talking about it, lest evil spirits would envy their
luck and try to interfere with it. Thus, when discussing their
good fortune, people knocked loudly on their wooden walls. The
noise was meant to drown their conversation and prevent any
ill-meaning eavesdropper hearing what they were saying about
their luck.

However, the custom most probably stems from pagan times,
when trees were deified. The fact that lightning often struck
trees led to a belief that divine power had entered them, and
they were soon identified with particular deities. It was thought,
for example, that the oak was the dwelling place of the god of
lightning and thunder. Hence to touch its timber would get
magic results.

THE LUCKY FOUR-LEAFED CLOVER

The origins of the belief that a four-leafed clover is lucky are
lost in antiquity. Only a legend that offers an explanation survives. This relates that when Adam and Eve were expelled from
Paradise, Eve took a four-leafed clover with her, which flourished
in the Garden of Eden. She wished to retain at least something
that would remind her always of her happy existence in the now

lost Paradise. That is how its presence in one's own garden came to be looked upon as an omen of good luck.

THE LUCKY HORSESHOE

There are several explanations as to why horseshoes are thought to be lucky.

Best-known is the legend about St. Dunstan. He was noted for his skill in shoeing horses. One day, the Devil himself, in disguise, called on him "for repairs", presenting his single hoof. But St. Dunstan recognized the "evil one". He fastened him tightly to the wall and then set to work so roughly that the Devil roared for mercy. St. Dunstan, however, did not let him go until he had promised never to enter a home on which a horseshoe was fixed.

Much more likely is the theory which associates the horseshoe superstition with an early and widely held belief in witches. All over the world and until late in the Middle Ages, men feared them and their nefarious work. It was commonly supposed that one was immune from their evil spells while in the open air, but that they could do harm in the home. It was believed that witches feared horses, for which reason they rode on a broomstick. It followed that a horseshoe at the door of the house would be a protection, as the mere sight of it would frighten away the witches.

The horseshoe has always been considered lucky. Its shape was that of the crescent moon, in which primitive man saw a sign of good fortune. It indicated fertility and the increase of all that was good.

The ancient Romans held that evil could be nailed, and the hammering of nails on the doors of their houses was a means of curing or diverting ill luck and disease.

The horseshoe cannot be hung just any way. It should be fixed with its points upward, lest the luck run out.

THIRD TIME LUCKY

The proverbial saying that "third time's lucky" is not just an encouragement never to give up trying — "If at first you don't succeed, try, try, try again." It has its ancient and sacred asso-

ciations and is based on the belief, spread throughout the West
and East, in the significance of the figure three.

The Greek philosopher Pythagoras in the 6th century B.C.
called 3 "the perfect number". It was the sign of completion and
fertility. That is why in some languages the figure 3 and the word
tree have the same root, meaning the power of reproduction. In
Arian tongues, 3 is the first expression of plurality and the
multiplication of things.

This concept of "the perfect 3" is inherent in man's thinking
and imagination. It can be found as much in ancient mythology
as in modern psychology. That is why all through the history of
mankind the idea of the essential triangularity of matter, and of
the trinity of the spirit, has prevailed. Shakespeare wrote that
there is luck in odd numbers, especially three.

In most prescriptions of folk medicine three ingredients are
necessary to ensure a cure. Indian philosophy speaks of the three
worlds — heaven, sky and earth. We ourselves speak of the
three parts of man — body, mind and soul.

In ancient mythology Neptune appears with the trident, and
Jupiter with three-forked lightning. Mankind itself, according to
biblical tradition, is descended from the three families of Ham,
Shem and Japhet. And in our time Professor Freud distinguished
in man the three aspects of super-ego, ego and id.

THE BREAKING OF A MIRROR

The superstition that the breaking of a mirror means bad luck
is so old that it leads back to times when mirrors could not be
broken because they were made of metal or — even earlier still
-- were of water.

The first mirrors were the still water of lakes and pools. When
people looked into them they did so, not out of vanity, but to
view their fate. The way their image appeared on the surface
was interpreted as an indication of what the future held for them.
If the face seemed distorted, broken into many pieces, as it were,
it was taken as a definite portent of evil, of the forthcoming dis-
integration of the viewer's life. Unfortunately foes could easily
disturb a calm and pleasant reflection by throwing pebbles
maliciously into the pond.

Other beliefs were soon added that made the breaking of a mirror even more ominous. Mirrors were used for divination, just as today people gaze into crystal balls. Primitive man imagined that the picture he saw was not the reflection of his personal image but of the soul which, he was convinced, had an independent existence, could detach itself from the body and thus actually be in the mirror. If this were broken the soul, too, was shattered, and thus the very substance of existence destroyed. By losing his soul through the shattered glass, the man or woman was bound to die.

Belief in magic further increased the unfortunate associations with the breaking of mirrors. It was assumed that any injury done to the reflection would affect the person whose likeness it bore, just as people believed that by piercing the eyes of a foe in his picture, they would cause him to go blind in fact.

There was yet another fear that the breaking of the mirror would anger the spirit dwelling in it so much (because it had been hurt) that it would seek vengeance on the offender, or one of his family.

Also, as mirrors were used to foretell a man's future, their being broken was interpreted as intentional, and not just an accident. It was an act deliberately committed by the gods themselves, who wished to prevent a man from being informed (and forewarned) of coming disaster.

Chinese people used to fix mirrors over idols they kept in their homes. The mirrors, so they firmly believed, were a potent power against evil spirits which, seeing themselves in the mirror, were scared away. Thus, if a mirror were broken, the only defence against malevolent powers was lost, and the home was wide open for them to take possession.

Though nowadays we decorate the home with numerous kinds of mirrors both to beautify it and to see ourselves, when broken, they still reflect our ancient superstitious past and out of the shattered pieces the spirit of old rises again. As Bernard Shaw has said, one of the laws still ruling even our modern age is the conservation of credulity.

It may be that beyond those many irrational fears and phobias a very mundane consideration has made people afraid of break-

ing a mirror — it is costly to replace and the risk is great of injury
by the glass splinters.

WALKING UNDER LADDERS

It is commonly held that to walk under ladders is unlucky. At
first sight it seems a logical deduction. Accidents do happen and a
painter working on top of the ladder might splash down some
paint or even drop the pot itself. Or we might be even more
unfortunate and become the unintentional target of a dropped
tool or a tile.

Such explanations, however logical they might appear, are
not the real ones, but what psychologists term rationalizations.

The true origin of the superstition leads back to the ancient,
pre-Christian belief in the sanctity of the trinity. A ladder, lean-
ing against a wall, forms a triangle. This has always been the
most common symbol of Holy Trinity. To pass through its area
would be tantamount to defiance of sacred power and an intrusion
into sanctified space. It would be a dangerous play with supernatural forces. Even worse, such action might disturb, if not
annul, the trinity's potency as a guard against satanic forces
which, thus released, would immediately start their evil work.

Another explanation relates to an ancient taboo, still observed
by some primitive races. This concerned man's head, which was
considered not as the seat of his wisdom but of his guardian
spirit. By walking under a ladder, this spirit would take offence
and, simultaneously, become ineffective, thus delivering the tres-
passer to malevolent agencies. A similar superstition led the
Burmese to decry as undignified to walk even under an awning.

Early Christian tradition took due cognisance of the superstition about ladders. However, trying to interpret it in its own
way, it pointed to the fact that because a ladder was used in
connection with the crucifixion of Christ, it has been associated
ever since with evil and death.

GETTING OUT OF BED ON THE WRONG SIDE

We say of people whom we find suddenly ill-tempered that
they must have got out of bed "on the wrong side". But when we

do so, we have not the slightest inkling that the phrase has any deeper meaning or ominous sense. We use it merely in the way of picturesque speaking. But in reality, and originally, it was meant quite literally. People firmly believed that the way they rose in the morning affected their mood and dealings throughout the ensuing day. The simple act of getting up was therefore of almost magic significance.

Matters were aggravated further by the fact that the most important question was left unanswered. If there was a wrong side from which to get out of bed, which was it? From long ago two different interpretations were given.

First, people assumed that it was inviting disaster to get up the same way as they retired. They must complete the "magic circle" and rise from the opposite side of the bed.

A more deeply rooted belief was that, no matter which way we had gone to bed, in the case of rising the left side was always the wrong side. Getting out of bed we must put down our right foot first.

In all ages the left has been linked with evil and, therefore, with superstitious fear. This might have been caused by people's experience that the average person's left hand was less powerful than the right, and even clumsy.

For centuries left-handedness has been associated with debility of mind. Even a criminologist of the standing of the Italian Cesare Lombroso claimed that left-handedness was a common occurrence among the insane and criminal.

The ancient Romans already had identified the left side with the "evil one". Therefore they considered it unlucky to enter a house with their left foot first. To avoid any such possibility, noble families employed a servant whose sole duty it was to ensure that guests entered his master's home right foot first. Appropriately, this slave's office became known as that of a *footman*. We still retain the title but have forgotten its original meaning.

Our own word *sinister*, likewise, dates from Roman civilization and the identical superstition. It was the Latin word for the *left* side. Its very association with evil caused it to become, in our vocabulary, a term denoting what is underhand, base and bad.

LIGHTING THREE CIGARETTES WITH ONE MATCH

The Holy Trinity, commercial interests and self-protection in time of war, are cited as the direct cause of aversion to lighting three cigarettes with one match.

Three is the symbol of the trinity. To make a mundane use of it was to defile its sanctity and to transgress the holy law. Man would invite disaster and put himself into the power of the "evil one". Thus, a match, trebly used, would light the fires of Hell for one's own soul.

Another, less fearful tradition claims that the superstition first arose among British troops during the Crimean War. They learned from Russian captives of the danger of using any light for a threefold purpose. They were told that it was the sacred rule of the Orthodox Church that the three candles on the altar were not to be lit from a single taper, except when the High Priest used it.

However, a more likely explanation of the origin of the custom is that British soldiers, entrenched against Dutch foes in the Boer War, learned by bitter experience of the danger of lighting three cigarettes from one match. When the men thriftily used one match to serve three of them, they gave the Boer sniper time to spot the light, take aim and fire, killing "the third man".

Ivar Kreuger, the Swedish match king, certainly did not create the superstition, as has been alleged, but he made the widest possible use of it to promote sales. People, innately superstitious, did not mind wasting a match. After all, there might just be something in it! Certainly there was millions of pounds of profit for Mr. Kreuger who thus, by fostering for his own purpose a realistic wartime precaution, was able to increase his sales manifold.

OPENING AN UMBRELLA INDOORS

It is a common superstition that opening an umbrella inside a house brings bad luck. A belief in magic and in the right order of things may have given rise to it.

An umbrella is meant to be a shield in the open air, no matter whether it is used against the rain or the sun. Therefore, to open it where it does not belong is, as it were, a defiance of natural order and an insult to the spirit of the umbrella which, thus personified, would surely take revenge. God intended umbrellas to be employed out of doors and will punish those who do not respect but scorn His intention.

There was also an ancient fear of having an unjustified cover over the head. People believed that evil forces enveloped them all the time, watching out for every possible opportunity of doing harm. But beneficial mystical powers protected them by their invisible radiation. Opening an umbrella indoors, however, put up an impenetrable screen against the rays of good fortune.

In modern times practical considerations reinforced the ancient superstition. An open umbrella in a room obstructs vision and can easily cause breakage, damage and injury. Even the most enlightened man, therefore, is well advised to deem it "dangerous" to open his umbrella indoors.

STUMBLING

People about to embark on a new venture instinctively and superstitiously look out for signs, which will either encourage or deter them. A bride on her wedding day will welcome sunshine and a blue sky as a happy augury. To stumble, on the other hand, has been associated with bad luck and "explained" as a warning of misfortune to come. As early a writer as the Roman Cicero mentioned the fear as one of the many omens at which weak minds are terrified. Seventeen hundred years later, Shakespeare could still record the identical obsession:

> For many men that stumble at the threshold
> Are well foretold that danger lurks therein.

Historical and biographical examples, ancient and modern, seem to support this superstition.

Tiberius Gracchus stumbled on the threshold of his home and died the same day.

When leaving his tent pitched on a battlefield, Antigonus slipped. His men immediately interpreted the accident as a revelation of the gods' ill will. And to all appearances they were confirmed in their opinion because Antigonus was killed that very afternoon.

Napoleon's horse stumbled one day during his invasion of the

East. The General, so it is said, defied the sign. Ridiculing it, and considering himself above Fate, he continued his campaign — with disastrous results.

About to embark on his second — and fatal — expedition to Africa, Mungo Park took leave of Sir Walter Scott. Immediately afterwards, on crossing from the moor to the road, his horse stumbled. Sir Walter, watching the incident, expressed his fear and tried to stop his friend from proceeding. But Park rejected the warning, saying that "omens follow them who look to them". He was never seen again.

Such examples, however numerous they are, prove nothing. They are mere rash rationalizations. After all, how many people have stumbled and nothing has happened to them! On the other hand, how many people who had never slipped did not return from their ventures, or died tragically.

Originally, stumbling was taken as a revelation of the agency of unseen, evil forces, determined to frustrate a person in the task on which he was about to embark. Therefore they made him stumble, as it were, to give him a last warning. If he still did not heed the sign and refused to turn back, they would see to it that their will was done.

Common sense offers a more obvious explanation. Stumbling is perilous at all times. A man who trips up or, worse still, whose horse misses a foothold, might easily break his neck.

Modern psychology, however, points to a much more rational answer. A close relationship exists between body and mind. Feelings can condition our actions. The way we approach a task — with confidence or with fear — will greatly determine its final execution, its success or failure. Hence, people who are not sure of themselves and hesitant in what they are doing would come to grief even without stumbling. But subconsciously they miss their footing. Their stumble is not a superstitious omen but a symptom of their own mood. No wonder therefore that eventually, already preconditioned to defeat, they miss their objective.

MEETING A BLACK CAT

To meet a black cat is considered both lucky and unlucky: it all depends in which country you live.

The belief that — in certain circumstances — black cats are lucky goes back to Egypt. There all cats, but especially those that were totally black, were looked upon with utmost reverence. They were even deified.

The cat was sacred to the goddess Isis. The goddess Bast or Pasht, the daughter of Isis, was represented with the face of a cat. A cat was thought to be so holy that any one who killed it, even by accident, was put to death. Frequently, mummified cats were buried with their worshippers. Cat cemeteries were found by archaeologists in Egypt and a shipment of embalmed cats was taken to England. Thus, the belief that a black cat that crosses your path brings luck is rooted in Egyptian mythology.

A tradition which arose in the Middle Ages in Europe made the black cat not a god, or one of its associates, but a companion of witches and even their familiar. People believed that a witch could assume the form of a black cat. Therefore, all black cats were suspected of being transformed witches. Thus, to have a black cat cross your path came to be regarded as an omen of bad luck.

In Lincolnshire, England, a popular story was told of a father and his son meeting a black cat which they suspected was a witch. They pounded it with stones. Next day they encountered the witch in her real form. Her face was bandaged and she died soon afterward.

Thus the two contradictory beliefs about a black cat are the result of two strands of tradition: the Egyptian idolized cat and the European witchy one. It is just a matter of geographical circumstances whether the black cat you meet augurs good luck or warns you of impending misfortune.

A RABBIT'S FOOT FOR LUCK

Widespread is the belief that a rabbit's foot brings luck. Children were brushed with it at birth, and well-wishers used to present one to young actors when first they appeared on the stage, to be used ever after when applying make-up. The rabbit's foot was deemed a guarantee of good fortune, and its loss a threat of disaster. As with numerous other customs and superstitions, many and various causes made the rabbit's foot a lucky charm.

The superstition may be a survival of ancient Totemism, which preceded monotheistic faith. This claimed (anticipating Darwin by many thousands of years) that man was descended from the beast. But, differing from scientific opinion, these early evolutionists thought that each tribe had its own kind of animal ancestor, which they worshipped, refrained from killing, and frequently used — either as a whole or only in parts — as their lucky charm. They called it their totem.

This ancient concept can be traced in biblical literature as the root of many dietary laws which prohibited certain (totem) animals being eaten. In much the same way, the modern regimental mascot, whether sheep or goat, is believed to secure luck for the regiment.

It is probable that the rabbit, too, is a long-forgotten totem which became the guardian spirit of its descendants. Thus, its foot is still considered a bringer of good luck.

But then, again, rabbits were taken to be evil, an opinion possibly quite feasible to those accustomed to speak of the Australian pest. The story was told of a ship's crew of God-fearing men who landed on an island. Being hungry, they chased and killed rabbits. When they sailed for home, their ship was lost on the high seas — "because of the rabbits!".

The rabbit's burrowing habits undoubtedly further contributed to the suspicion with which it was once regarded. What was the animal doing down under? People asked themselves that question and some surmised that the rabbit had a secret communication with the underworld's evil forces. So it was that rabbits were said to have the power of the evil eye, an assertion reinforced by the erroneous notion that young rabbits were born with their eyes wide open.

It was the rabbit's fecundity that helped to give its foot an association with good luck and prosperity. The rabbit was so prolific that people considered it the outstanding example of all that was creative, and it became symbolic of an abundance of life.

After that it did not take people long to assume that by carrying part of a rabbit, its proximity or touch would transfer to them the rabbit's good fortune. The choice of the foot was not accidental. Even before Freudian sexual interpretations were known, a foot was recognized as a phallic symbol and regarded as a sure means to foster fertility.

THE LOCKET OF HAIR

To give a lock of one's hair to a cherished person is a beautiful custom. But its real meaning is much more profound.

A locket of hair is now considered an ornament or, perhaps, a charm — a constant reminder of someone we love. Originally, however, it was worn or carried to dominate the donor.

The gift of a lock was an act of surrender. It was based on the ancient superstition that the hair was the seat of one's vital spirit. Whoever had even a single strand of it was able to influence, even bewitch, the person who had grown it. Thus, if you bestowed a lock of your hair on a chosen person, you entrusted to him (or her) your very life. Certainly, nothing could surpass such testimony of love and trust.

WHISTLING AT SEA

In the old days of sail the sailor's calling was especially hazardous and it was small wonder that superstition permeated much of his life. In numerous ways seafaring men tried to ensure that the sea would be friendly. They left nothing undone that might help them to escape disaster by propitiating the many invisible, hostile forces on whose good will they depended so much and whose whims they could not guess. These agencies, sailors believed, hovered all over the sea and peopled ships. They could cause terror and destruction.

One way of dissuading them from evil intention was sympathetic magic, of the potency of which primitive man was firmly convinced. Thus, some African tribes would never heat milk. If they did so, they imagined that the cow which had provided the milk would suffer, in sympathy, from the heat and perish.

Gales were one of the most frightening hazards at sea. To avoid them by every possible means was a matter of common sense. Sailors believed it was possible to call up a gale by the accidental use of sympathetic magic — if a noise like a storm were made, a storm would come.

The sound of whistling resembled that of a gale in the rigging and for that reason it was assumed that any one who whistled magically started a gale. Whistling on board ship was thus considered an invitation to bad luck.

Of course, when the sea was calmed circumstances changed and on such an occasion a whistle could become the right charm. However, sailors who then whistled for the wind did so with utmost caution lest they roused the wrong type in both strength and direction. They whistled softly and only towards the point from which they wanted the wind to blow.

The view that it is "common" and wrong for a woman to whistle, whether on land or at sea, is rooted in the same belief in the magical power of a whistle. It was considered that a woman's place was in the home and that for her to meddle in male concerns was dangerous at the best of times. But if she did so with a whistle, it could prove fatal. She could rouse winds from the wrong direction and in destructive, gale force.

Apart from that, a woman who whistled usurped a male privilege. An old-established custom gave a man the right to "whistle up" a girl he fancied. This was not, as it is today, a rather vulgar way to attract her attention. As in the case of the wind, it was thought that a man's whistle magically brought the girl to him.

THE HOWLING OF DOGS

It is a long-held belief that the howling of dogs portends misfortune, if not death. People were convinced that everything has a cause and they could not imagine that a dog would howl just for the sake of howling.

It was assumed that the dog, a friend of man, tried to give him a message. The dog's prolonged doleful cry, full of wails, suggested that the message was of a calamitous nature. This is the most obvious explanation of how people began to believe in the clairvoyance of dogs and to credit them with the faculty of seeing ghosts and spirits. There were other contributory factors.

A dog's perception, at least in part, extends beyond that of a human. Its senses of smell and hearing excel by far those of its master. Thus, it took note of many things which, to man, did not seem to exist.

Unable at first to find a natural explanation to this phenomenon, people endowed dogs with supernatural gifts and mysterious instincts. These, it was thought, gave them the power not just to "sense" spirits and ghosts — especially the approaching figure of death — but literally to *see* them, even though man could not perceive their presence. To warn him that death was hovering over his home, the animal began to howl. It was the least it could do.

Many examples of such "supernatural" gifts of dogs can be found in literature from the earliest times. Best-known is the account given in the Odyssey, where it is told how the dogs of the swineherd Eumaeus, "with a low whine shrank cowering to the stalls' far side" in the presence of Athene, whom Telemachus was unable to see because "the gods in no wise appear visible to all".

Again, there is the story of Hecate, associated in Greek lore with the realm of the uncanny and ghosts. Hovering at the crossroads, she foretold death. But only dogs were aware of her. They gave warning by their show of terror and barking.

It is hard to determine whether the numerous tales of that sort were the result or actually the origin of the superstitious notion. At all events, they certainly helped in spreading it. Gullible man, not always capable or willing to differentiate between fact and fiction, soon took the myth for reality.

There may be a much simpler and more rational basis to man's belief in the ominous nature of the dog's howl. When rabies was rampant, the whining and howling, no doubt, were linked with the dog's going mad. By its bite, it transferred the sickness and consequently caused death. Unaware of the medical facts, man considered the symptom of the disease as a supernatural omen of death.

AVERSION TO RED HAIR

In some parts of the world there is still a prejudice against red-haired people. It may be that one of its causes is the psychological law of the dislike by the like for the unlike. Certainly, red-haired men and women almost everywhere are in a minority.

But the unjustified, irrational attitude has other significant foundations as well.

It has its historic roots. Anglo-Saxons dreaded their red-haired, Danish foes. In the subconscious memories of many English people the otherwise long-forgotten association of hostile invaders with red hair lingered on.

Even nature itself has played a part in rendering red an ominous colour. Red-yellowish sand was found in the desert which spelled drought, thirst and disaster to many. That is how Egyptians first came to depict one of their evil gods in a red-yellowish sandy colour.

A medical fallacy has equally been quoted as the virus which poisoned people against red-haired neighbours. Doctors used to diagnose illness by the patient's colour and, at some time, a red complexion was considered a symptom of a "gross humour" and ill blood. Possibly scared of infection and because illness was regarded as the result of sin, people shunned and despised those with red hair.

It has been suggested that neither fear of sickness nor horror of sin created the prejudice, but pure envy. Red hair, this much more pleasant fallacy claimed, was an indication of the purest blood, a most clarified spirit and, consequently, the finest of intellects. Red hair showed the best balanced constitution, poised exactly halfway between the blond (phlegmatic) and the black (melancholic), the fickle and the authoritarian.

It was for this reason that other people, lacking such a gift, jealously derided and abused those who by the very colour of their hair could not disguise their superiority. An Italian proverb asserted that "face without colour, either a liar or a traitor".

There are biblical sources as well. Scarlet was the colour of sin, and artists therefore painted evil men with yellowish-red hair. The best examples are those of murderous Cain and treacherous Judas Iscariot. And it may have been their portrayal most of all that was responsible for the antipathy toward red-haired people.

SPITTING

The habit of spitting on things for luck has a sacred origin. It leads back to belief in magic and the story of the Gospels.

Ancient man regarded spittle as representative of his soul. To expectorate, therefore, was like making an offering to the gods who, in return, would extend protection to the spitter.

On the other hand, primitive races believed that if they could get hold of their foe's spittle, they would be able to bewitch him. That is why on the Sandwich Islands, for instance, chiefs were accompanied by a servant who carried a portable spittoon. He carefully buried its contents every morning at a secret spot, lest sorcerers used it for their nefarious purpose.

Human saliva served as a charm against witchcraft and enchantment and was considered a potent antidote against every type of poison. The magical rite of spitting thus found its place in primitive medicine, especially in treating the eyes.

In pugilistic bouts in ancient days, fighters spat on their hands, expecting that this would magically increase the strength of their blows.

Authorities quoted by Pliny asserted that the pernicious powers of toads, frogs and serpents were rendered innocuous by spitting into their mouths. Tacitus recorded how Vespasian healed a blind man in Alexandria by wetting his eyes with spittle.

Above all, it was the narrative of the Gospels that spread among Christian nations the belief in the miraculous power of spittle. It is told in several passages of the New Testament how Jesus, by its use, worked wonders in restoring sight and speech:

> "And they brought unto him one that was deaf and stammered . . . and he took him aside from the crowd, and put his fingers into his ears, and touched his tongue with spittle. And looking up to heaven, he sighed and said to him, 'Be opened!' . . . and straightway his tongue was loosed, and he spoke plainly." *(Mark VII, 32f)*
> "And they brought a blind man unto him . . . and he took the blind man . . . and he spat into his eyes, and put his hands upon him, and asked if he saw anything, and he looked up, and said, 'I perceive men . . .'." *(Mark VIII, 22f)*
> ". . . he saw a blind man from his birth . . . he spat on the ground, and made clay of the spittle, and anointed his eyes with the clay; He went away . . . and washed, and came seeing." *(John IX, 1-7)*

It was stories of that kind, both sacred and profane, which were remembered by the people. They hoped that what had worked once might prove successful again in their own case.

Eventually spitting was credited not only with possessing the power of curing disease, but with acting as a general prophylactic against evil of any kind. And as it could ward off misfortune, so it would attract good luck.

POINTING

It is considered rude to point at people. This is merely a rationalization of an ancient superstition and a primitive practice.

In some parts of the world to point at a celestial body was taken as an affront to divine power, which would punish the offender. His action could not harm the sun, moon or stars but only himself. By a natural development the dangerous import of pointing was generalized.

Pagans, while worshipping idols, pointed at their image. It was thus a natural reaction for Christian people to view with disfavour any type of pointing.

However, black projective magic is the most likely source of the disapproval. Wide-spread and most feared among savage people was the practice of pointing. It was a supernatural way of killing. Possibly at first the savages pointed at an adversary whose death they desired. They did so with a bone taken from a dead man's body, believing that with it they could best express and attain their aim.

Survival of this magical death ritual among primitive races, including Australian Aborigines, rendered the act, if no longer fatal, reprehensible. To avoid any possible ill effect, yet (consciously or unconsciously) not wishing to admit knowledge of the original murderous background, any sort of pointing was decried as uncouth.

CHAPTER II

BIRth anд its customs

BIRTHDAY celebrations are rather a paradox. Who but a child would be happy because a calendar date reminds him that another year of his life has gone?

Originally, birthdays looked into the future and their celebration was regarded as ensuring continuation of life. It was held that life was renewed on that day, which was thought magically to repeat one's actual birth. If properly observed, the birthday ritual meant life, health and prosperity for the next 12 months. This is why the birthday wish is for "many happy returns of the day".

THE STORK AND BABIES

Dutch, German and Scandinavian mothers especially tell their children that babies are brought by the stork. They say, too, that the stork, when depositing the baby, bit the mother's leg, causing her to stay in bed for some time.

In its very name the stork carries a tradition of love. The English word comes from the Greek *storgé,* meaning *strong natural affection,* and in the sacred language of Hebrew the stork appears literally as *the pious one.*

Several factors combined in creating the belief in the stork as the bringer of babies. First, there was the bird's remarkable tenderness towards its young and old. Legends grew up which described how the young ones looked after the aged, blind and

weak parents; how they carried them around on their own wings
and fed them.

People watched the stork's care in making its home and noted
how it loved to return to the same spot each year. Soon, the
stork's very presence was considered a sign of good fortune.
Indeed, German peasants often encouraged it to build its nest on
the roof of their house, putting a waggon wheel there for a
foundation. The stork soon used it for that very purpose.

The bird's regular trip abroad added to the mystery. At the
time, people knew nothing of the migratory habit of birds, and
legend assumed that during the winter storks went to Egypt
and there changed into men. It was believed that the stork
once had been a human being.

Finally, there was the fact that storks loved water and frequented swamps, marshes and ponds. Ancient tradition held
that it was in those watery places that the souls of unborn
children dwelt.

It was easy to link all these beliefs and superstitions, to make
the stork, so conspicuous in appearance, all-important in the
propagation of man.

BLUE FOR BOYS AND PINK FOR GIRLS

An explanation of the custom of dressing boys and girls in
different colours is linked with their sex. Babies all look alike,
and what better means of identifying them readily than by
colours — blue for boys and pink for girls? This colour scheme
has been adopted all over the world. But who would ever suspect that in the blue ribbon is tied up a terror-crazed past and
a haunting fear of anxious parents, deeply concerned with their
baby's future?

From the days of antiquity it was believed that evil spirits
hovered menacingly over the nursery. It was thought further
that the evil ones were allergic to certain colours, of which the
most potent was blue. It was considered that the association of
blue with the heavenly sky rendered satanic forces powerless
and drove them away. Even in our own time Arabs in the
Middle East continue to paint the doors of their homes blue to
frighten away demons. Thus, the display of blue on a young

child was not merely an adornment but a necessary precaution.

Girl babies were regarded as vastly inferior to boy babies and it was assumed that evil spirits would not be interested in them. That is why blue was reserved for boys. Any distinctive colour for girls was deemed unnecessary.

Possibly later generations, unaware of the original cause of "blue for boys" but very much conscious of the neglect of girls, introduced for them the new pink-look.

European legendary tradition suggests another beautiful explanation of the colour scheme for babies. This tells that baby boys are found under cabbages whose colour — on the Continent of Europe — was mostly blue. Baby girls, on the other hand, were born inside a pink rose.

THE PRAM

Mothers may not know it, but they owe a special debt of gratitude to monarchs for having eased considerably their burden. Strange though it may seem, the adoption of our modern pram is due, in no small measure, to Royal example.

Since babies are the hope of man, it is not surprising that from prehistoric times every care was taken to protect the young child physically, psychologically and even magically.

Mothers were not so lucky. For thousands of years it was considered their pre-ordained fate, biblically attested, to bear children in pain. Even after the birth, little was done to case the mother's lot. It was almost symbolic that, among primitive tribes, the father went to bed at the birth of a child to rest there for days, if not weeks.

Women were expected not only to bear children but, afterwards, to go on carrying them — in one way or another. The husband's only concern was that this did not interfere with her other work. Thus, North American Indians carried their babies in cradle boards tied to the back. An Eskimo mother put her child in the hood of her fur jacket. Bedouin women fixed their children securely high on the shoulder. Many a native woman in Africa still carries her youngster on her back in a blanket wrapped around her own body.

The modern pram is a little more than 100 years old. It was

first constructed in New York City by Charles Burton in 1848. His new-fangled idea did not catch on, mainly because the pram collided with too many pedestrians.

Burton, however, was determined to make a success of his invention. He went to Britain and opened a factory there. And the change of site brought him a change of luck. His pram appealed to the common sense of mothers and became fashionable when Queen Victoria (and later Queen Isabella of Spain and the Pasha of Egypt) ordered the new type of baby carriage for their families.

The choice of the word perambulator for the new baby vehicle is interesting. Its literal meaning, derived from the Latin, is to *walk through*. Actually, the term was first used to describe a machine which measured distance by "walking" along it. The shortened version, "pram," first appeared in the vocabulary in its new sense in 1857.

BIRTHDAY CAKE AND CANDLES

The purpose of birthday candles is to honour the birthday child and to bring him good fortune for the ensuing year.

The custom goes back to the ancient Greeks. According to the writings of Philochorus, worshippers of Artemis, goddess of the moon and hunting, used to put honey-cakes on the altars of her temple on the sixth day of every month, which was her birthday. The cakes were round like the full moon and lighted with tapers.

No further record of this custom exists between the days of those Greek moon-worshippers and its re-appearance among German peasants in the Middle Ages, who again used to light candles on birthday cakes. This was done at the moment the child wakened. The candles were kept burning until the cake was eaten at the family meal. If necessary, they were replaced by new ones. The number of candles indicated the age of the child. An extra taper representing the light of life was always added.

Like sacrificial fires, burning tapers were endowed from earliest days with a mystical significance and it was believed that the birthday candle had the power to grant a wish and ensure a happy year for the child. However, the wish, which had to remain secret, would only come true if all the candles were blown out with one puff. The candle lost its magical power if the wish was uttered aloud.

The old belief that the candle symbolized life is retained in many sayings. Thus we warn people of not "burning the candle at both ends" and Macbeth spoke of life as a "brief candle".

THE QUEEN'S BIRTHDAY

That the British Sovereign has two birthdays every year — one on the actual date and an official one in June — has nothing to do with Royal privilege. The custom was introduced during the reign of King William IV and the idea behind the Sovereign's official birthday was, and is, to bring happiness to the greatest possible number of people. This will appeal specially to Australians who transfer mid-week public holidays to a Monday in order to enjoy an extended weekend.

While the present Queen was born on April 21, her official birthday always falls in June. Then it is midsummer in Britain, theoretically the best time for the people to spend the day in the open air.

Another example of how concern for the public interest determines the date of the official Royal birthday was the decision in 1959 to conduct the celebrations on the second Saturday in June because London's dense traffic would have made it very difficult to Troop the Colours on a weekday.

There was another practical consideration for selecting June as the fixed, official Royal birthday season. It is an established tradition of British Royalty to bestow titles and decorations twice annually — an Honours' List is published on New Year's Day and the Queen's birthday. By making the latter fall always in June, it was ensured that the two occasions would never clash; in fact they were kept as far apart as possible.

Thus even the very birthday of the Queen and its duplication reveal the thoughtfulness and democracy of British Royalty and its concern with the happiness of the people.

CHAPTER III

the Ritual of courting
and marriage

THE HISTORY of courting is a mirror of human civilization and technological advance. Its duration and speed have varied enormously. Its time and pace have fluctuated between the 14 long years it took Jacob to woo Rachel and the lightning speed of our times.

The range of its intensity, likewise, has differed greatly. It extends from the reticence of young lovers making polite conversation in the presence of ever-watchful chaperons in Victorian parlours to the impetuous petting of modern teenagers in the complete privacy, propinquity and mobility of their car.

Even the choice of one's partner has undergone many significant changes. There were times when the bridal couple met for the first time on the day of their marriage, which had been arranged — independently of their own wishes and desires — by the tribe or the family. Then marriage brokers took over the task, on a strictly commercial basis, yet they were not unaware of human factors. Rome had its lottery for lovers.

For the sake of marriage God gave Eve to Adam. Ever since people have married. They have made many mistakes and have often taken the bond for something that it is not.

We speak of wedlock and imagine that a marriage is something that locks people up and chains them together like prisoners. The original *lock* is no lock at all but the Anglo-Saxon for *gift*, as *wed* means a *promise*. Wedlock thus pledged the finest of all gifts — the happiness of a man and a woman. To achieve that aim, numerous customs have been followed down the ages.

The story is told that ever since God created woman out of one of Adam's ribs, men have been rushing all over the world, seeking their missing rib.

Some never get hold of it and they rationalize their failure by calling themselves confirmed bachelors. Others actually find "a rib". But it is not theirs and that is why it does not really fit, and both parties concerned experience much anguish and pain. But then there are the lucky ones. They retrieve the rib which belongs to them and thus become once more "complete", with all the happiness this implies.

Beautiful and romantic are the numerous customs we now associate with courtship and marriage. Nearly all of them can be traced to primitive ritual and early practice designed to ensure — by magical rites and armed force — the fertility of the union.

THE KISS

Western civilization takes the kiss for granted. Greek poets called it "the key to Paradise". Other people and ages have condemned the kiss as vulgar, indecent and a social sin. Japanese never kiss (except parents their children) and have not even a word for it. Chinese regarded a kiss as suggestive of cannibalism and in Indo-China mothers used to frighten their children by threatening them with the white man's kiss.

The origin of the kiss leads back to the earliest stages of human existence and even beyond. Some authorities claim that the kiss developed because primitive man believed that the air he exhaled had magic power. It was an emanation of his true self. By kissing each other men and women mingled their souls.

Others have assumed that the mouth kiss was only the last stage of a long evolution. It started with face touching face (just as Eskimos and Maoris still rub noses) and one man smelling the other (as Indian tribes used to say "smell me!" instead of "give me a kiss!").

Touch has been called the mother of senses and experiments have shown that even the slightest contact with another skin excites the brain. Many animals touch and feel each other and those of whom they are fond. Cats and dogs rub their heads against their owners; birds stroke beak with beak and elephants intertwine trunks. Even insects caress each other with their antennae and snails with their horns. Man's most sensitive touch-zone is the mucous membranes of his lips, and that is how in the search to express deepest affection mouth found mouth.

Another ingenious explanation links the mouth kiss with our earliest ancestors and animal forebears. The mother, so it is said, used to warm and premasticate the food in her own mouth before transferring it — by way of a "kiss" — to her infant. It was the subconscious memory of this pleasant association of the far distant past that gave us our present-day kiss.

X FOR A KISS

The use of an X to signify a kiss began in the Middle Ages, when the majority of people were illiterate and unable to sign even their own name. Having to testify documents, they put a cross in place of a signature. Without it a contract or agreement was considered invalid. And to affirm their sincerity, they solemnly kissed it, in the same way that they used to kiss the Bible when taking an oath. Eventually the kiss and the cross became synonymous.

The choice of the cross was not accidental or, as might be thought, merely caused by its simple shape which could be traced by anyone. It was the sign of St. Andrew and implied a sacred guarantee and promise to fulfil one's obligation in that saint's name.

Everybody can write these days. But the early link of the cross and the kiss survive, and St. Andrew's mark, far removed from early illiteracy, medieval legal practice and theological tradition, has become a universal shorthand of love and affection.

SPOONING

Three possible explanations offer themselves for the use of the word spooning to describe courting.

Far from being slang, the term recollects a beautiful custom. Young men in Wales used to carve a wooden spoon which they presented as a token of love to the girl of their choice. Often this took the place of an engagement ring. If she accepted the spoon, it was as good as a promise of marriage.

The spoon itself was elaborately carved. Frequently it was decorated with intricate floral patterns, both on handle and bowl. It was stained and embossed with the lovers' initials, suitably intertwined.

Only the progress of civilization with its mass production of spoons discontinued this lovely mode of courting. Engagement rings, easily purchased and comparatively impersonal, took the place of the spoon, now merely retained in the way of speaking.

A less romantic interpretation relates the spoon to childish behaviour, and implies that spooning couples are not serious about their love-play.

Lastly, there is the suggestion that spooning refers to the lying closely together of two people, as spoons fit into each other.

THE VALENTINE CARD

On February 14th millions of Valentine cards are sent out to people of the opposite sex. Once individually written and now mass produced, they are light-hearted missiles of love. Either in prose or in rhyme they voice amorous feeling. Mostly they are humorous, sometimes vulgar and often accompanied by illustrations.

It is all a play of love, strongly spiced with sentimentality and fun. Who would think that this gay and harmless custom of budding romance began many thousands of years ago and has its origins in pagan tradition about the love-life of birds, an ancient lottery for sweethearts and, most of all, the martyr's death of a Christian bishop? The Valentine cards' popularity also testifies to the early Church's successful endeavour to Christianize heathen practice.

Long before the advent of Christianity, the middle of February was considered propitious for love. It was the season of Spring and birds started mating.

Roman mythology associated the day with the goddess Juno, worshipped especially by women at all crises of life. She was the "venerable ox-eyed" wife of Jupiter and the queen of heaven.

Identified with the Greek Hera, she became the guardian of
women and marriage, though significantly also a goddess of war.

Part of the pagan ritual honouring Juno was a unique kind of
lottery. Young girls wrote their names on slips of paper and these
were placed in a drum from which the boys drew their luck.
There were no blanks. The girl drawn by a young man became
his sweetheart until the next annual draw.

All the world loves a lover, and Christianity was unable to
uproot a day dedicated to the enjoyment of life and love. Therefore, the early Church appropriated February 14th for its own
calendar, linking it with the martyrdom of St. Valentine.

Originally, Valentine was a pagan priest of the 3rd century
A.D.. He was converted to Christianity and became a bishop.
The story is told that at the time the Roman Emperor Claudius
had decided to abolish the institution of marriage, as he felt that
husbands did not make good soldiers. He tried to enforce the
new law with the utmost rigour.

Valentine considered such policy against the spirit of God and
of human nature. He secretly married young lovers, but not for
long. He was arrested, imprisoned and brutally murdered on
February 14th, 269 A.D..

Another (and more plausible) account relates that Valentine
frequently aided persecuted Christians, and that it was for this
reason that he was thrown into prison. But even there he continued his saintly work, miraculously restoring vision to his
gaoler's blind daughter. But he was doomed. On February 14th
he was clubbed to death. The date coincided with the ancient
pagan feast of Juno, and ever since has been celebrated as St.
Valentine's Day.

But the Church's desire to Christianize pagan practice did not
end here. There was still the most popular part of the feast —
its lottery for love. Those early theologians were men of the
world and certainly did not live in an ivory tower. They knew
only too well that one cannot suppress man's deepest urges,
including his love of gambling — no matter for what.

Therefore they retained the ancient lottery but changed its
prizes. The names of saints were substituted for those of girls!
Now the lucky winners were expected in the ensuing year to
match their life to that of the saint whose name they had drawn.

This bored the participants. The girls recaptured the lottery drums, putting into them once again their own names, and the ancient love-play started all over again.

Then a final development took place. People were no longer satisfied with having their sweethearts chosen for them by chance. Their own choice, they felt, should take the place of luck. So on February 14th they began sending a gift, a card or a set of verses to whomsoever they considered nearest their heart.

Often the cards were sent anonymously and it was left to the recipient to guess their author. Their text either stated briefly but to the point that "The honey's sweet and so are you" or went into most elaborate and passionate musings. Those who could not write their own words selected them from specially published handbooks, such as "The Young Man's Valentine Writer", which appeared in 1797. And that is how eventually the printed Valentine card came into existence. Its popularity was greatly fostered by the introduction of cheap postal rates.

It was only the new fashion of Christmas cards that ended the vogue of the Valentine. Though in its small and quiet way it still survives, hoping perhaps one day to recapture the imagination of young lovers.

LEAP YEAR PROPOSALS

The right of women to "pop the question" every fourth year goes far back into the past. The choice of a leap year is rather significant. According to ancient tradition, many things happened then that were topsy-turvy. It was even thought that beans grew the wrong way during that year.

That specially appointed day — February 29th — really was not counted and had no status in English law. It was because of this that it was "leapt over", which explains the year's name.

Just as the extra day every fourth year brought at least a partial correction of the discrepancy which developed between the calendar and the season, so the privilege of leap year proposals gave women an opportunity of correcting, temporarily, a state of affairs that was one-sided and completely unjust. Especially at a time when there was a surplus of females, they could try to ensure that they were not left on the shelf.

The origin of the custom has been explained both as the result of a specific (but fictitious) Royal Act and rebellion by some nuns.

It is alleged that in 1288 Queen Margaret of Scotland decreed through her Parliament that in a leap year any woman could propose to any man she liked. He could refuse her only if he was already engaged. In all other cases he had no choice. But if, defying the law, he still insisted on preserving his single state and rejected the woman's advances, he was liable to a fine of £100, reducible only in cases of hardship.

From the Scots the rule was adopted in Genoa, Florence and France, though at no time — at least officially — by the English themselves.

Yet in spite of the fact that this so-called Act of the Scottish Parliament has been quoted numerous times, investigation has proved it to be a myth and non-existent. Thus for hundreds of years women based their "right" on a legal fiction.

Scottish people are renowned for their wisdom. No wonder, therefore, that their men were not slow to guard themselves from being taken unawares by a female pursuer. They conceded that women had the privilege of proposal during leap year, but stipulated that they indicated their intention by wearing a scarlet petticoat with a clearly visible hem. This gave bachelors warning and a sporting chance to get out of the way.

Celibacy among priests and nuns was not always the rule. Certainly not at the time of St. Patrick, which makes at least a little more feasible an otherwise completely outrageous myth.

One day Patrick was approached by St. Bridget, who was in tears. The nuns under her supervision, so she related, were in revolt. They strongly resented the unfair institution that gave only men the right to propose and barred women from taking the initiative in selecting a mate.

Patrick himself had vowed to stay single. Nevertheless, he sympathized with the rebellious women and saw their point. Total equality was out of the question. Hence he suggested that they should be permitted to propose during one full year every seven years.

Bridget was still dissatisfied and did not see her way clear to accept the offer. She knew men's weakness and threw her arms around Patrick, calling him "my jewel" and saying that she dare not go back to the nuns with such a proposition. "Make it a year in four!" she begged.

The future saint had rather enjoyed her embrace and promised that, for another of those "squeezes", he would accede to her request. Moreover, he undertook to make it not only every fourth year but the longest at that — the leap year.

The agreement took effect at once. St. Bridget was not slow to take advantage of it for herself and immediately proposed to Patrick. Having taken a vow of celibacy, he could not help but refuse. However, to soften the blow, he gave her a kiss and a silken gown as a consolation gift.

From this legend came the custom, observed until recent years, of acknowledging the right of a rejected woman to claim as compensation a new dress of pure silk.

THE BEST MAN

The Best Man has always been the bridegroom's best friend, but for different reasons. Originally, his duties were neither pleasant nor particularly safe.

At the beginning of history a bridegroom's Best Man had to excel in many qualities which are now completely unnecessary and even forgotten. Then he was chosen for being strong, brave and a good fighter. He accompanied his friend as an armed escort to help him in capturing a bride! No wonder, therefore, that he was called the *best* man. For such a purpose only the best was good enough.

In some parts of the world warriors considered it undignified to woo a woman themselves. They let others do the job for them. When all was ready for the marriage they set out with their companions — to wrest the bride from her original groom. That is why the actual wooer surrounded himself with an armed guard, his "best men". They were there to repel any attacks and defend the goods, so richly deserved and already paid for.

Times changed. Men no longer captured their brides, either from their homes or their rightful "owners". And yet, on the day of the actual wedding, they needed extra protection and support. There still was the danger of a rival who, at the last moment, might carry off the bride. To avoid this the Best Man was in attendance, armed and on the alert.

It was for this reason, too, that Scandinavians used to hold their weddings under the cover of night. Behind the High Altar of one of the Swedish churches, so it was said, were kept lances with sockets for torches. These served the Best Men in their hazardous task, as weapons and sources of illumination, to detect and repel possible abductors.

At first, as is only logical, the Best Man accompanied not the groom but the bride, whom obviously he was there to guard and retain. Only when rough times increased vulgarity on the part of the men, and brides seemed even less safe under their protection, a separation of sexes proved advisable. From then onward the Best Man was always near the groom, whilst bridesmaids closed their ranks around the bride.

BRIDE ON LEFT SIDE OF GROOM

Procedure at a wedding follows definite rules. Its processions and paraphernalia are therefore carefully studied and rehearsed by all parties concerned.

The bride and groom stand and walk together in a way that is traditional. At the altar, the bride takes her place at the left hand of the groom. After the ceremony, her husband places her hand within his left arm to follow the clergyman into the vestry to sign the register. Finally, on the way out, the bride passes down the aisle, once again on the *left* arm of the bridegroom.

That on each of these three occasions the groom offers his left arm and hand to the bride is not just a matter of meaningless etiquette. It is the result of ancient and most anxious considerations. Once, he did so purposely and not merely because it was "the right thing" to do. He placed her on his left not to honour but to secure her. It enabled him to keep his right (and sword) hand free: to be ready to defend her (and himself) from attack and capture by jealous rivals.

THE BRIDE'S VEIL

A complexity of old traditions, fears and obsolete social conditions are interwoven in the bridal veil.

The bridal veil is also a relic of the early custom of capturing a wife. Naturally the newly acquired "goods" were safely wrapped up before being taken away. What now consists of a thin lace or net covering was once a large sheet big enough to envelop the body.

As the times grew more polite, the veil began to assume more subtle and psychological meanings. It indicated a woman's original complete submission to her husband. She should not even be seen. Hidden goods tend to appear more precious and attractive than those openly on display. That is why in ancient times (and still today in some primitive groups) the bridegroom was not permitted to set eyes on his bride until the very moment when they were about to consummate their marriage.

The veil used to express also humility on the part of the bride. It certainly retains the ancient biblical tradition of Rebecca who, when she first met Isaac, her future husband, shyly "took a veil and covered herself with it".

Man is most superstitious at moments when great happiness is about to be his. Fear of jealous demons who might carry off a lovely bride led to the custom of disguising her identity — and hiding her face behind a "curtain". This was also thought to be effective against the "evil eye", once considered to be an ubiquitous and potent malevolent force.

It is for that reason, too, that Moroccan brides are expected to shut their eyes throughout the wedding ceremony and that in Korea they used to cover their faces with the wide sleeves of their garments. This same fear made couples in primitive societies wear specially dirty clothes just before their nuptials — a disguise to foil evil spirits.

Yet another interpretation points to the use of a veil not only at weddings but on all occasions when a person assumed a new identity. Thus initiates into religious communities are veiled, and even the dead as they, too, enter a totally new group of associates.

The bride, likewise, by the fact of man and woman becoming "one flesh", was considered to change completely her personality. The veil "shut out" magically her old former being. She was now to be a new person altogether — "for better or worse".

Finally, the veil might be the last relic of the "care-cloth", as it was called among Anglo-Saxons. This enveloped both bride and groom. Aware and afraid of higher powers, the couple thus acknowledged their presence and, even more so, tried to protect themselves from them.

ORANGE BLOSSOMS

Flowers have expressed, without words, many a significant message, not the least on behalf of a bride on her wedding day.

The orange blossoms that traditionally adorn her were originally not merely a decoration. They were used to tell — in silent language — facts and hopes which it would be too difficult and embarrassing to voice in so many spoken words.

The white blossoms were, first of all, a symbol of innocence and purity. They were worn to announce publicly that the bride was a virgin. But then, as few trees bear greater crops, the orange blossoms were meant to express equally the fervent prayer for future fruitfulness on the part of the bride as well. Even more so, they tried magically to ensure the realization of this wish.

Only on rare occasions does life bestow on man all he desires. Mostly it is a question of one thing or the other. Various qualities are thus distributed among different individuals, and only in the most fortunate cases combined in one person.

In former days a man hoped to wed a wife who was not only beautiful in both looks and character but, at the same time, prolific, the future mother of many children.

The orange tree, an evergreen, was one of the few plants which produced both fruit and flower simultaneously. Therefore its blossoms could most suitably voice the hope and wish that the bride, too, far from being merely "a worthless flower of beauty", would be blessed with the two virtues of the orange tree.

Orange trees are a common sight in countries of a warm climate. But in Northern Europe they were known as something exotic. They were rare and costly. Hence only the rich could afford to import them. For this reason their blossoms were chosen to adorn brides from the wealthy and noble classes. Consequently they became a symbol of high rank.

To imitate the rich has always been the desire of those less fortunate. They were anxious to do so especially on their wedding day, when only the best was good enough. That is how all the brides, no matter at what cost, began to adorn themselves exquisitely with the rich and noble men's orange blossoms.

In England, the custom is of a comparatively recent date. It was introduced from France about 1820. The French had adopted it from the Spaniards who many centuries earlier, so tradition says, received their first orange trees from the Moors.

A beautiful legend tells the story of the origin of the custom and associates it with a poor Spanish girl. Soon after the trees had been introduced into Spain, the then reigning monarch planted them in his palace garden.

There was especially one tree he treasured most. The French ambassador often expressed the wish to obtain an offshoot for himself. But, possibly jealous of his possession, the king refused.

His gardener's daughter knew all about this. She was in desperate need of a dowry to marry the man she loved. Her father was too poor to give it. Secretly, the girl cut a slip from the prized tree and sold it to the ambassador at a high price.

On the day of her wedding she felt that, somehow, she had to acknowledge her debt to the tree to which, after all, she owed her happiness. For that purpose she took some of its blossoms and put them into her hair. Thus she inaugurated the fashion which became universal.

Though the custom's origins, as a symbol of virginity and a magical aphrodisiac, were crude and selfish, this story lends it the romance and beauty it so much deserves. It interprets the orange blossoms as an expression of exuberant joy and deep gratitude.

THE WEDDING RING

The ring, now an essential for the wedding ceremony, is just over 1000 years old. It was adopted by the Christian Church in the 9th century, from the pagan world. Its origin leads back to ancient superstition, to magic, and the kidnapping of one's wife. Its shape was both utilitarian — best adapted to secure a precious property — and symbolic. In the Egyptian hieroglyphic script the circle represented eternity and marriage was seen as a permanent bond.

The ring originated in the East, whence it was copied by the ancient Greeks. Then it was taken over from them, like so many other customs and traditions, by the Romans. Finally, it was introduced all over the world. Now a small ring worn around a finger, it developed from huge bands that circled the wrist, the ankles, or even the waist.

Primitive man believed in magic. He bound a rope around the woman he chose for himself, being convinced that this "magic circle" would fetter her to him and cause his spirit to enter her body. Thus she was tied to him by supernatural forces which could never be broken.

Yet another primitive belief saw in the ring an amulet that would ward off evil spirits hovering around the bride to threaten her marital bliss.

The early custom to capture one's wife survives in many a legend. The ring thus also leads back to that primitive beginning of matrimony, when the man bound fetters around the wrists and ankles of the woman he carried away to become his property and servant.

Actually the wedding ring developed from the engagement ring. It was an earnest of future intentions and, therefore, it is also closely connected with the purchase of women, once prevalent and still remembered by the dowry, given to or for the bride.

The ring, bestowed in this manner, was an old Roman custom confirming betrothal. It was a commercial pledge that the contract would be carried out. In modern terminology the ring served as the first instalment of a lay-by plan. From the moment this had been paid, the ring, conspicuously displayed, told all other men that this woman was no longer "for sale".

Among the Jewish people the ring was first introduced in the 8th century A.D.. It replaced the custom of handing the bride a small coin as a promissory "note" of the husband's ability to meet all future financial obligations toward his wife.

The ring's very shape was not ornamental in purpose, but a practical means to enable the woman not to lose (or lose sight of) that precious token.

From early antiquity onward, as excavations and biblical

records testify, rings had a signet. This provided a seal with which orders were signed. To hand such a ring to another person symbolized, and actually carried out, a transfer of authority. That is why Pharaoh took off his ring and handed it to Joseph, so that "You shall be over my house and according to your word shall all my people be ruled".

To hand one's wife the signet ring implied, likewise, that she had come to share all responsibilities and had been admitted as an equal partner in the management of the home. Its circular shape indicated the lasting character of the contract.

It was only Pope Nicholas who — in 800 A.D. — first distinctly referred to the Christian use of the ring. Once adopted by the Church, it came to represent not merely a commercial trans-action but a token and pledge of fidelity, a sacred covenant. Its shape now signified "the eternity, constancy and integrity of love". It was there perpetually to remind the wife and others of the sanctity of wedlock. As the circle symbolizes harmony and perfection, and its lines are endless, so the ring was now fit to indicate the continuity of the sacred bond and to remind the couple that their mutual love and affection should flow from one to the other in a circle, continually and forever.

Psychoanalysis, with its early sexual interpretations of almost every aspect of life, saw in the finger a representation of the male and in the ring of the female which — at marriage — were joined together.

THE RING FINGER

The choice of the ring finger is of unquestionable pagan origin. It is due to a combination of varied causes. These include, apart from a little romance, an error in anatomical knowledge, a sur-vival of woman's inequality, the dogma of trinity and a safety measure — in more senses than one.

That the woman's left hand became the proud wearer of the matrimonial sign and symbol is the result of a humiliating tradi-tion. It retains the assumption that the man is the master — the "right hand" of the family — and the woman his slave. The "right hand" always stood for power and authority, while the left hand expressed submission and serfdom.

Ancient Greek and Roman anatomists wrongly believed that a vein or nerve led straight from the heart to the third finger. This gave rise to its ancient description as the "medicated" or "healing" finger. Doctors, when preparing drugs, used it to stir their mixtures as, so they imagined, the presence of any noxious ingredient immediately would be made known to them in their heart by means of this direct line.

No wonder, therefore, that this finger, too, was selected to wear the ring attached to matters of the heart. When, later on, the absurdity of this view was discovered, other additional considerations kept the ring in its place.

Completely utilitarian was the explanation that the third finger was the least active of the whole hand. Used so sparingly, it was easily available and accommodating for the purpose of matrimony. The ring placed there, indeed, inconvenienced its wearer least, and there was less likelihood of its being worn out or damaged.

The third finger was the most prominent of all the hand. A ring put on it was always in view and could not be hidden. Conspicuously it announced to all the engagement.

An even more practical consideration certainly contributed, if not to the choice, to the retention of the ring finger. Whereas every other finger can be stretched independently, the third one cannot be extended to its full length on its own. To do so the co-operation of the rest of the hand is needed. This was a good safety measure as the ring thus cannot easily slip off this finger, which is usually slightly bent. By its lack of independent action, therefore, the third finger was almost preselected for such a precious object.

Nowadays at the marriage ceremony, the bridegroom puts the ring immediately in its proper place. But that was not always so. In the ancient ritual of the Church (still practised in the 16th century) the pronouncing of the Trinitarian formula was accompanied by a systematic moving of the ring from the thumb to the third finger.

The bridegroom first placed the ring on the top of the thumb with the words: "In the name of the Father". Then, saying: "In the name of the Son", he moved it to the forefinger and then to the middle finger, adding the words: "and of the Holy Spirit".

Finally he left it — as we continue to do — on the third finger, with the closing word "Amen", which sealed the marriage bond.

THROWING OF CONFETTI

The word "confetti" comes from the Italian, being of the same root as the word "confectionery". It refers to "sweet meats" — a recollection of the time when nuts and sugared almonds were thrown over the bride and groom.

This custom in turn derived from the ancient pagan rite of showering the happy couple with grain. Most of the wedding ritual was designed to *ex*pel evil. But in this case at least the intention was to *im*pel bliss. The missiles of grain or rice were a standard feature of pagan marriage. Their purpose was not just symbolically to express wishes for a fruitful union. It was believed the fertility of the seeds would be magically transferred to the pair on whom they fell.

Confetti is the inexpensive paper-substitute for the rice, wheat or nuts originally thrown on the newly-weds. It is strange to imagine that our age, which has become so proficient in birth control, still enthusiastically applies — in its paper version — the ancient magic of birth promotion! A generation so conscious of the use of contraceptives showers the couple with confetti, the original purpose of which was the exact opposite — the boosting of fertility.

THROWING OF OLD SHOE

In our days the throwing of a shoe, or the tying of it to a carriage, is restricted to wedding celebrations — when a bridal couple is about to go away on the honeymoon. It expresses people's wish for good luck to the newly-weds. Not so long ago, however, people threw shoes after anybody starting on a trip. Ben Jonson could thus say:

> Hurl after me an old shoe
> I'll be merry whatever I'll do.

Who would guess that such a simple custom as throwing a shoe contains a wealth of meaning, good and bad? It was observed as a magic means of ensuring plenty of children and lots of luck. The shoe is an ancient symbol of fertility. Eskimo women, for instance, used to carry a piece of an old shoe to make themselves prolific. At some time shoes were part of a man's wages and greatly esteemed as such for the same reason.

The choice of an old shoe for throwing was not a matter of economics. On the contrary it was a most thoughtful selection. People believed that a man's soul lived in his shoes. These preserved the essence of the life of the person that wore them. Therefore, to throw them, or just one of them, after a bridal couple or, better still, to tie them to their carriage, gave to those embarking on a new life all the additional good luck and experience of the shoes' former owners. Indeed, it was not only the cheapest but the most precious of all gifts.

For thousands of years slippers and shoes have also served as an emblem of power and possession. To cast one's sandal on a piece of land, actually meant to take possession of it. Holy Scripture itself supplies an example when it makes God say that "Over Edom itself I cast My shoes". Still prevalent in various languages is a phrase that speaks of having a person "under one's slipper" or "under one's heel", meaning that one dominates him.

In case of a sale or the transfer of property, the former holder would take one of his sandals or shoes and give it to the new owner. The shoe was the ancient equivalent of the modern title deed to goods or property. The ceremony was therefore a legal procedure, not restricted to marital occasions alone.

In antiquity a wife was considered a man's chattel. Her parents sold her to her future husband and the transaction was confirmed in the then customary way of a business deal, in which a sandal was given as a token of good faith and of the transfer of property. By throwing shoes after the bride, parents indicated — in the presence of witnesses — that they had relinquished all rights of dominion over their daughter who now legally belonged to her new master.

Yet another explanation links the custom with the ancient institution of capturing one's bride. In this case the throwing of shoes is a last remnant of the old (but later merely mock) battle between the bride's family, anxious to retain the girl, and the bridegroom's party, set on abducting her.

There are two further interpretations. Throughout marriage, the wife formerly had to present shoes to her husband. She thereby re-affirmed symbolically her inferior position and his lordship. To help build up a stock of shoes, friends tossed some on the day of the wedding.

It has also been suggested that not men but unmarried women were the original shoe-throwers; out of happiness and in self-congratulations. The shoe was the symbol of women's serfdom to men. But they had — so far — escaped from that fate and preserved their liberty. Happy for themselves, but sorry for the bride, they cast shoes after her as she was being carried off as a slave.

THE WEDDING CAKE

Even the wedding cake has its history and its present sugar-coating, like the veil, covers up quite an exciting past. It first appeared among the Romans, where it was used only at the nuptials of the upper class, the Patricians. It was part of a ceremony known as the *confarreatio*, meaning "eating together".

First, the bride and groom shared a small part of the cake, which was a sort of unleavened scone made of flour, salt and water. This was thought to secure for them a life of plenty, in both children and happiness.

Then the cake was broken over the bride's head and the guests scrambled for the fragments, believing that they, too, would share in the blessings these symbolized.

Only children born of a marriage solemnized in this fashion, with a cake and in front of ten witnesses, qualified for the high sacred offices in Roman life. The cake thus provided not only the guests with some tasty morsels of food (and a little extra luck) and the couple — magically — with future fertility, but even their still unborn children — legally — with opportunities for advancement!

The wedding cake rites, with the food symbolizing fertility, were followed all over the world, with local variations and developments. American Indians used the simple, scone-type cake, which the bride herself had to bake and present to her groom. The early Anglo-Saxons supplied at a wedding a huge basket of small, dry biscuits. Each guest took one and any remaining were distributed among the poor. Later on, guests began bringing their own cakes. These were often spiced buns, which were piled into an enormous heap. If the bride and groom were able to kiss each other over the mound, it was considered a good omen for their life-long happiness.

Eventually, around the time of King Charles II, the many buns were combined into one big cake. Legend credits the inspiration for this to a French chef visiting Britain. Watching the cumbersome way of piling numerous little cakes on top of one another, he decided it would be more practical to ice the mound of buns into one mass. Out of this grew the tradition of the elaborately decorated, many-tiered wedding cake of today.

CARRYING THE BRIDE OVER THE THRESHOLD

The custom of carrying the bride across the threshold has been found among the ancient Romans, the Redskins of Canada, the Chinese and the Abyssinians.

Several reasons could account for it. All of them date back to a superstitious past or do not reflect favourably on the beginnings of matrimony. This custom, too, might be a recollection of the days when wives were captured. They did not come willingly but had to be taken by force into the man's house.

Psychologists may even think that it is a wise and not-so-romantic way to make the woman realize who runs the house and who determines where to go. On the other hand, it is a common experience that even a sham opposition creates greater desire, and perhaps the bride loved to appear as if she entered the new home under compulsion.

A superstition, dating back to almost prehistoric times, makes people afraid of stumbling. It was thought to be a sign of ill luck, especially if you fell over your own doorstep. To avoid any possibility of such an ominous accident, that might doom the marriage from its very beginning, the cautious bridegroom carried his bride across.

In ancient Rome the threshold was sacred to Vesta, the virgin goddess. Therefore, it was considered not merely bad taste, but sacrilegious, for a woman, who was about to leave her maiden status, to touch the threshold.

Indeed an ancient belief in the sanctity and evil properties of the threshold may account most of all for the custom. People assumed that demons dwelt there and to avoid touching it they jumped over it. To propitiate those evil forces, they buried still-born babies under the door or smeared blood on its lintels. To save his wife from any possible contact with the demons lurking under the doorstep the young husband carried her across.

THE HONEYMOON

There are several opinions as to the origin of the honeymoon. Its true meaning depends on whether we take it very literally or merely as a beautiful picture.

The moon gave birth — on the loom of language — to the "month". In ancient days (and still today among Arabs and Jews) the duration of a month coincided with the period of revolution of the moon. You had only to look at the moon to ascertain the approximate date. A new moon always signified the first day of the new month. Hence the honeymoon was the first month of marriage, when all was sweet.

Other lunar observations turned away from the sunny side of the moon — and life — and noted their ever-changing character. The moon never appears the same. It is always different. According to this dismal way of thought the honeymoon refers not so much to the period of one month as to the eventual waning of love, after the first white heat of passion. Indeed, not a few misanthropes explained that the honey was bound to change — like the moon — but to water and gall . . .

> But of all the lunar things that change,
> The one that shows most fickle and strange,
> And takes the most eccentric range,
> Is the moon — so called — of honey.
> *Thomas Hood*

However, the most likely origin of the phrase is an old Scandinavian, and generally Northern European custom, of drinking honeyed wine or other kinds of diluted and fermented honey as an aphrodisiac during the first month of marriage.

THE HELPMATE

When we speak of a helpmate, we really should pronounce and spell it help-meet because that is its original spelling and mean-

ing — man's most *suitable* companion, meeting all his requirements, to *assist* him in life.

It all started with the creation of woman herself. We owe
helpmate to the second chapter of Genesis and to a later, rather
confusing, English translation of the original Hebrew text.

At first, man was all alone. But soon God realized that solitude
was not good for him. Man was meant to be a social being. So
God decided to revise His creation and to give man a companion
to share his life and help him in his work.

According to the biblical story, man had been formed out of
the dust of the earth and it seemed appropriate to use the same
material in the creation of his mate. Thus God moulded, equally
out of the clay, the animals and the birds and then brought them,
one by one, to man, hoping that he would find among their
number some creature fit to share his life.

But the experiment failed. Man took no fancy to any of them.
God saw that someone different was needed. To be made out
of the same clay, obviously, was insufficient. Man's companion
must be of his own flesh and blood, as it were, part of himself.
And that is how God, in His solicitous search for the right mate,
succeeded. He made woman from one of man's ribs. The very
intimacy of relationship is expressed even in the choice of the
name of wo*man* which still, literally, contains man as part of
itself.

The passage which explains God's intention to find the right
type of companion for man was also responsible for the creation
of the word helpmate. The actual Hebrew term is most difficult
to translate. It speaks of woman as a help who acts as man's
"opposite", someone to be "at his side" and hence a being both
similar and supplementary.

Even words have a life of their own. Most of them live, as it
were, forever. But others suddenly, and for no known reason,
die and are forgotten. Only the dictionary may continue to list
them with the telling remark that they are "archaic" and hence
obsolete.

In a few cases, however, such dead words survive; not in
everyday speech, of course, but in the time-honoured text of
documents, proclamations and sacred writings. The fact that they
once found their way into a greatly revered and guarded text,

preserved them long after they had lost their meaning and use-fulness. Unfortunately, many people coming across such words cannot make them out. Consequently they not only mispronounce them, which would not matter so much, but try to guess their meaning with often erroneous results.

That is exactly what took place in the case of the word *meet*. During the reign of King James I it was commonly used as a synonym for *suitable*. Therefore anyone, who at that time wanted to say that anything was fit, employed this expression.

When, at the king's authorization, a group of scholars prepared a "modern" English translation of the Books of the Bible, they encountered great difficulty in rendering correctly and in the idiom of their own time, certain Hebrew terms. Among them was the passage which referred to God's creation of Eve as Adam's companion.

The scholars rejected an earlier translation by Wycliffe which made God say: "Make We to hym help like hym". Neither did they favour Miles Coverdale's choice of words in his version of 1535, describing Eve as "an helpe, to beare him company". Adopting the then current word *meet* (for suitable), they rendered the passage as saying: "I (God) will make him (Adam) an helpe meet (suitable) for him".

By the time this new "Authorized Version" of the Bible was published — in 1611 — people had stopped using "meet" in the sense of suitable. But as it was now part of the new English Bible, which had been given official status throughout the English-speaking Protestant Churches, people were reluctant to replace it, even by a word that would make sense and be intelligible to the average person. Thus, for hundreds of years, the Bible went on printing a text that was incomprehensible and perplexing. Those who read the word and could not make it out eventually imagined that somehow it must be a special term for a wife.

In 1673 Dryden tried to improve matters by using a hyphen, rendering the obsolete term as *help-meet*. Later generations, still in search of a meaning yet more puzzled than ever, again dropped the hyphen and fused the two words into one — the *helpmeet*. The stage was set for just one more change: less than another 50 years later, *helpmeet* became *helpmate*, with a new meaning as well as spelling. It is a word born of misunderstanding and former generations' reluctance to bring even words up-to-date.

THE MARRIAGE CERTIFICATE

Originally the usual form of contracting a marriage was the simplest. The mere act of cohabitation made a man and a woman husband and wife. With the refinement of taste, the growth of moral consciousness and the development of a sense of social responsibility, this type of union came to be considered legally insufficient and shameful.

At first a woman counted for nothing. She was captured or purchased as a mere chattel and became her husband's property. The price widely differed, depending on supply and demand, on the girl's qualities (again assessed differently according to tribe), her age and her family's status in the community.

Central Africa's Nandi tribes, for instance, considered six cows a fair price for a good wife, 14 years old. Most expensive among African Bantus was a girl who was already an unmarried mother, as she had proved that she was able to bear children.

The purchase-price led to the certificate. This is not mentioned in the Bible. Its antiquity is shown by the discovery of a document of this type, possibly the earliest "marriage certificate" in existence. It was found among Aramaic papyri, relics of a Jewish garrison stationed at Elephantine in Egypt in the 5th century B.C. .

The Book of Tobit, which is part of the Apocrypha and was written in the 3rd century B.C., explicitly tells how on the marriage of his son Tobias to Sarah, the father-in-law "took a book and wrote an instrument and sealed it". Though what it contained is unknown and left to our imagination.

The certificate had become a regular document among Jewish people well before Christian days. Its text was influenced by pagan marriage contracts of similar nature, some of which, dating back to that early period, are still preserved. In them the husband agreed to give his wife all the food, clothes and amenities she needed, and the wife, on her part, pledged to conduct herself blamelessly.

The marriage certificate was officially introduced among the

Hebrews in the 1st century of our era. Jewish religious law then stipulated that a marriage without the contract having been drawn up was not properly consummated.

This was not a mere formality or the result of ecclesiastical bureaucracy, but due to important considerations. These took into account that a woman was still without rights of her own and completely at the mercy of her husband, who could disown or dismiss her on the slightest pretext. To safeguard her for all eventualities and to give her a more secure status, the new kind of marriage certificate was demanded.

Its dual purpose was clear. First, it defined the husband's duties toward his spouse, giving a promise to honour her, work for her, maintain her and honestly provide her with everything necessary for her comfort. But as its most significant part, it provided for his wife, should he divorce or predecease her.

The terms laid down in the certificate made any husband think twice before sending away his spouse as, ridding himself of a companion he no longer desired, he also had to surrender a considerable part of his fortune! Likewise, the document guarded a widow against greedy heirs who might try to deprive her of sustenance.

The original marriage certificate was thus most realistic. Though presented at the couple's very pinnacle of happiness, it lacked all romance. At the moment of marriage, it was concerned with the possibilities of an untimely end to the relationship by death of the man or divorce.

Its text was rigid, following prototypes of Roman law. First of all, it had to detail date and place of marriage. If this was celebrated in a small village, it was essential to add the nearest town and any river on which it was situated.

The partners' names followed and, as at the time surnames were unknown, bride and groom were carefully identified. Next came the statement that the man had actually sued for the bride's hand and pronounced the traditional formula that she should "be consecrated unto him according to the Law of Moses and Israel" and that she, in turn, had accepted him.

Final clauses specified the dowry received and provisions in case of divorce or the husband's passing. They further guaranteed the bride maintenance, cohabitation and burial!

The writing of the certificate was the groom's responsibility. It had to be read out publicly at the wedding. Two men, unrelated to each other or either of the partners, had to witness and duly sign it. No signature was required from bride or groom.

The wife was expected to keep the document in safe custody for future reference, should that unfortunate necessity arise. In case of loss, she could demand a new copy. She could still collect the moneys promised 25 years after her husband's death or divorce, even in the case of her own remarriage.

The Christian Church early adopted and adapted its text, adding an obligation on the wife to "love, cherish and honour" her husband, who on his part had to do all that a free-born wife expected from a worthy husband.

Yet from the 6th century onward its use among Christians lapsed, except in the case of marriages between persons of high rank. The Jews — always conservative in their habits — still, even after 2000 years, use almost the identical form of the ancient marriage certificate.

As if to compensate for the legal and dry nature of the document, people began to ornament it. They added, apart from the portrait of bride and groom, all kinds of artistic creations, including nude figures representing Adam and Eve in Paradise.

BILL OF DIVORCE

Divorce among primitive and pagan people was free and easy, lacking any kind of documentation. It was devoid of all formalities and purely a private matter, with which tribal and "state" authorities were unconcerned.

In Tonga, for instance, a man divorced his wife by just telling her to go. Arabs did not leave the actual choice of words for her dismissal to private initiative. But the formula they prescribed was so simple that no husband could err. It consisted of only one word, to be repeated three times: *ittalak*. Its meaning amounted to the wish that she should "go to the devil". Eskimos merely moved into another igloo. Altogether, there was at first no necessity of explaining or giving reasons.

Anglo-Saxons, on the other hand, demanded grounds for divorce. But it was not too difficult for a husband to find an excuse. He had the right to dismiss his wife for good and all if she was barren, passionate, luxurious, rude, habitually drunk, quarrelsome or abusive.

Early Romans considered a spouse's dislike of his partner reason enough to terminate their union. Later Roman law continued to view divorce, just like marriage, as a private affair between two parties. All that had to be done was for the one spouse to send a letter to the other, through a messenger or in the presence of seven witnesses. This private "writ" had both to express the intention to terminate the marriage and to state that in future the other may keep his or her own property. A judicial inquiry took place only when the parties disagreed regarding the future of their children or the division of their assets.

Not so with the Hebrews. Certainly, they permitted divorce. But a merely private or oral declaration, however formal, was insufficient. A written official statement was essential for them.

The Bible itself mentions the writing of a Bill of Divorcement, which is all the more surprising as it does not do so regarding a marriage certificate. A husband who wished to dismiss his wife had to place the document into her hands. We are not told its actual text. Since those early biblical days, a divorce certificate has become an established condition. Still, no public trial was then necessary. The sole formality consisted of the presentation of the "bill" to the wife, who had to accept it.

Post-biblical Jewish ecclesiastical authorities soon felt the need to make divorce proceedings more difficult and to lay down the precise wording of the writ. They issued minute instructions on procedure and the writing of the bill.

Divorce could take place only before a Court of three Judges and in the presence of two witnesses. The document had to be written by an expert-scribe during the Court session. The names of the parties as well as the place where the Court met had to be identified beyond any possibility of mistake. The bill had to be written legibly and could not be corrected. Any mistake made necessitated the destruction of the copy and the writing of a new one.

Once the document had been drawn up, the two witnesses had to examine and then to sign it. No signature of either divorcee was demanded.

With the bill thus having been duly read and attested, the chairman of the Court presented it to the husband who, in presence of witness, had to place it into the hands of his wife. Simultaneously, he had to repeat the traditional divorce formula: "Here is your Bill of Divorcement. Take it. From now onward be divorced from me and free to marry any man".

However, the wife did not keep the document. She had to return it to the Judge in charge of the case who retained it but, first of all, tore it partly across, lest it be used again for fraudulent purposes.

This earliest divorce decree — still used among Orthodox Jewish people — thus read:

"On the .... day of the week, the .... day of the month ....
in the year .... in the city of .... situated on the river ....
I .... the son of .... with the surname of .... who today
am resident at .... do hereby consent of my free will and
without any restraint, to release, set free and put away my
wife .... who at present resides at ....

"Up to this moment you have been my wife. But now you
are released, set free and put away, so that you may be your
own mistress, and may marry any man you may desire. No
one may hinder you from doing this, as from this day forth
you are free to marry any man.

"Thus you received from me this Bill of Divorcement, a
document of release, a Bill of freedom according to the
Law of Moses and Israel."

CHAPTER IV

δeath anδ mourning

LIFE is a continuous progress toward death. The latest drug
may extend man's life-span by many years, but it cannot remove
the inevitability of his passing. Thus, Victor Hugo could comfort
the condemned criminal, standing in the shadow of the guillotine,
by saying that "all men are condemned to death — only the date
of execution is uncertain".

The mystery of death puzzled and haunted the primitive
savage as much as modern man. Was death merely a portal to
a further existence, a gate through which man had to pass, or
complete extinction?

Mourning is a universal reaction to death, but the way we
express our grief varies widely. Likewise, several factors account
for man's sorrow which is not just, as we believe, the result of
piety and loving remembrance of the departed.

There are psychological reasons. These include an unconscious
but healthy desire to externalize sorrow which otherwise might
cause serious harm to the bereaved.

People are sorry for themselves. They have lost a companion
and are all the poorer for it. Ashamed to admit that it is for
their own selves and their loneliness that they mourn, they
rationalize their grief.

Many of our present mourning customs, however, are a legacy
of obsolete fears of the dead and of their power to haunt and
harass the living.

TO KICK THE BUCKET

The term "to kick the bucket", as a description of man's passing from this world into the next, might seem on the surface to be mere slang. But it has, in fact, an interesting history.

The ancient Egyptians used the bucket not only in the construction of their pyramids but equally in the symbolism of their faith. It became the sign of death. Hieroglyphic script employed it as the representation of a body without life.

To kick, in this context, had nothing whatsoever to do with our modern "striking out with the foot". It is an ancient Egyptian word that, as if it were mummified, has survived in our modern way of speaking. It is the Egyptian *khekh,* meaning to "return", to "send back".

Therefore, to "kick the bucket" really means to send back and return the empty bucket — a lifeless body.

Another interpretation of the phrase dates back to the late 16th century and to British farm life. Farmers usually killed their own cattle and pigs, using a heavy three-legged contraption with a pulley in the centre. The animal's legs were tied to a wooden beam which was hoisted by a rope. As this reminded the farmer of pulling a bucket from a well, it was not long before the beam itself was called a bucket.

Often, as the animal was being lifted, its feet were thrown against the beam or bucket. This gave the impression that it was kicking it. But as in reality by that stage the beast had become a carcass, the phrase "to kick the bucket" assumed a deadly significance.

A third derivation of the term comes from the act of suicide. A common form of killing oneself was always by hanging; in former times men frequently stood on a bucket to adjust the noose around their necks. When they were ready to die, they kicked the bucket (away). Soon the description of this suicidal method was adopted for any kind of dying, no matter who cut the thread of life.

TO GO WEST

The saying "he has gone west" became especially popular during World War I. However, the origin of the phrase goes back to most ancient days. Its obvious reference is to the setting sun, which "goes west" to expire there.

There are various other claims as to the origin of the saying. The Egyptians of old considered the West as the home of departed spirits. Thus, mourners standing on the banks of the Nile, as if to speed and guide the dead in the right direction, used to call out to them: "To the West . . .".

Another suggestion links the phrase with early American history. First, so it is told, the Red Indians used it. They said that a man who had died had "gone west" to meet the setting sun.

Then, in later years, bitter experience of the white pioneers gave the phrase a tragic meaning. Prospectors, advancing westward beyond the Mississippi, often failed to return because Indians, anxious to keep their territory for themselves, had murdered them. Thus, to the friends of anyone who was reported missing, the words "gone west" soon became synonymous with his having lost his life out there.

According to an English claim, the phrase was first introduced in London in totally different circumstances. It was used by criminals who went on their last trip — to the gallows. West was the actual direction of their final journey.

Newgate Prison, built in the 13th century, was situated near the New (western) Gate in the wall surrounding the City of London. Just outside that gate, at the site of the present Marble Arch, was the famous Tyburn Tree, London's execution place for 600 years.

Men and women sentenced to death accordingly were led out of the prison to the gallows, due West. Hence to "go west" assumed its lethal meaning. Somehow the term became so general that by the year 1592 it was applied to all who had died and it lost completely its ignominious significance.

STOPPING OF CLOCKS AT DEATH

Clocks and watches have been linked closely with human life and its vanishing hours. No wonder, therefore, that they have stirred man's imagination for centuries and given rise to many a fallacy and superstition.

Some people claimed that the "electricity" of their body made it impossible for them to carry or wear a watch. Others refused to turn back its hands because they thought — wrongly, except in the case of striking clocks — that this would damage its works.

The superstition that some clocks stopped at the moment of their owner's death is deep-rooted. It sounds so sentimental and, as it were, assumes that even a clock can feel or, among the more primitive-minded, that it was regulated not just by an intricate mechanism but by sympathetic magic. Several factors and considerations — apart from "magical" agencies — account for the belief.

First of all, though exceedingly rare, there is always the possibility of a mere coincidence. It might just have happened that, accidentally, a clock stopped at the hour of death. And who could blame people, already emotionally upset, for regarding sole chance as a matter of cause and effect? They would tell the story to others, and tales of that kind are always easily spread and accepted as accurate by those susceptible to the mysterious.

A more feasible theory relates the superstition to facts. Once a clock was a rare and precious possession. Hence its owner — who was always the head of the house — treasured it and it was his jealously guarded privilege to perform — like a solemn regular rite — its winding up.

It was only natural that at his death his family was confused and harassed and forgot all about the clock and its needs. But even if they did remember the necessity of winding it up, they still refrained from doing so. They were reluctant to undertake — at least immediately — a task so long reserved for the head of the house. Otherwise it might appear that he was not being missed and that his passing had not really upset the smooth running of the home. With its works run down, the clock inevitably stopped.

Visitors could not help but notice that in the house of mourning time was standing still. They did not draw the obvious conclusion that this was due to natural causes. Gullible, ignorant and in awe of the dead, they saw in the stoppage a supernatural phenomenon. They further assumed, and later asserted, that the occurrence had actually coincided with the exact moment of death.

In many places it was believed that a clock must be stopped

at the hour of death or bad luck would stay in the home. The
gesture was prompted by deference to the dead and a wish to
express symbolically that, in this home at least, life itself had
come to a stop and the world was at an end.

It was a moving custom. Yet its original purpose was not
concerned with the dead. The clock was stopped not to honour
the deceased but to guard the living. The action told Death to
get out of the house; that, having done his nefarious work, the
time of his rule there was over, and a new era of life was about
to begin.

Man's memory is short and indulges in rationalizations. That is
why the true sequence of events is often forgotten. Possibly
driven by some unconscious urge, people came really to believe
after some time that not they themselves but Death had stopped
the clock!

BLACK FOR MOURNING

To wear black for mourning in Western countries is a custom
that dates back to pagan days. Its origin had nothing to do with
piety or a wish to show grief. On the contrary, it expressed fear.
It arose not out of respect for but dread of the dead.

People put on black as a disguise, so that the ghost of the
deceased might not recognize and then start haunting them. The
same purpose, it is thought, applied to the mark of Cain, which
was put on him after his brother's death, lest he be recognized
by his victim's spirit.

The wearing of black, and sometimes even the veiling of one's
face, was also believed to act as a protection against one's own
death, since it was designed to confuse any demon still hovering
around and bent on snatching more lives. Among some races the
painting of the face white or black was supposed to trick the dead
into the belief that the mourners themselves were ghosts and
not living creatures to be envied.

Indeed, there is no real difference in intention between the
wearing of black and the even more primitive custom of gashing
the flesh and tearing the clothes.

The modern explanation of the use of black for mourning is a
superb example of man's way to spiritualize and rationalize
ancient superstitions. Black is symbolic of the night, and the

absence of colour seemed best suited to express a person's abandonment to grief. The colour of mourning also served as a constant reminder of the loss one had suffered. To the people one met, it indicated one's state of mind, making them in turn considerate, and reminding them to refrain from saying anything that might hurt or offend. The dark colour itself not only reflected the sorrow of the bereaved but created inward tranquility and serenity.

Black has never been the universal colour of mourning. Henry VIII wore white when "mourning" Anne Boleyn, just as many Chinese do. Burmese chose yellow and Turks violet. Ethiopians preferred a greyish-brown and the South Sea Islanders a combination of white and black stripes perhaps to symbolize how joy and grief, darkness and light, are always intermingled in life.

In some parts of China, however, the traditional mourning colour was purple. This influenced American trade in a most unexpected way. When one U.S. manufacturer of chewing gum changed its wrappers from green to purple, its export sales to China dropped alarmingly. It was subsequently discovered that the Chinese believed that the gum was meant to be chewed at funerals only!

THE MOURNING BAND

The wearing of a black band around the left sleeve as a sign of mourning in British countries is now reserved to military forces on the death of a monarch, or at funerals. Once, it was a common expression of grief.

The custom is a survival from the days of chivalry, when the Sovereign Lady used to tie a scarf around the arm of her chosen Knight. She did so to bind him symbolically to serve her. Nothing would make him part with the cloth.

Eventually, a black band became a token of a man's loyalty to the departed, with whom he was linked for ever, even beyond the portals of death. The days of chivalry passed but their insignia of devotion thus remained.

HALF-MAST

The flying of a flag at half-mast is an international sign of mourning. Tradition demands that the flag should first be hoisted to the top of the mast, stay there for a moment, and then be lowered.

The custom had its origin in early naval battles. At first it was possibly not just the defeated vessel's flag which had to be lowered, but its top sail.

The beaten foe had to haul down his flag (halfway) so that the victor's colours could take its place and show his superiority.

It was with this background that in later years the lowered flag became a mark of respect, especially to one of superior station. The practice developed, also, of passing ships dipping the ensign as a gesture of courtesy. The original practical purpose to make room for another flag above was completely forgotten.

That is how, finally and far removed from its first martial context and naval warfare, the flying of a flag at half-mast became a token of respect to the dead, expressing the homage people wished to pay to a worthy departed.

CANDLES AND DEATH

Ingeniously and in every possible way man has tried to defeat his last and greatest enemy — death. With that aim Egyptians first built their majestic pyramids, learned to mummify bodies, and composed the "Book of the Dead", which has been called "Everyman's Guide to Immortality".

Jews and Christians alike believe that burial in consecrated ground helps to ensure resurrection. The washing of the corpses was not entirely a reflection of cleanliness: hygiene even after death. It was based on the superstition that demons and witches had an aversion to water. Therefore, by its application to the bodies of the deceased, they were kept at bay.

The vocabulary associated with death has its own story to tell. A *sarcophagus* originally consisted of a type of stone which, the Greeks believed, consumed the flesh and bones of the dead, with the exception of the teeth, within 40 days. Thus they called the coffins made of stone by the Greek word meaning "flesh-eaters".

A *cenotaph* now is a monument, erected to honour the dead fallen in battle. Its name, too, is derived from the Greek and signifies an "empty tomb". However, originally, a cenotaph was any monument that did not contain actual human remains or marked their final resting-place. It was built in memory of any person whose bones had been lost, or had been buried elsewhere, or who had drowned at sea.

Different people and faiths have chosen their own terminology to describe the special site where they buried the dead. The original Greek *cemetery* described man's "dormitory" or "sleeping place". Germans call it *Friedhof* — a "courtyard of peace". Among Hebrews, the cemetery is known as "the house of eternity".

The undertaker is of recent date. He owes his existence to modern man's dislike of the unpleasant. It was in search of an innocuous title that those concerned with the removal of bodies assumed the name. As it was their task to *undertake* funerals, they chose "undertaker" as their so dignified-sounding description, ignoring the fact that many other and much more pleasant things may be "undertaken". However, today even undertaker has lost its original value as a term of dignity and is being replaced by funeral director and, among Americans, grief therapist.

The burning of candles or lights has been linked with death and the dead from primitive times. They are still used to light a bier and to give special expression to grief.

Catholics light votive candles on All Souls' Day in memory of the faithful departed. Jews burn a lamp for 24 hours every year on the actual anniversary of the death of a loved one. Japanese celebrate the Feast of Lanterns.

A perpetual light burns on Christ's tomb in the Church of the Holy Sepulchre at Jerusalem. When, in the 16th century, the tomb of Tullia, Cicero's daughter, was discovered in the Via Appia outside Rome, it was said that a light had been burning inside it for nearly 1500 years. This was not necessarily an incredible, miraculous tale, but could have been accounted for by a supply of natural gas or oil.

The word *funeral* itself has been derived from the Latin *funus*, meaning "torch". It was believed that torches and lights at a funeral could guide the departed soul to its eternal abode. Lamps, it was considered, aided the dead to find their way through the darkness.

Later times rationalized the flickering light of a candle as a simile of human life and saw in its steady glow a symbol of the soul, itself a spark from the never-dying flame of the divine.

Originally, however, candles, torches and lights near a corpse or grave served a completely different purpose.

Above all, they were a relic from the days when fires were lit around the dead to frighten away supernatural evil beings anxious to reanimate the corpse and take possession of it. Their domain was darkness and they were afraid of light.

The same considerations accounted for the rite of demon-repulsion, practised at the birth of a child. The ancient Romans lit tapers to keep evil spirits away from a woman in labour. For the same reason, Parsees and Hindus burnt fires in the room where a child was born.

As with a new-born child, so too with the departing spirit, the powers of evil were ready to take their toll. But as they could operate only under cover of darkness, a simple light rendered them harmless.

The ghost of the departed itself was believed to be afraid of light and thus, by the burning of candles, was prevented from returning to haunt the survivors.

Another early source of illumination at funerals was the wish of primitive man to provide the dead with the very comforts they had enjoyed in life. Among these was light.

Fear of the dead themselves also was responsible for the use of tapers. The burning flame was to show the deceased that he was well remembered by members of his family and therefore he had no reason to attack them for any forgetfulness. On the contrary, the light, kindled in his honour, should remind him to guard them in reward for their loyalty.

Also it was thought that the dead loved to re-visit their old haunts, especially on certain days, not least the anniversary of their passing. To guide them home and light their way, candles were lit.

THE COFFIN

The English word *coffin* stems from the Greek *kophinos*, meaning a "basket". The ancient Sumerians and Egyptians used to enclose their dead in a structure of plaited twigs which resembled a basket.

From earliest days, a kind of wooden coffin, in its most primitive form, was equally known. It was a tree (often an oak, which

was considered sacred) split into two. One half served as the bed
for the dead and was suitably hollowed. The other half was
used as a lid.

Such early tree-trunk burial had its roots in ancient, pagan
belief. It was linked with the myth that man had grown out of
a tree. More significantly, there was a striking resemblance
between this "tree of the dead" and the dug-out, the primitive
form of canoe. The original coffin was not just a "bed", but a
boat, ready to transport the dead on the last journey across
the waters.

The modern commercialization of death has taken due advantage of the coffin. To be properly "boxed" has become almost a
status symbol and thereby has added further to the cost of dying.
Many people are led to believe that it is the right thing to
enclose their beloved dead in a substantial "casket" (which is the
modern, American-born term, replacing the outlived "coffin").
This has to be of the finest wood, highly polished, with comfortable lining within and precious ornamentation without.

Nevertheless, this is not a recent development either. Hundreds of years ago, a "chested burial" was considered to be an
attribute of the privileged classes alone and, therefore, reserved
for people of wealth and social standing. The poor had to be
satisfied with a coffin only for a short time, as a temporary
place of abode. It conveyed the body from the house of death
to the graveside. There, the corpse was removed and put in the
grave, wrapped only in a shroud. The coffin, aptly described as
a death-hamper, was returned empty, to await further use in
other funerals.

Apart from the social significance of the casket, many other
reasons account for its use. They lead back, through the centuries, to prehistoric times. No doubt, they reflect the various
stages of civilization, religious belief and human attitudes. They
can be divided into two main objects — protection of the corpse
and safeguarding the living.

There is first of all — especially so in more recent times — the
wish to pay due respect and deference to the dead. To preserve
the body from decay as long as possible, it had to be enclosed in
a chest. This protected the corpse against the weather and
microbes in the soil, for a time at least.

But other dangers threatened the body. Wild animals might dig it up. During the early days of anatomy, when religious authorities frowned on the dissection of human remains, corpses were at a premium. Body-snatchers were active but coffins hampered their activities.

The ancient belief in bodily resurrection, which is still observed by the orthodox sections of many faiths, was a contributory reason for using coffins. At the end, all the dead would rise again. Therefore everything possible should be done to keep their bodies in perfect condition. A suitable chest was the first and most obvious means, and the more durable it was, the better it was.

But if we dig deep enough in search of the original coffin, pious considerations for the dead suddenly change into crude self-interest on the part of the living. Indeed, this was the prime motive in its invention.

Survivors were concerned to protect themselves from anything their dearly beloved could do to them, now that he had moved to realms beyond their power. Thus, everything had to be done to prevent a dead person from returning and haunting the living. Frequently, his feet were fettered and sometimes, for the identical reason, even his head was cut off and placed between the legs.

On the way to the graveside, devious means were employed further to bamboozle the dead person, lest he find his way back to his family and former home. He was carried out of the house feet first and, in many communities, not through the usual door but by way of a hole in the wall made for that one occasion and immediately closed up again. Then, the longest and most circuitous route was chosen.

It was for this reason — to keep the dead away — that coffins were first introduced. Often they had heavy stone lids to make doubly sure that the departed stayed inside. Nailing down the lid served the same purpose!

THE WREATH

The story is told of a soldier who in a foreign land visited the grave of a former comrade, to place flowers on it. On his way, he

met a native who was carrying an offering of food to his ancestors' tomb. The soldier stopped him and pointed out the absurdity
of his action. "When do you think," he asked, "your relatives will
come out of their graves to enjoy the meal?" "At the same time
as your friend will come up to smell the flowers!", was the
immediate retort.

To send a wreath to a funeral and to lay it on the coffin or the
grave is a relic of ancient superstition and idol worship. The
early Christian authorities did their best to stop the custom. But
they did not succeed. The floral wreath is a survival of the belief
that it was necessary to provide comforts for the departed.

The flowers were also regarded as, literally, a floral offering,
a sacrifice to the dead. They were meant to keep them happy,
lest, being dissatisfied, they might haunt the mourners.

The wreath was a magic circle to keep the dead man's spirit
within bounds and away from the sorrowing family and friends.

The Egyptians used wreaths thousands of years ago and kept
special gardens to grow flowers for that purpose only. They
crowned mummified bodies with chaplets of flowers or leaves in
order to assure them a triumphant and safe passage into the
other world.

The wreath for the dead was also a continuation of the Greek
and Roman habit of crowning with laurels emperors, victorious
generals and distinguished athletes. Its evergreen leaves not only
symbolized but ensured an existence that would never fade or
wither — eternal life. The wreath was a floral tribute not so
much to the dead as to the vegetation spirits which, it was believed, resided in its very flowers.

None of these various early roots are remembered. There is no
magic left in the wreath, and to "say it with flowers" has become
an established custom in the Western world, though other
nations and races still prefer to put small stones on their dear
ones' graves.

THE HEARSE

Originally the hearse was not a vehicle to transport the dead to
his last resting place but an agricultural implement. Hearse is a
French word signifying a *harrow*. That is exactly what it was in

the very beginning. It consisted of an iron, triangular frame, to which spikes were attached. Roman peasants were the first to use it. The French adopted it from them.

Its earliest "harrowing" use (not to be confused with the grievous connotation of the word) is reflected in the modern theatrical term, *rehears*al. Like a farmer the actor harrowed the field of his memory over and over again, until the part he had to play was so deeply ingrained in his mind that he would not stumble over his words.

In the 13th century, ingenious peasants discovered that their harrow, when not used to rake the fields, could serve another purpose. Turned over, it became a multiple candlestick. The rake's spikes were just right to impale the tapers. Thus, the hearse took on the additional function of an inverted chandelier, decorating and illuminating the farmer's house. Soon it was found especially useful on religious occasions, particularly at funerals. That is how eventually the hearse was transferred from the home to the church.

With the passing of time the original, small harrow grew ever larger. Its height extended to six feet and it evolved into a magnificent, elaborate construction. Indeed, such was the rake's progress that it became a masterpiece of fine workmanship, worthy of adorning and lighting the burial service of the most noble.

Its development did not stop there. From each of the hearse's three corners, supports were erected. These were joined at the top, thus forming a framework. This was draped with black cloth on which mourners and their friends pinned tickets with poems and epitaphs on them, in honour of the departed.

Numerous ornaments were added and the number of candles impaled became so large that the flickering lights were compared to the stars. Then the inevitable happened. The very width and height of the hearse suggested that the coffin be put on its summit. The whole structure was next surrounded by a rail.

The hearse was still stationary. It remained in the church, even after the body had been removed from it to be carried to the grave. It served as a shrine to honour the dead. The bereaved continued to light votive candles on it in memory of their beloved, long after his remains had been laid to rest.

Later, the hearse itself, with the dead still reposing on it, was carried to the grave. Soon wheels were added and the mourners pulled the "harrow" like a cart. The hearse had become a death waggon.

In modern times, horses pulled the deceased on his movable bier to his final destination. Then, with the invention of the internal combustion engine, came the motorized hearse, in which nevertheless are still entombed many remnants and traces of its thousand-years' growth. The hearse has certainly travelled an exceedingly long way since the Ancient Roman days when it was but a crude rake.

THE FUNERAL PROCESSION

There is an old belief that a corpse must proceed to its grave without stopping or hindrance. The smooth and unhampered progress of a funeral cortège is much in keeping with the solemn occasion. Even modern traffic authorities suspend some of the regulations in the case of a burial.

A funeral procession must in no circumstances be split up. Once the hearse has passed an intersection, even if the traffic lights have changed to red, the rest of the cars may follow through. Similarly, it is considered an offence for other vehicles to cut in. Equal care is taken for a cortège to move at the slowest possible speed.

All this expresses unwillingness, as it were, to part from the loved one, and pays due respect to his mortal remains. Yet, even those sentiments are rationalizations.

Reluctance to impede a funeral procession goes back to ancient superstition. People feared that some dissatisfied spirit, averse to leave this world, might take advantage of the halt. Seizing the opportunity, it might escape from the body and start haunting and harming the living.

The slow pace of the cortège is not just a mark of respect. It recalls those earlier days when the dead person was carried by friends on a bier and a cross-bearer headed the solemn procession. The rate of progress was controlled by the mourners' strides, and it is this pedestrian pace that still restricts the hearse's speed.

THE TOMBSTONE

The practice of putting a stone on a grave arose not from piety, but from atavistic fear; its origin was not respect for the dead but the motive of self-protection. Even after all other precautions had been taken, the living were still afraid that the dead person might return and act against his former community. To make absolutely sure he stayed in his tomb, they weighed the soil down with a heavy stone.

At first, people were buried anywhere, generally near where they had died or been killed. Thus graves could be found in most unexpected places.

Primitive society looked on a dead body as something impure. To touch it, or even pass over its burial place, defiled. Thus, they marked graves with stones. These were meant to be a warning to passers-by to keep well away. At times, to make the stones stand out more clearly, they were coated with lime.

The identical consideration led to the origin of the cemetery. Special fields, removed from human habitation, were set apart to isolate the dead in order to protect the living from contamination.

A later development was the worship of graves. The tombstone was looked on as an abode of the deity or the spirit. At this time, people were no longer worried about getting defiled, but about the grave being desecrated. They heaped stones on it to prevent animals from digging up the body.

Inscriptions on headstones and monuments came later. Initially, they were reserved merely for people of rank, to draw special attention to their last resting-place and to invite passers-by to pray for their soul.

CROCODILE TEARS

We say of the hypocrite displaying grief that he sheds crocodile tears. This picturesque phrase dates back thousands of years to ancient fable and a sort of archaic science-fiction. It was believed then that crocodiles used guile to trap their prey. Lying camouflaged in slimy water or mud, they spat mouthfuls of water on to the soil near the lair, to make it so slippery that people or animals aproaching would miss their footing and fall. Unable to get back on to their feet quickly enough, they would be caught by the crocodile and duly devoured.

Another interpretation discovered in the (non-existent) crocodile tears an ingenious ingredient which the reptile itself supplied to add to its daily diet, to make otherwise indigestible parts of its victim soft and palatable! It was thought that the crocodile spurted its tears to soak the skull of its prey, macerating the hard substance and preparing it for a tasty meal.

This piece of folklore was soon embroidered upon. People attributed to the beast the most evil cunning, believing that it attracted its daily "bread" with bait of a most unethical kind. The myth-makers now alleged that when hungry, the creature deliberately sobbed and sighed, simulating a human in distress and so luring prey to the slippery river-bank. From sobbing and moaning it was only a short step to dreaming up real tears.

To add insult to injury, it was further assumed, that whilst eating its victim, the crocodile continued shedding tears. But now it did so out of pity for the unfortunate fool.

The fact is that crocodiles never shed tears, but they do make peculiar groaning noises. Once upon a time, the crocodile's tears were a traveller's yarn. But credulous people eagerly lapped them up and believed in them. Though nowadays crocodiles no longer cry, even fictitiously, before or during meals, their tears have not completely dried up. They survive even among the most civilized people: in their conversation, especially when they talk of the humbug and hypocrite.

THE GRASS WIDOW

In his famous Dictionary Dr. Samuel Johnson explained that a grass widow is a corrupted form of a grace widow. But this theory has now been discarded. Certainly, a wife temporarily parted from her husband may be a widow by grace or courtesy but, literally, the term goes down to the grass roots, either of the Indian highlands or the Californian hills.

According to one version, grass widows made their first appearance among Anglo-Indians about the middle of the past century. British forces were stationed in the coastal plains of India. But the sweltering heat during the summer made life there well-nigh unbearable for people who were unaccustomed to such a tropical climate.

To spare their womenfolk unnecessary hardship, the soldiers sent them during that season to the hills. There cool breezes prevailed and, by contrast with the plain's parched earth, the grass was green. This, indeed, was the most noticeable feature of the hill country at that time of the year. The men began jokingly to refer to sending their wives "to the grass", and that is how a spouse separated from her husband came to be known as a grass widow.

Another less kind and gracious explanation links the grass widow with the Californian gold rushes that took place almost at the same period, though on the other side of the world. Possessed by gold fever, many prospectors felt that their families were an encumbrance. Therefore they boarded their wives in other people's homes.

Rather crudely they compared their action to that of a farmer who put a horse out to graze, when it was not wanted or useful for work. "I have put my wife to grass!" they laughingly remarked to their mates.

Even though those fortune hunters kept everything they found to themselves, they still, unknowingly, presented a word as a free gift to the English-speaking world.

CHAPTER V

everyday courtesies

COURTESY is derived from the courtier's customs and used to define a way of living and manners befitting a prince. But this explanation is only partly true.

Politeness is not as civil as at first it appears. Behind it is a history of discrimination and terror, of people living in constant mutual suspicion, afraid of attack and assassination. Most customs of courtesy are thus the product of a defence mechanism. Their original purpose was to fortify oneself against attack either from men or supernatural forces.

Codes of etiquette have varied from time to time and nation to nation. They are geographically conditioned and the outcome of a specific climate of nature and thought.

Anyone belching after a good meal, for instance, would horrify us. We would rightly call such a person's behaviour rude and crude. But when one dines as the guest of an Arab, it would insult the host if a hearty belch were not given in approval of the meal.

Courtesy has been described as a lubricant which smoothes human relationships and prevents friction. In fact, however, good manners are survivals of evil times, as an inquiry into their origin soon reveals.

ETIQUETTE

Etiquette is a French word, signifying label or card, which gave birth to the English "ticket".

Centuries ago, guests at royal receptions were handed little notes, giving detailed instructions on conduct. These tickets were known as etiquettes. A widening of their application led to the word's modern use.

Another explanation is that officers in the French forces used to publish their daily orders on small sheets posted around the camp. They were called etiquettes.

A Scot, who had served in the French army, became the chief gardener of King Louis XIV at the Palace of Versailles. In his efforts to lay out a beautiful park, he was continually frustrated by the carelessness of visitors, who walked across new lawns and flower beds, destroying young plants before they had a chance to take root.

Remembering the "etiquettes" of his army days, he had notices put up all over the grounds directing visitors where to walk and where to keep off the grass. From these small posters at Versailles, it is said, the word found its way into the English language and described the right kind of behaviour everywhere.

SHAKING HANDS

Suspicion and stark fear are the source of the apparently harmless and polite gesture of shaking hands.

People once were haunted by the many dangers which threatened them both from beasts and other men. You could trust no one. Thus, in a spirit of self-defence, men moved about well armed. Primitive man carried a club and more civilized man his sword.

Meeting with a stranger aroused immediate suspicion. Neither man knew the other's intention. Four possible reactions offered themselves. Both men could turn and make their escape without waiting to find out what might happen. They could stand their ground and fight. Grasping their weapon all the more firmly, they could proceed on their way, perhaps giving each other the widest possible berth. Or, they could remain peaceful and, perhaps, become friends.

To do that they first had to make sure that there was no possibility of attack. That is why they laid down their weapons or kept their hands well away from them, displaying their empty palms. But to be doubly sure, and to prevent the other man from suddenly grabbing his sword, they clasped hands firmly.

The hearty handshake, therefore, did not in the beginning show friendship but distrust. Nor did the customary use of the right hand originate by chance. It was a precaution to immobilize the other man's weapon hand.

RAISING ONE'S HAT

The raising of one's hat to a lady, not inappropriately, dates back to the age of chivalry. Yet its origin was not courtesy but an assurance of peaceful intentions. Knights in armour lifted the vizor to indicate they were not afraid of being attacked. Eventually, it became the custom for a knight to stand bareheaded in the presence of a lady.

The doffing of the helmet in a home showed that the protection of the host was relied on and in a church that one was not afraid of an enemy in the House of God. Friendly knights raised their vizors to each other, and the removal of the helmet indicated friendship and utter trust in a hostile world.

Going beyond this chivalrous interpretation, the raising of the hat can be traced to the early days of primitive warfare when captives were stripped. Their nakedness was to proclaim complete subjugation. Gradually, this symbol of serfdom was restricted to the baring of only the upper part of the body, down to the waist. Finally, all that remained of the early stripping was the removal of whatever served as a hat. "I am your obedient servant!" is thus the implicit message from the days of slavery, when silently a man greets a lady by baring his head.

Women have always been exempt from the custom. However, this does not really imply that they have been considered the master. It does not show lack of courtesy on their part either. Perhaps it reflects man's complete trust in the female sex, or his feeling of superiority — that he has nothing to fear from a mere woman.

THE CURTSY

The curtsy in our time is a slight bend of the knee and lowering of the body. It is a custom reserved for women only.

It is the last remnant of the days, not so long ago, when woman was considered inferior to man and was expected to bow down in his presence as a sign of subservience. The curtsy, as practised now, is the last relic of complete genuflection.

Curtsy and courtesy seem such near relatives. They almost sound alike. But in reality they are worlds apart. A curtsy belongs much more to the shameful history of female degradation than to books on etiquette. Perhaps Lewis Carroll was not just being funny when, seeing "Through the Looking Glass", he explained that a woman, while curtsying, may think what to say, which would save time.

"GOD BLESS YOU" WHEN SNEEZING

A sneeze nowadays is considered merely a symptom of a common cold and nothing to be specially scared of (except as the possible spreader of germs). That was not always so. To primitive man, and in biblical and Greek times, a sneeze was regarded as a sign of great personal danger.

Possibly because sneezing had been a frequent occurrence during the great Athenian plague, people assumed it was the first indication that a person had a dreaded disease.

Actually, fear once associated with the sneeze was world-wide. Romans saw in it an evil omen. Parsees felt that the sneeze indicated the threatening presence of evil spirits.

The ancient Hebrews believed that when a man sneezed, he was nearest to death. The fear was based on an erroneous but widely held notion. Man's soul was considered to be the essence of life. The fact that dead men never breathed led to the fallacious deduction that his soul must be breath. This was supported by the biblical tale that God, when creating man, fashioned his body out of the dust of the earth but "breathed into his nostrils the breath of life", which made him a living soul.

No one could deny that a sneeze expelled a considerable amount of air. And if air were the substance of the soul and so much of it left so suddenly, was it not understandable that people became afraid that, deprived of this essence of life, death might be inevitable?

Soon other ideas enforced the belief. One was that, originally, after the Creation, God decreed that every man should sneeze only once, and at that very moment his soul should expire. Indeed, it was said that Jacob the Patriarch died by his first sneeze.

It is thus not surprising that from the earliest days people learned to respond to a sneeze with apprehension and the fervent wish to the sneezer that God may help and bless him and preserve his life.

Somehow in medieval times this early origin of the custom must have been forgotten because it was Pope Gregory the Great who was credited with having introduced the saying "God bless you", to anyone who sneezed. During his reign the Roman population was decimated by a plague believed to have been caused by contamination of the air. This, it was thought, made people who sneezed "give up the ghost" immediately. It was then that the Pope prescribed a special form of prayer and the wish for all sneezers that God may keep from them any evil effect.

Yet another explanation of seeking God's help for sneezers is founded in Irish lore. It tells the story of a brother and sister who lived in Erin at the time of a Black Plague. Being observant people, the two soon noticed that victims of the scourge were first attacked by a bout of sneezing. Therefore, whenever they themselves had to sneeze, they uttered a prayer, "God help me". Because of this supplication, the story continues, they were allowed to live — the sole survivors in the district.

HAND IN FRONT OF MOUTH WHEN YAWNING

It is sometimes very difficult to suppress a yawn. However, it can be concealed behind the hand and failure to do this is decried as uncouth and rude.

The fact that people feel so strongly about it indicates that there must be a much more deeply rooted significance in the custom than so-called good manners — a wish to cover up the unpleasant-looking cavern of the mouth and to shut off possibly bad breath.

Primitive man was convinced that an unguarded yawn could make all the difference between life and death, for two reasons.

Man's spirit was identified with his breath. The mouth was its most obvious place of entry and exit. Primitive races assumed that the soul actually departed via the lips, with the last breath. This was responsible for the biblical custom of kissing the mouth of a dying person, so catching the departing spirit to transmit it to future generations. People of some races used to hold the mouth and nose of a dying friend. By doing so, they imagined, they prevented the ghost from escaping and thereby preserved the man's life.

Thus, covering the mouth while yawning was, first of all, a safeguard against the soul's issuing prematurely.

Equally, however, a gaping mouth gave access to unwelcome guests. It was, as it were, an open invitation to lurking evil spirits and demons. Moslems regarded the very wish to yawn as the work of the Devil, anxious to take possession of a man's body. To chase away the "evil one", Hindus snapped their fingers loudly in front of their open mouths. In some parts of Spain and France, Christians make the sign of the cross for the same reason.

CHAPTER VI

table manners
and eating habits

SOME PEOPLE love eating. Mere mention of food is sufficient for their body to begin the process of digestion — the mouth starts watering. Of them it could be truly said that the way to the heart is through the stomach.

Others could not care less about what, when and how much they eat. Percy Shelley, the great English poet, could never understand why people wanted more than plain bread. His wife sent meals into his study, but he frequently forgot to eat them. Joining her later, he would inquire, "Mary, have I dined?".

Originally, people gorged themselves like beasts. They ate whenever and as long as they had food. The introduction of regular meal times was one of the great stepping-stones in the history of civilization.

The present generation is highly food-conscious. The right kind of diet, with enough vitamins and not too many calories, is a feature of all our menus. Beyond the facts of mere nourishment, early philosophers already appreciated the effect on us of the food we eat. The Germans have a pun, *Der Mensch ist was er isst*. — "Man is what he eats."

Menus have differed in various ages and they still change from country to country. It has rightly been said what is one person's meat is another's poison. Every country has its national dish — Irish stew, Italian macaroni, German Wurst, Scottish haggis, English roast beef, Australian steak and eggs, and so on.

Thus every age and nation have had their own food fads and taboos, the dishes they craved and abhorred. Few people, however, realize that generally accepted eating customs have a history set against a background of national traditions and sociological considerations, of irrational superstitions and practical intentions.

THREE DAILY MEALS

It is surprising that the basic pattern of our three daily meals — breakfast, lunch and dinner — has been established only since 1890. It is the result of a development through many centuries.

Meal times have differed in various countries and epochs. They are the outcome of many circumstances, such as climate, occupations and general working conditions.

Originally, Anglo-Saxon tradition knew of only two meals a day — breakfast and dinner. In the 16th century, breakfast was a snack, with no fixed menu. Its only purpose was to *break* one's *fast*. But 200 years later it had become a sumptuous meal; not just for the family, but for plenty of guests as well. It was a social occasion, which commenced at 10 a.m. and often lasted till 1 p.m. Then breakfast began to deteriorate. It became — comparatively — meagre and was taken at a much earlier hour. By 1850 it had retreated to 8 a.m. and shrunk to a family affair.

Dinner, however, went the other way. In the 16th century it was eaten at 11 a.m. Years afterward, it moved to the early afternoon, then to 5 p.m. By 1850 it had reached 7 p.m. or 8 p.m.

Lunch is a relatively recent innovation. It first appeared on the time-table as a snack to fill the gap between breakfast and dinner. In his Dictionary of 1755, Dr. Johnson defined it, "As much food as one's hand can hold".

The literal meaning of *lunch* retains its early frugality. It denotes a *lump* — a piece of whatever you may choose to swallow. As breakfast became ever earlier and dinner later, lunch assumed an important position and developed into a big meal. The division of the working day in the Victorian age into two periods — from 9 a.m. to 1 p.m. and from 2 p.m. to 6 p.m. — finally made luncheon an institution.

That is how the three daily meals, as they are known today, came into existence. It is quite possible that, with ever shorter working hours, lack of domestic help, calorie-consciousness and popularity of precooked dishes, the pattern and rhythm of our meal times will change again.

KNIFE AND FORK

Knives have always been used. They had a place in the equipment of the Stone-Age man.

Forks are mentioned as far back as in the Bible and, as excavations have shown, were used by the Anglo-Saxons in 796 A.D. However, it seems that forks lost their popularity and disappeared from use.

A book on how good children should behave, written in 1480, says: "Take your meat with three fingers only and don't put it into your mouth with both hands. Do not keep your hand too long in the plate".

And yet, forks were referred to in Italy in the 11th century, and Thomas Becket, Chancellor of England under Henry II, knew of and introduced them to royal society. However, it seems that his innovation died with him as, some 450 years later, in 1611, an English traveller, Thomas Coryate, observing their use in Italy, re-introduced forks into England. But people ridiculed him and scorned them as finicky and effeminate. Priests condemned their use as most unsuitable and almost irreligious. An angry preacher told his congregation that to eat meat with a fork was to declare impiously that God's creatures were not worthy of being touched by human hands!

Savages of the South Sea Islands used forks — but only to devour their enemies. Their religion did not permit them to eat human flesh with their fingers.

At first, forks were two-pronged. It was only toward the end of the 18th century, when also the lower classes started adopting them, that the four-pronged fork became standard. Iron forks were first mass-produced for table use by a German artisan in 1846.

THE CROSSING OF KNIFE AND FORK

The custom of putting knife and fork side by side on the plate on finishing a meal has practical and religious explanations.

The position of the knife and fork gives a message to those waiting on us that "we have finished eating and you can take away the plate". Crossed cutlery indicates, very quietly and politely, that "there is still room for more".

Crossed knives and forks can easily fall off when the plate is removed. That is not so when they are placed next to each other, a position which also facilitates picking up the cutlery and stacking the dishes.

The sign of the cross is a sacred symbol which should be reserved to its proper place, which is certainly not a dirty plate. Nor would anyone wish to see as the constituent parts of the cross such menial instruments of eating as a dirty knife and fork.

However, there are always exceptions and Browning mentioned people who specially crossed their knife and fork as a pious act.

CHOPSTICKS

The Chinese give much thought to their food. It must have perfect flavour, crispness, tenderness and delicacy.

It is said that Confucius divorced his wife because she did not fulfil his expectations as a cook. He demanded that meat should always be served in its proper sauce, be cut perfectly square and have exactly the right colour. For him, even the choicest of rice was generally not white enough, and minced meat rarely fine enough.

The Chinese are fastidious too in the way food is eaten. Meals, they reason, have to be prepared properly in the kitchen. Once served, they have to be completely ready for eating. To have to cut meat into small pieces at that stage not only would be uncouth, but barbarian. "We sit at table to eat, not to cut up carcasses," is an often quoted Chinese observation.

It was among the cook's duties to dish up the food in convenient size. The process of eating consisted of graciously lifting the morsels from their bowl and transferring them into the mouth. Chopsticks served just that purpose and, if dexterously applied, did so smoothly and at high speed. This is recalled by their name which means "the quick ones".

Made of ivory, bone or wood, they obviously had to be used in pairs and, as the Chinese soon discovered, they could also serve as a code between host and guest. Anyone wishing to leave the table, for instance, placed the sticks across the bowl.

According to another explanation of the origin of the chopsticks, the Chinese initially made proper use of cutlery. But one of their emperors, fearing an uprising and assassination, forbade his subjects to own any kind of utensil made of metal.

Knives and forks came, of course, in that category. As the Chinese were loath to eat with their fingers, they invented chopsticks.

THE SERVIETTE

For the many centuries when forks were unknown, man's hands carried food from plate to mouth. This naturally caused the hands to become greasy and dirty. Thus, washing and drying them after the meal, and still at table, became a custom. It was for this purpose that the napkin was introduced, and assumed the practical role of a small towel at every meal.

However, once forks were adopted, the napkin became redundant. But it was retained nevertheless, yet with a different objective in mind. It changed from an indispensable adjunct to the dinner table, serving human cleanliness, to a decoration. Hosts vied with each other in displaying napkins in fantastic shapes. The various foldings were meant to appeal to the diner's aesthetic taste.

Long lists are still in existence which suggest numerous ways as how to fold the napkin. Instructions of the year 1682, for instance, give 26 different shapes. These included serviettes folded in the form of Noah's Ark, of a hen and her chickens, a carp, a tortoise and two rabbits!

Today the wheel has turned full circle. The rabbits and tortoises, made of cloth, have disappeared from the dinner table and the napkin, much smaller and less conspicuous, again serves a utilitarian purpose — mostly to protect the diner's clothes.

THE DIFFERENCE BETWEEN TEA AND COFFEE POTS

The present-day shapes of tea and coffee pots seem designed to produce the best brews. A low, wide pot provides for the maximum expansion of the tea leaves which, being light, tend to rise in hot water. On the other hand, soon after boiling water has been poured on coffee, the grounds sink to the bottom and pure clean coffee is left in the rest of the pot. Its narrow, high shape thus serves it best.

Originally, however, there was no difference between coffee and tea pots. When first introduced in England, each was circular and tapered towards the top. It was only several years later that the tea pot diminished in height and increased in diameter. This actually resulted from a wish to get a Chinese atmosphere. It became fashionable to copy the wide and bulky Chinese porcelain tea pots. Their shape has been maintained since.

THE SUNDAE

A strange mixture of piety, hypocrisy and legal subterfuge make up the Sundae — ice cream with syrup, fruits and nuts. Its name is an obvious and even intentional mis-spelling of Sunday.

One tradition erroneously asserts that it referred to Sunday's left-over ice cream dishes, sold, possibly at a cheaper price, during the following week. So that a customer would not think they were freshly made and thus be deceived, they were specifically called "Sunday's".

In reality, we owe the first Sundae to the United States of America and the business acumen of a drugstore owner. However, where exactly it was first concocted is still a matter of controversy and various claims.

Some say that the Sundae was invented in Evanston, Illinois. Others are equally definite that the pride of place belongs to Norfolk, Virginia, where to this day people point to a certain store as "the birthplace of the Sundae".

No matter where it was first made, all accounts agree on the reason for it. It was purely a matter of circumventing the law! Sunday, the Lord's Day, had to be strictly observed in many, and sometimes peculiar ways. Puritan tradition made it a solemn and sombre occasion. Children's swings had to be chained and barred. The reading of books was banned unless they were religious in theme. Theatres were closed. The "blue law" of Virginia outlawed even soda drinks on the Sabbath!

But people were still thirsty and not satisfied with mere water. In this, an ambitious drugstore proprietor saw his chance, both to give customers a refreshing dish on the Lord's Day and to increase his takings to a considerable degree.

If to serve ice cream with soda was illegal, why not offer ice cream with syrup? He began to sell this new and permissible formula every Sunday. And no guardian of the law could object. Appropriately, he named his concoction after its birthday — Sunday.

Still, the authorities took exception, not to the dish itself but to what it was called. To name it after the Lord's Day was sacrilegious, they contended. In consequence, the drugstore owner changed its spelling and his "Sunday" became overnight the "Sundae". It still sounded and — most of all — tasted the same. It did not take long for the sweet to become popular all over the world and soon people asked for Sundaes even on weekdays.

WELSH RABBIT

A proverb says that "toasted cheese has no master". The Welsh rabbit has been considered the national dish of Wales and accordingly had been described as "the Welshman's delight" and "Davies' darling".

Many people like Welsh rabbit. It is a simple but tasty dish of toasted bread covered with toasted cheese and smeared with mustard and pepper. People still wonder how the rabbit got into this savoury which is completely vegetarian and lacks even the slightest resemblance to a bunny, in taste or shape.

The appetizing morsel owes its name, and perhaps existence to human antagonism, a former condescending dislike of the Welsh by the English. At a time when the English looked down on the Welsh and were contemptuous of everything that came from Wales, it was not by chance that the well-known rhyme "Taffy was a Welshman, Taffy was a thief, Taffy came to my house and stole a leg of beef", was coined.

The Welsh, so it was thought, were a poor lot in every sense of the word. Their country lacked almost everything, even rabbits, which were numerous elsewhere. As they could not afford to buy them from England they were forced to find a pauper's substitute, their own kind of synthetic rabbit. This they made from the cheapest ingredients available, bread and cheese. Disdainfully, the English thus called this national "delicacy" of the Welsh their "rabbit".

> Jenny ap-Rice, hur could eat nothing nice.
> A dainty Welsh Rabbit? — go toast her a slice
> Of cheese, if you please, which better agrees
> With the tooth of poor Taffy than physics and fees.
> A pound Jenny got, and brought to his cot
> A prime double Gloster, all hot, piping hot —
> Which being a bunny without any bones,
> Was custard with mustard to Taffy ap-Jones.

An old anecdote illustrates this one-time attitude to the Welsh and their (lack of) food. It tells of a bragging Welshman relating how his father entertained 12 guests and employed no fewer than 12 cooks. But the listener would have none of it. Sarcastically he remarked: "Ah, I suppose every man had to toast his own cheese!"

Inevitably Welshmen came to resent deeply all that was associated with their "rabbit". They soon claimed that they themselves had never spoken of a rabbit at all. How could they have done so? Actually, the Welsh "rabbit" was the result of bad enunciation on the part of jealous Englishmen. In reality the course of melted cheese had nothing to do with the common rabbit but, on the contrary, was a "rare-bit" of delicious food.

Alas, the chronology of philology contradicts this. As attested by the Oxford Dictionary, the Welsh *rabbit* appeared first in 1725, whilst its refined version, the *rare-bit*, came into existence exactly 60 years later, in 1785.

Perhaps the change of terminology was due, after all, to some fair-minded Englishmen. Regretful of an earlier generation's bad taste toward a brother race, they may have tried to modify the name by taking the sting out of the rabbit.

PEACH MELBA

The stage has enriched human life in many ways. But it was left to an Australian prima donna to add two dishes to the culinary enjoyment of man. Years after Dame Nellie Melba's voice has been silent, people still talk of her, when they crunch a certain type of thin toast or order a special kind of dessert.

Only the best was good enough for her. "If I'd been a housemaid," she once said, "I'd have been the best in Australia. I couldn't help it. . . . It's got to be perfection for me." She wanted to show the world that Australia could produce more than sheep and boomerangs. Even in the choice of her stage name, she gave world-wide publicity to Victoria's capital, where she was born.

One thing worried her — that not her artistry, but her culinary tastes might be remembered longest. But that is exactly what happened. Melba is still listed among the great sopranos of the world, but her name is spoken most around the dinner table. Peach Melba and Melba Toast have immortalized one of Australia's greatest singers to a larger extent than her glorious voice.

Peach Melba as it is served now, is a far cry from the original, spectacular sweet. This was a blend of beautiful colour, attractive shape and delicious taste which combined the flavours of raspberry, peach and vanilla. It was devised by a great culinary artist.

George Auguste Escoffier, Officer of the Legion of Honour, has been called the king of cooks. He was a perfectionist whose principle was that nothing in food should ever be camouflaged. He fought sham and make-belief in the kitchen. Yet, small of stature, he wore high heels to make himself taller.

His taste extended beyond the delights of the palate to the world of art. He worshipped Dame Melba, who herself was one of his patrons.

During 1892-3 she was staying at the Savoy Hotel, London, when he was its chef. He often went to the theatre to listen to her, and enjoyed especially her performance as Elsa in Lohengrin. That night at the opera was to him an unforgettable occasion which, somehow, he wished to perpetuate in his own creative way.

The brilliant singer was to dine at his hotel on the following day. To surprise her and show his appreciation, he resolved to serve her a completely new dish — a dessert in her honour.

From a block of ice he shaped two wings of a swan and coated them with icing sugar. Between them were peaches resting on a bed of vanilla ice cream. Obviously, the dish was to recall the most famous scene in Lohengrin and, at first, he called the sweet *pêches au cygne* — "swan-like peaches".

Later, on the occasion of the opening of London's Carlton Hotel, he improved the sweet by adding raspberry sauce. It was then that he renamed the dessert and, recalling the moment of its first creation, gave it the description it has carried ever since — Peach Melba.

MELBA TOAST

Melba Toast made its debut as a mere accident. On one of her visits to London, Melba once again stayed at the Savoy Hotel. She was keeping to a strict diet to control her weight and mostly ordered nothing but dry toast.

One day she again asked for "the usual". The head waiter was busy and left its preparation to one of his men. Somehow things went wrong, and the toast served was much too thin and dry.

When the chef noticed the error it was too late. He rushed to Melba's table, profusely apologizing and expecting a vociferous complaint. To his surprise, Melba did not mind at all. On the contrary, she complimented the chef on the "exquisite toast", the like of which she had never tasted before. The chef was over-joyed and there and then called the toast by her name.

He continued to serve the new "invention" as long as Melba was at the Savoy. Soon other guests asked for it and "Melba Toast" became a favourite, low calorie delicacy in fashionable restaurants the world over.

A second, much less exciting story, relates Melba Toast not to an accident but to yet another of Escoffier's inventions. He created it first not for Melba but a friend, Madame Ritz, who had complained to him that the usual toast served was much too thick. It so happened that at the time Melba was a guest at the Savoy and known to favour toast. This gave Escoffier and his friend the idea that the toast should bear the singer's name.

THE ADAM'S APPLE

The Adam's apple is the little projection in the neck, which is formed by the thyroid cartilage. It seems to move up and down

the throat. When early anatomists were legally permitted to dis-
sect corpses, they were greatly perplexed in identifying it. In
spite of their scientific outlook they had to go on calling this
firm but elastic tissue the Adam's apple.

Ancient folklore said that when Adam committed his "original
sin" and, at Eve's invitation, ate of the forbidden fruit, a piece of
the apple stuck in his throat. Some assert that this happened
when he swallowed his first bite. It is a claim which, from a
psychological point of view, is most feasible. Ever since, all of
Adam's descendants, but especially the males, have been born
with that lump in the throat as a constant reminder of man's
first sin and a warning to resist any future temptations.

Adding insult to injury, it is now realized that Holy Scripture
never identified the forbidden fruit. Nowhere in the Bible are we
told that it was an apple. Most of the authorities now agree that
probably it was an apricot. Being so much softer than an apple,
an apricot is less likely to get stuck in one's throat, so that the
"Adam's apple" has fallen to the ground.

Yet an unscientific name, based on an erroneous notion about a
fruit that was not eaten and did not even exist at the time and
place in question, got stuck in speech!

TO EAT ONE'S HAT

Hunger and curiosity have driven men to eat almost anything.
Cannibals ate human flesh. They did so however, not, as most
people think, for the sake of eating. Feeding on man, they
imagined, did not only nourish their bodies but, much more so,
their souls! By eating another human being, they believed, they
also magically acquired his strength, brains and courage. That
was the chief reason for their choice of the inhuman human diet.
— Aborigines delight in witchetty grubs, whose taste — if raw — is
like cream, or — if cooked, rolled in warm ashes — like pork rind.

Frenchmen love horse-meat and those of us who loathe even
the thought of it should know that there is nothing really wrong
with it. Our distaste stems from forgotten days when the horse
was worshipped and, because of its sanctity, people were afraid
to kill and eat it.

But in spite of those various and exotic tastes, whoever would think of eating his hat, whether of straw or felt? And rightly so, because the kind of hat of which we speak, when trying to impress on others our incredibility and amazement, was never the sort of hat we know. It is just a confusion between millinery and gastronomy.

Its place has always been in the cookery book and not on our head. This is testified by one of the earliest publications of recipes. It relates that "*Hattes* are made of eggs, veal, dates, safron, salt, and so forth". The ingredients suggested leave no doubt that a dish of that type would hardly be palatable. Most likely to eat such a hat, or even the wearable kind, would be beyond one's digestive capacity.

PORK AS FORBIDDEN FOOD

One of the best-known food prohibitions is that of eating pork. It is carefully observed by Jews and, for that matter, Arabs as well. At times of religious persecution, they preferred martyrdom to partaking of the flesh of swine.

It is a mistake, however, to assume that the pig was singled out as the only animal forbidden by Jewish dietary law. It is not fit for human consumption, according to Hebrew tradition, because it does not fulfil one of the two requirements of the Bible for animals which it is permissible to eat — that they chew the cud and have cloven hoofs. Both the cow and the sheep qualify, but not so the pig, and this only because it does not chew the cud.

But there must have been other weighty reasons that led the Hebrew people and other groups in the Middle East not only to exclude the pig from their diet but to view it generally with abhorrence. It was a combination of factors that rendered swine unclean to the Jews.

The pig was taboo, at first, for significant religious reasons. It was worshipped by primitive races who also sacrificed it to their idols and ate its flesh in sacred meals. This fact especially, of the pig's association with alien gods and rites, made Jews, in their passion for a monotheistic, spiritual faith, reject the pig and decry it as unclean.

Man often scorns even the best of things, if he is not accustomed to them. The unfamiliar is under suspicion even today. It is no wonder, then, that primitive groups faced the unknown with horror. They believed that the eating of strange foods was fraught with grave danger. These were avoided not because of possible food-poisoning — something completely unsuspected at that time — but for the terrifying possibility that they carried magical, harmful forces which, once absorbed by the body, could cause irremediable damage.

Primitive races imagined that they became what they ate, and acquired the qualities of the animals they consumed. Thus, to become swifter, some tribes favoured venison and refrained from eating the meat of the clumsy bear. The Caribs did not eat pork because they feared that if they did, they would grow the pig's small eyes, while Zulu girls shunned the pig lest their children grew to resemble it.

Although the ancient Egyptians reared and ate pigs, they regarded them as unclean. Herodotus, the Greek historian, recalls how anyone touching a pig had to plunge with his clothes on into a river, and that swineherds, though Egyptian by birth, were the only people excluded from the sanctuary. Socially, they were so ostracized that they had to choose wives from their own class.

As pigs seem to revel in filth and to consume almost every kind of dirt, they were regarded as contaminated and too dangerous to be eaten.

It is unlikely that in the initial stages of civilization hygiene prompted the devising of laws and customs. Modern notions are often wrongly applied to primitive man. That is why it has been deemed fallacious to suggest as yet another reason for the prohibition of pork that the animal was frequently infected by microbes and that, therefore, fear of disease, specifically trichinosis, led the ancient Hebrews wisely to reject pork as part of their diet. Nevertheless, human instinct works in wondrous ways and in many cases anticipates, by centuries, future knowledge. Perhaps that was true of the early banning of pork.

Certainly, aesthetic and ethical reasons have played their part in creating contempt for the pig. In addition to its supposedly filthy habits, it was known to devour its young, and such infanticidal tendencies rendered the beast all the more abominable to people trained in the reverence for life.

A further theory sees in the aversion to the pig, even in pre-

Hebrew times, survival of early antipathies of pastoral groups to settled, agricultural races. The nomads thought themselves a better breed and despised people bound to a permanent home and leading a regulated life which seemed to lack adventure.

The raising of pigs was part of the early agricultural pattern and pastoral people soon came to regard swine as an expression of settled existence. Later, they transferred their contempt for a way of life to its symbol, the pig. They decried it as unclean and avoided its flesh.

Finally, totemism has been cited as the earliest cause of rejecting the pig as food. Primitive races recognized in the animal the symbol of their group, indeed their ancestor, whom to kill would have been fatal to themselves.

CHAPTER VII

ᕍRINKING CUSTOMS

Of THE "ISMS" that threaten the world, one of the most dangerous is alcoholism. Yet spirits, ever since their first appearance, have not only haunted man but helped him to relax, to rejoice and to instill good will. Drink makes some people jolly and others depressed. It can sharpen the appetite, help digestion, or act as a tranquillizer.

Drink has been used from earliest times as part of communion with gods. Alcohol is mentioned in the Bible 165 times and, it is well to note, in most cases favourably. Wine was served at the Last Supper. Indeed, the ancient Hebrews used to bless and thank God for having created the fruit of the vine. On the other hand, some ancients and moderns have decried it as the worst of all evils, a gift of the Devil.

Alcohol is one of the most volatile spirits that have roused human passions. In America bootleggers fought the police and prohibitionists fought governments. The teetotaller fought himself. Scots and Irish still fight each other if, for nothing else, for the credit of having invented whisky, whose name derives from Gaelic, meaning so aptly "the water of life". Rum used to be called the motive power of the British navy, but in Australia it became the earliest currency.

Whether drink is good or evil is a matter of degree. It has been pointed out rightly that first the man takes a drink, then the drink takes a drink, and finally the drink takes the man.

A legend relates that when God created the first grapes, He was assisted by three members of the animal kingdom, the lion, the ape and the pig — who, each in turn, sprinkled some of their own spirit on the young plant. That is why up to the present day anyone who drinks just a little grows in strength like a lion; he who imbibes several glasses starts resembling strongly his simian ancestor; and he who does not know when to stop eventually lies under the table like a pig.

HOST POURING WINE INTO HIS OWN GLASS FIRST

Ancient and modern, civil and gruesome, are the two reasons that account for the custom, which is now etiquette, of a host's first tasting the wine. It has nothing to do with the assumption that it was to ensure that the wine was of the best quality and right temperature — thus good enough for his guests.

That before filling their glasses he pours a few drops of the drink into his own glass first, nowadays has the obvious purpose to remove any pieces of cork that may have fallen into the bottle whilst it was being opened. This thoughtful gesture, however, goes back to much earlier times, when it was made in different circumstances.

Before the introduction of corks, the Italians used to top the wine with oil, which filled the neck of the bottle. In serving drinks, therefore, it was necessary first to pour off its liquid protection, the oil. To make quite sure that none of the guests received in his drink any drops, which might still be floating on top of the wine, it was only natural for a considerate host to fill at least part of his own glass first.

The custom leads back still further — to medieval times when conviviality frequently was mixed with assassination, and the drinking of wine offered an occasion to poison one's foes. It was thus not merely as an act of courtesy that the host sipped the offered drink before everyone else but as a kind of life assurance in its most literal sense. It was to kill all suspicion (and not his friends), that he did so. The company was assured they had nothing to fear, and could relax. Perhaps this background of the custom explains why Jewish people, for thousands of years, have been using for their toast the wish, "For Life".

THE TOAST

In recent years motorists have grown accustomed to "additives" which are said to increase the power of petrol. In former times, and long before the invention of the internal combustion engine, people used to apply additives to certain liquids reserved for the inner man.

People used to put a piece of bread "parched with heat" — which is the literal meaning of the word toast — into a tankard of beer or glass of wine. By doing so, they believed, they improved the flavour. Such additives are still customary at some Universities in connection with their Loving Cup.

Eventually, the toast additive was found to be of no real value and was again left out of the drink, and we have forgotten all about it. Drinking the health of a person or cause is still called a toast, reminiscent of the now vanished piece of parched bread.

Further, to add an element of romance to the toast, the story is told that in reality it originated in Bath at the time of King Charles II. On a public holiday, when spirits were gay, a famous beauty was taking her bath in the public baths of that city.

One of her many admirers watching her, took a glass of the water in which she was standing and drank her health. Another of the revellers, anxious to outdo the man and, as those who tried to excuse his behaviour liked to point out, slightly inebriated perhaps, offered to jump into the bath himself. "I do not like the liquor so much," he explained, "but I should love to have the toast." — indicating the lady.

THE CLINKING OF GLASSES

The clinking of glasses at toasts nowadays is considered a sign of conviviality and friendship. But this has not always been the case.

The custom itself dates back thousands of years to our superstitious past. People were afraid that with the drink the Devil might enter their body. It was a thought which was not particularly far-fetched, considering the effects of intoxication. That is why, before actually indulging in the drink, they made a loud noise first. The sound was meant to frighten away the evil spirit. It is for the same reason that Congolese natives and other primitive races, before emptying their cup, used to ring a bell, and Bulgarians make the sign of the cross.

A modern rationalization of the custom explains it differently and so much more pleasantly. To enjoy our drink to the utmost, it is not sufficient merely to drink it. All our senses must join in the pleasure. We must not only taste the drink, touch, smell and see it, but hear it as well. And it is for this purpose that we clink our glasses.

THE COCKTAIL

America is the home of the cocktail, but no one is sure about the first concoction — either of its name or ingredients. Cocktail parties have become a social institution the world over, with plenty of people standing all the time, talking inanities and leaving none the wiser but richer in some kind of spirit.

The earliest reference to the cocktail appears in 1806 in an American periodical, inappropriately called "The Balance", which defined the drink as "a stimulating liquor, composed of spirits of any kind". Indeed, the cocktail may be a mixture of many things and there is as great variety of ingredients as there is of explanations as to the origin of this drink.

First of all people sought for a solution of the mystery of the cocktail in its literal meaning. They tried to fathom any connection (real or imagined) between the cock's tail and the drink. However, the plumage of the rooster in itself did not supply the answer.

It was the dictionary which revealed that a certain type of horse, used mostly for hunting and drawing stagecoaches, at some time had been referred to as a "cocktail". And for an obvious reason. The horse's tail was generally cut so short, that it stuck up like a cock's tail. Those horses were never thoroughbreds but a mixture, just as the drink:

"Perhaps it's made of whisky, and perhaps it's made of gin:
Perhaps there's orange bitters and a lemon peel within . . ."

More likely than horsebreeding as the source of the cocktail are certain historical events associated with the ancient Aztecs, Mexicans and American forces of the Southern states.

The ancient Aztec civilization is renowned for many of its achievements and, not surprisingly, it has been given the distinction of having made the first cocktail as well. An Aztec nobleman, so the story goes, brewed a drink out of the sap of the cactus plant. This he sent as a gift to the emperor by the hand of his daughter, Zochitl, a fact which — no doubt — made it all the more intoxicating.

The emperor tried it and liked the drink and the daughter so much that he acquired both! As it was Zochitl, his newly-wed wife, who first introduced him to the world of intoxication, he thought it only fair to call the beverage by her name. Pronounced with the royal Aztec accent, it came to sound like Octel.

All this took place generations before the establishment of the United States and gave the drink time to take root. When, many years later, the American army under General Scott invaded Mexico, they were impressed not only by the country's brave warriors but by their spirit, which soon conquered the would-be conquerors.

They carried it back to the States as their most potent and lasting booty, assimilating its name into their own tongue by changing Octel into cocktail. Thus a relic of the Mexican war still fights many a battle inside numerous men all over the world.

Another explanation also links the birth of the drink with American soldiery but relates it to the time of the War of Independence. A young widow named Betsy Flanagan then kept a popular tavern close to New York. She called it "The Four Corners" and not without reason, as both French and Americans and coming from all directions, made it their haunt. They were attracted by the friendliness of the inn and the charm of its hostess but — most of all — by its drinks.

Patrons spent many hours there playing cards and gulping the sparkling liquor, which Betsy herself mixed according to a formula she jealously kept secret. Mrs. Flanagan's "bracers" became known far and wide, and no other tavern had a chance to compete with them.

It happened that adjacent to the inn was the property of an Englishman, a loyalist and the soldiers' inveterate foe. He excelled in farming chickens, and his fowls, like Betsy's drinks, had no equal. What a pity that they could not meet — at least inside her guests!

Betsy was a good hostess and a good sport and loved to join in the fun of the soldiers. Soon it became her habit, when the spirit in the tavern reached intoxicating heights, to promise that one day she would serve her guests, free of charge, a meal of fried chicken, stolen from the finest coop in the country — next door.

This became a standing joke but eventually it was taken seriously. Officers, visiting the inn, began to inquire when they could expect the promised meal. Then, one day, Betsy made good her promise. To celebrate the occasion (and the theft) Betsy decorated the inn's jars and bottles with the feathers of the roasted roosters.

One of the soldiers, who craved a bracer, noted the decorated bottles and asked for a glass "of those cocktails". His call soon was taken up by others and the trophy of a theft became perpetuated for all time by being linked with Mrs. Flanagan's drink.

That same night, a further tradition says, one of the soldiers, surfeited pleasantly with fowl and drink, remarked: "We are drinking the beverage that offers the palate the same charming sensation as the feathers of the cock's tail offer the eye." At once, it is said, a Frenchman proposed a toast: "Long live the cocktail!".

That is how from "The Four Corners", from a theft, a war and an early antagonism between British and Americans spread a new name and concoction to the four corners of the earth. At that early stage it showed how British and Americans, though they may differ in some things, by joining forces around the table can create an invincible spirit.

There is yet another interpretation which associates the first cocktail with the American-Mexican war. But this time with its final phase.

A truce had been called, and both the commanding general of the Southern armies and King Axolotl VIII had agreed to meet. The negotiations took place in the royal palace. The two men, accompanied by their officers, were seated ready to commence the talks when the king, in a convivial mood, suggested as one man to another they first should join in a drink.

The American guest gladly agreed and the king ordered that a drink should be served at once. A girl of striking beauty appeared, carrying a magnificent golden goblet, which contained a potion of her own brewing.

What had been meant as a friendly gesture now assumed a

critical aspect. A hushed silence fell over the party and it seemed that the fate of the war was in the balance. There was only one cup. Who should drink of it first? Whoever it was, his precedence was bound to insult the other. It was a delicate situation.

The girl quickly assessed the implications of the single cup. With a smile she bowed to her king and the general, and then drained the cup herself. Her presence of mind and female intuition had saved the situation.

Before leaving, the general asked the king who the tactful young lady was, whose beauty equalled her wisdom. In reality Axolotl had not the slightest idea. He had never seen her before. Nevertheless he told the American that she was his daughter Coctel. On hearing this, the general replied: "I shall see to it, your Majesty, that your daughter's name will be honoured by my army for all times." The general not only kept his promise but through the American forces "Coctel", now spelled "cocktail", conquered most of the world.

Some people who indulge in drink explain that they do so for medicinal purposes only. In the case of the cocktail, so yet a further claim asserts, it was actually the medical profession that was responsible for its invention. An American "ancient print", quoted by a New York paper, stated that doctors used to treat certain diseases of the throat with "a pleasant liquid" which they applied by means of the tip of a long feather, plucked from a cock's tail. Patients soon referred to the treatment as that of "the cocktail".

At first only used for painting the throat, the liquid was later prescribed as a gargle, with its original name still clinging to it. Possibly to make its taste more pleasant still, several "appetisers" were added. No wonder that soon the sick swallowed the gargle! Eventually, the cocktail became completely divorced from sore throats and assumed its social function.

BEER

Man began his modern drinking habits with the imbibing of beer, his oldest alcoholic drink. He did not invent its production but discovered it in the process of nature. Possibly some bread crumbs fell into water and started fermenting. Tasting the product, primitive man rather enjoyed it and, long before the development of his scientific mind, started his own research — with intoxicating results!

The history of brewing goes back well over 10,000 years. It began long before the Egyptians had started building their first pyramid. It almost coincides with the beginning of agriculture and the first making of bread. Indeed, baking and brewing thus went together.

Beer not only belonged to man's original diet, but helped him in serving his gods. The very origin of the beverage was considered divine. It was the spirit of the corn and was used as a sacred libation. It was poured into the ground to appease the gods so that they would bless the fields with fertility. Without this ritual, primitive man was convinced, nothing would grow.

The brewing of beer was so sacred that, among some tribes, men engaged in the task were kept isolated from their womenfolk. Otherwise, it was believed, the magic transformation of Corn into Spirit would not take place.

One of the most ancient clay tablets in existence, dating back to Babylonian lands and the year 6000 B.C., depicts a crude type of beer-making for sacrificial purposes. Babylonians actually specialized in a bread reserved for fermentation. By 4000 B.C. they had learnt to produce 16 different types of the beverage. Brewing was a privilege set aside for their kings and restricted to temples. Thus the earliest breweries were places of worship!

The Egyptians attributed the introduction of brewing to Isis, their goddess of nature. Beer became their national drink, as popular with the living as with the gods and dead. Peasants and workers were allotted a daily allowance of four loaves of bread and two jugs of beer! An ancient hieroglyphic temple-inscription records that Pharaoh Rameses III consecrated 466,303 jugs of beer to the gods.

From Egypt, the art of brewing spread to Greece and then to Rome. However, it is quite likely that the people of Northern Europe discovered the drink separately. Beer had been established in Britain at the time of Christ, and was found and enjoyed there by the Roman invaders.

Its early religious association lingered on through the ages. Medieval monasteries excelled in making beer and provided different brands for the monks and their guests, each of whom was given a gallon a day.

Churches sold beer to raise funds. It became the most popular drink at weddings where it was poured by the bride herself. Thus it became known as the *bride's ale,* accounting for the word *bridal!*

People soon saw many qualities in beer. It nourished them and, so they imagined, saved them from the plague. It buoyed up their spirits and relieved fatigue. Water became stagnant and deteriorated on long trips across the seas, whilst beer not only kept its taste but remained wholesome.

Beer even made history. It was because their casks were almost empty that the Pilgrim Fathers, sailing on the Mayflower, decided to cut the voyage short and look for a port, ahead of schedule: "For we could not take time for further search and consideration, our victuals being much spent, especially beer."

WINE

Wine, this "living blood of the grape", comes second: not in quality but in age. It was already produced in Mesopotamia before the year 3000 B.C..

Though not dating back quite as far as beer, wine rejoiced men's hearts almost from the beginning. It was considered not only a gift of the gods but a part of the gods themselves, and drunk as such. Wine was their blood, and with the wine the god entered the human body. Thus, the drinking of wine initially was a sacred ritual, and intoxication was regarded as the presence of the divine spirit, mysteriously working within man. — Egyptians saw in the black and purplish grapes, so round and lustrous, the divine eyes of Horus.

All evidence points to Asia Minor — and especially to the Caucasus — as the vine's original home. It did not take long for man to learn to cultivate the wildly growing grapes. The very name of wine stems from that region and at least from the year 1500 B.C.. It has been found in cuneiform-script on Hittite clay tablets of that time. Both wine and its name spread from there all over the world.

The Bible gives Noah the honour of having invented wine and planted the first vineyard. It further relates that he did so almost immediately after the Flood, when he had alighted from the Ark. This had landed on the summit of the Ararat mountain range — the highest part of the Caucasus!

Accidents happen and mistakes are made all the time. Sometimes, however, they proved not a bane but a boon. Hence it is very likely that a Persian legend is correct in its claim that we owe wine to human error. In fact, wine at first was considered a waste of precious grapes and almost poured away as a poison.

Grapes were plentiful around the city of Persepolis, whose founder, Jam-Sheed, was exceedingly fond of them. He wanted to enjoy them even when they were out of season, and anticipated modern methods of preserving by having grapes bottled and stored.

But one day an accident happened. The luscious round grapes were crushed. Their juice duly fermented and its taste was so strange that Jam-Sheed had it poured into a separate jar. This he immediately marked POISON, but somehow forgot to throw away.

One of his servants had grown tired of life and was determined to commit suicide. By chance she saw the labelled bottle. It was exactly what she was looking for. Secretly she drank of the juice, yet with most unexpected results.

When she came to, she drank some more. No one really knows whether she did so imagining that she had taken too small a dose for the poison to do its work properly, or because she was getting the taste of it and rather enjoyed that strange kind of dying. She repeated the procedure until the jar was empty. Far from dying, she had experienced most world-affirming sensations.

She confessed her deed to her master. By uncovering the prohibited jar, she had discovered wine. This soon became known all over Persia and was described as "the delightful poison".

Wine's popularity spread far and wide. Soon the wild vine shoots were cultivated all over the world — climate permitting. The use of wine increased steadily and was glorified in proverbs and hymns of both pagan and Christian nations. Mohammedans, officially asked to abstain from the drink, excelled in singing its praises.

CHAMPAGNE

Champagne started with a bang. A bottle of wine burst and a wise monk asked, "Why?". At least that is the traditional tale. The champagne recalls an Eastern province of France, famous for its vineyards and generally known as "The Garden of France".

Dom Perignon, a Benedictine who in 1668 was put in charge of his Abbey's cellar, was not satisfied with just looking after the wine. He tried to improve it. His dream was to blend the best of the grapes growing in the vineyards around him, and have his new creation surpass everything else in taste, colour and fragrance. He spent countless hours experimenting.

One day, so the story goes, there was an accident. One of the bottles of wine exploded. Perhaps it was nature herself who, in her peculiar ways, tried to point out with a loud bang what had so far escaped Dom's attention.

Investigating the damage, he noticed that strange bubbles were rising in the wine left in the bottle. He readily assumed that these were somehow related to what had happened. He sipped the wine. Never before had he tasted a drink like it! Excitedly, he called out to his brethren, "I am drinking stars!".

Here was the answer to his quest. All that he needed was to find out what had taken place. Once he had traced the source of the magic bubbles, he would be able to produce the effervescent drink. He reasoned that something inside the bottle must have built up such a pressure that it burst. The bubbles pointed to some kind of secondary fermentation. Soon his research was successful, resulting in the "invention" of champagne.

It may be that all this is just a beautiful story to give additional lustre to the dance of the sparkling atoms. Perhaps the birth of champagne was much more prosaic, yet no less exciting. The fact remains that we owe its discovery to Dom Perignon.

The drink's popularity began with one of those unexpected events which abound in life. At one of his lavish banquets, the Marquis of Sillery wished to offer his guests something unique.

He chose the new champagne. When the party was well in swing, a dozen girls appeared on the floor. They were dressed in the guises of the drunken revellers who once danced and sang in honour of Bacchus, the Greek god of wine. They carried flower-wreathed bottles whose corks suddenly popped. The champagne, fizzing out, was poured into huge glasses specially made for the occasion.

Its taste enchanted the guests who, soon after the feast was over, spread the tale of this wondrous drink wherever they went. The court once again had set the fashion. Ever since, the serving of sparkling wine has become an indispensable part of all ceremonial occasions throughout the world.

THE TEETOTALLER

The Bible not only gives Noah the credit of first making wine, but tells also that he was the first man to discover the mystery of the new plant. After having tasted the fermented juice of the grape, he became drunk and began to act strangely. He behaved most improperly, even according to the primitive standards of ancient morality. He committed the offence of indecent exposure.

No one could blame or condemn Noah for his drunkenness. How could he have known the evil effects of wine on his nervous system and moral inhibitions?

Thousands of years ago, some people decried the use of fermented grape juice. The prophet Hosea, for instance, bitterly attacked those indulging in wine which "took away the heart". Isaiah, too, pointed out, in words whose implication could not be misunderstood, that even the priests and prophets had erred and stumbled in judgment "through strong drink".

Early on thus small groups of men began to dedicate themselves to shun and oppose the drinking of liquor. One of these, the Rechabites, was highly commended by the prophet Jeremiah.

Thus prohibitionists and the temperance movement have their roots in the distant past. And those who sign "the pledge", just like those who enjoy their drink — like the Devil — can cite Scripture for their own purpose.

The description of people who refrain from taking alcohol as *teetotallers* is of much more recent date. Nevertheless, this has not prevented a controversy as to the origin of the name. It was first used in 1834 by Richard Turner, a Lancashire working man, in a speech advocating total abstention from intoxicating drink. However, opinions differ as to how Turner first came to use the term.

Some say that he stuttered. As is usual in such cases, his impediment showed itself specially badly at moments of nervous tension. Passionately pleading his cause, he wanted to end his address by saying that "nothing but *total* abstention will do — that or nowt!" It could have been a most eloquent peroration. But unfortunately Mr. Turner's stammer spoiled it somehow. The audience watched him struggle to articulate and heard him speak haltingly of *t-t-ttotal* abstention.

Opponents immediately made use of the incident. It offered an opportunity of ridiculing both the man and his movement, which they at once christened "t-totalism". But just as the Quakers made a description designed to deride them their name of honour, so total abstainers were neither upset nor annoyed. On the contrary, they adopted their new name and have borne it with pride ever since.

Others believe that it was not really a speaker's stammer but a preference for *tea* at temperance meetings which was responsible for the new word. Though the spelling itself slightly differs, the sound of tea can unmistakably be heard.

Even a game of chance has been quoted as a possible source of the term, though it can be disregarded as such. The *teetotum* was a small, four-sided, lettered disk or die, spun by a player. The letter which lay uppermost when it stopped spinning, decided the player's luck. "T" stood for *totum*, signifying that the player had won *all*, the whole lot. Certainly, teetotallers regarded *all* drink as evil.

GLASS

Glass was not invented. Like wine and champagne, it was discovered by accident. No one will ever know by whom, and exactly when. It is one of the many anonymous, chance-discoveries that have enriched human life. Glass has been in use for at least 6000 years.

The famous 1st-century Roman writer, Pliny the Elder, claims that it was first "found" on the sandy shores of Palestine. Phoenician sailor-merchants were camping there. One night they took from their cargo big lumps of carbonate of soda to support their cooking pots over the fire. Next morning, when raking the ashes, they discovered the first glass. It had been created by the melting sand in the presence of the alkali.

But archaeologists have shown that even this early claim was much too conservative. At the site of ancient Babylon Sir Flinders Petrie excavated specimens of glass, antedating the Phoenician "invention" by many centuries. The earliest examples of man-made glass are Egyptian stone beads coated with blue glass and dating from the year 4000 B.C..

At the beginning, and for a long time, glass was used only as a surface coating or to imitate precious stones and gems. Almost a thousand years passed before the first glass vessels were made. They were definitely in use in Egypt and Mesopotamia in 1500 B.C..

The most common method for making them was known as that of the sand-core process. A core of sand was formed in the desired shape of the vessel and then tightly wrapped in a cloth, which then was either dipped into, or covered by, a solution of warm, viscous glass. When this had cooled, the inner core was removed and the vessel was ready. Alternatively, glass was pressed into a mould or the vessel was ground out of a cool block of glass.

After another 1500 years — just around the birth of Christ and again in Palestine — a new and revolutionary method of making glassware was invented — blowing, whose essential principle has not changed ever since.

Mystery envelops even this comparatively late invention. Was it the result of ingenuity or again the outcome of chance? Tradition favours the latter view. It says that a glass maker found a faulty tube — it had been accidentally closed by the hot glass at one end. To remove the obstructing blob, he blew into the tube from the other end. But instead of the tube opening up, the blob of glass became a bubble. Thus the latest method of glass-working was born.

CHAPTER VIII

the history
of man's dress

BIBLICALLY, tailoring started in Paradise, when Adam and Eve sewed their first dress of fig leaves. But somehow this must have proved unsatisfactory, as soon afterwards the Bible records the first change in fashion, when animal skins supplanted the fig leaves.

Opinions still differ as to what man's first dress, at least according to biblical tradition, looked like. Some describe it as a simple girdle. Others suggest that the apron was man's first costume. A 16th century translation of Hebrew Scripture erroneously stated that Adam and Eve made themselves breeches!

From the very earliest times, men and women have covered their bodies, and the reasons why have become increasingly complex. Nearly everything we wear has had, at different times through the ages, a definite purpose, although today, in many instances, this has faded into obscurity.

Primarily, clothes protected the human body from the forces of nature. Man needed them in order to survive. A sense of modesty was another source. Associating sex with shame, man tried to hide the erotic zones of his body. However, dress was often designed also to impress others and arouse fear, admiration and desire. It is a form of attractive display (like the feathers on birds or the gay marking on animal skins).

Clothes were introduced to emphasize the difference between the sexes, to stimulate the senses, but to avoid promiscuity. On the other hand, dress was a means to stress class distinction. In the nude people are equal. But costumes removed this democracy of the uniformity of naked bodies. An outer skin could make all the difference and thus dress became much more revealing of human character than nakedness. It was the earliest status symbol, proclaiming the wearer's profession, power and social rank.

Always anxious to make the greatest use of anything they possessed, people soon employed their cloak for numerous other functions as well. It became their blanket, and even their bed. When the Hebrews left Egypt, they wrapped into their garments their kneading troughs and all they contained. Merchants used their robes as counters, on which they displayed their wares, and cloaks served as saddles and carpets as well.

To be properly dressed has meant many things to different ages. What was considered decent to one generation and quite in order, has sometimes shocked and offended another. Fashion certainly is a taste shared by a large number of people for a short time. There have been eras when dress has tried to conceal natural shapes and others when everything possible has been done to display them.

It becomes evident that man's wardrobe is crowded with intriguing revelations about his attitudes and reactions to life, society and the other sex. What applies to dress in general, is equally true of each of its peculiar features, with their contradictions, incredibilities and many surprises.

The leopard cannot change his spots. But man has the power to change his skin. And certainly he has made good use of it. There are few sayings truer than that "clothes make the man".

TROUSERS

Trousers were first worn by the Nomads of Central Asia, possibly a thousand years before Christ. We owe their invention to the horse.

Originally, people dressed merely by wrapping a piece of cloth or animal skin around their bodies. The warriors of the Asian steppes found that this sort of garment was uncomfortable on horseback and restricted their movement greatly. That is how they got the idea to clothe the lower part of their bodies with trousers. These were not as drab as ours. They were striped, checked and even embroidered.

And when the Nomads clashed in battle with their "civilized" neighbours, these recognized the usefulness of trousers, as their own long flowing garments put them at a disadvantage. They lost no time in adopting the barbarians' attire — not out of fashion but in order to survive in battle.

Thus from Central Asia, through war and the horse, the use of trousers was eventually adopted by the Persians, the Indians, the Chinese and found its way into Northern Europe.

When in 55 B.C. Julius Caesar reached Britain he specially remarked on the brightly-coloured trousers worn there by the men. It was actually the Romans' conflict with the barbarians of the North, that introduced trousers into their Empire.

However, at first there was much opposition, and the Romans despised the new garment, called it unworthy of noblemen and fit only for slaves. But in spite of it, the trousers' obvious advantages soon made them fashionable. So much so that an Imperial edict was issued threatening those freemen who wore trousers with loss of property and banishment. But it had no effect. Trousers had come to stay at least for a while.

Then, even in Northern Europe, they went out of fashion again. In their present form they were reintroduced in England at the end of the 18th century, superseding breeches and silk stockings. But even as late as 1814 the Duke of Wellington was refused admission to his club because he was wearing trousers.

Trinity College issued an order in 1812 that any student who appeared in Hall or Chapel and was clad in trousers, should be deemed absent. In Sheffield a special clause appertaining to clergy ruled that "under no circumstances whatever shall any preacher be allowed to occupy the pulpit who wears trousers". Indeed, any one so attired would not go to Heaven!

Modern times rendered the wearing of trousers a matter of life and death. During the French Revolution, they became a political symbol of the equality of man. Former aristocrats put on the blue linen pants of workmen, to try to escape the guillotine.

On the other hand, less than a hundred years ago rich men in England adopted the wearing of trousers. They suffered badly from gout and were convinced that this proletarian (and barbarian) attire would assuage the pain of their swollen legs.

TURN-UPS

An immaculate Englishman's concern with his dress on a rainy day in New York is said to have been responsible for the introduction of cuffs on trousers.

People have often wondered why trousers should have this peculiar fold at the bottom. What purpose did it serve, apart from collecting dirt and dust which, according to clothing experts, amounts to at least one ounce every year?

Some have suggested that tall men invented the cuff because it made them appear somehow shorter and less ill at ease. Others, more commercially minded, assumed that the cuff owes its existence to merchants to whom every inch of extra cloth sold meant more profit.

As far as records are available, cuffs on trousers were first seen in New York towards the end of the last century on the occasion of a big society wedding. This was attended by numerous dandies as well as by respectable visitors from the Old World. At the time Americans specially watched their English cousins, whom they then still tried to imitate, at least as far as their dress was concerned.

One of the overseas guests was late; he had been caught in a downpour which flooded the streets. The ingenious Englishman, so meticulously clad, did not want to spoil the hang of his trousers and so, to keep them dry, he rolled up their bottoms.

Due to the excitement and his late arrival, he somehow forgot to turn them down again and so, when ascending the church steps, conspicuously displayed his "cuffs".

Many took notice of them but, unaware of their real reason, took them to be the latest English fashion and eagerly copied the "turn-ups".

THE WAISTCOAT

Fashion has had a profound effect upon the waistcoat, a garment that has come and gone many times since its first appear-

ance in the 16th century. Its purpose was manifold and equally
subject to change.

In its earliest use it was an elaborate and costly apparel of
show, lending itself especially to the expression of individual
taste. It was worn purely as an ornament and it was most unusual to wear a waistcoat made of the same material as the coat.

Though worn under the jacket, it was meant to be seen and admired and had, therefore, to be — at least partly — visible. This
was made all the easier as at the time the sleeved coat was not
fastened at all: its buttons served only a decorative purpose.
Indeed, later on, coats were specially cut away in front so that
the waistcoat would show to better advantage.

It was made of the finest of materials, often with silver and
gold, and in all colours, the gayer the better. Frequently
quilted, embroidered and even fringed, the waistcoat was lavishly
adorned with delicate handwork.

An inventory of Henry VIII's wardrobe records a waistcoat of
"cloth and silver, quilted with black silk" and another of "white
satin, with sleeves embroidered with Venice silver". When the
Earl of Essex, the unfortunate favourite and victim of Queen
Elizabeth I, was led to his execution, he put off his doublet and
was seen to wear underneath a scarlet waistcoat.

Even so modest a man as the great Beethoven was anxious to
have an elegant waistcoat. In 1793 he wrote to a young lady of
whom he was fond, asking her kindly to help him in the realization of this wish: "that I may be lucky enough to possess a
waistcoat worked by you in goat's wool."

Gradually, however, the waistcoat was not only shortened in
length (at first having reached the dimensions of a jacket) but
was reduced in status as well. Instead of its original ornamental
role, it came to fulfil a strictly utilitarian function. Frenchmen
in particular stressed its purpose: "to protect chest and stomach
from the air" in winter and encourage "a healthy tendency to
sweat in the summer".

And even when medical opinions changed and sweat and the
exclusion of fresh air were no longer considered helpful but
harmful, the waistcoat still served man well. Its multiple
pockets were useful for carrying many small items.

Between the two World Wars the waistcoat lost both its aesthetic and practical appeal. It is only now making a come-back — once again as an ornament to brighten up man's drab clothes.

THE BOTTOM BUTTON ON THE WAISTCOAT

Custom decrees that a man should leave the bottom button of his waistcoat undone.

One explanation dates this strange fashion back to a member of the British Royal Family who appeared at a public function with his bottom button unfastened. Possibly he had dressed in too much of a hurry, or one of his aides had been neglectful in fulfilling his duty. No one could know (or would dare to guess) the reason. So that he should not be embarrassed, all the other men followed "suit" and the fad caught on. Once again, Royalty had set the fashion.

Another theory traces the undone button habit back to the stage where the dandies were wearing not one waistcoat but two, each of extremely precious and gaudy material, a scarlet one underneath, for instance, and a canary-yellow one on top. By leaving the bottom button of the top waistcoat undone, the wearer was able to show the fact that he had another beautiful and expensive garment on underneath.

Much less glamorous but more practical is a third explanation. Waistcoats were tight, especially so around the waist. Therefore some leader of fashion undid the last button in the interests of comfort and everyone followed his lead.

Waistcoats have lost their original close fitting. Tailors remedied the defect of tightness by inserting some extra cloth into the sides. But, as always in life, customs once introduced for definite reasons, are accepted to be right for all times and, therefore, they are thoughtlessly continued, even when they have become redundant.

BUTTONS ON SLEEVE

The obvious purpose of a button is to secure a dress for reasons of fit, or warmth and decency. None of these motives, however, seems to explain the small buttons on the cuffs of man's present-day jackets.

These buttons are really useless now. But when they were first sewn on sleeves, they served a definite purpose. Their origin was linked with the early long sleeves. The buttons were a simple and ingenious means of preventing them from hanging down and impeding movement.

In the 17th century, much money was spent on men's coats and naturally people tried to avoid anything that would ruin them. Most vulnerable, of course, were the cuffs. To keep them out of harm's way, they were turned back. And lest they slip down again, they were fastened with buttons.

Also the buttons could help a man to adjust his dress to suit the climate. If it was cold and windy, the wide sleeve could be tightened and closed around the wrist.

In centuries past, man was not as drab in his dress as in later years. Like his female partner he, too, liked to adorn himself and if possible to display his wealth by means of his costume. Buttons could serve just that purpose. They were hand-made in beautiful shapes and colours. They were both costly and decorative.

Buttons no longer were used to fasten sleeves to keep them out of the wind or dirt, but to boost the ego and attract attention. John Brandon, for example, who died in 1364, was shown with 40 buttons on the sleeve of his undervest alone.

The distinctive buttons on military uniforms are said to to have found their way there for totally different reasons. At least that is the story usually told. They started as the result of a king's displeasure when he saw some of his men wiping their noses on their sleeves. To make such behaviour impossible, he decreed the fixing of cuff-buttons. Any soldier who forgot to use his sneeze-rag and tried to wipe his nose on his sleeves, soon desisted in pain.

"TO LAUGH UP ONE'S SLEEVE"

To "laugh up one's sleeve" is certainly not a sign of good manners. Worse still, it shows not the best of character. After all, no decent person would laugh at another's expense and do so — cowardly — hiding his amusement.

Altogether the phrase itself seems so absurd. You laugh in front of a person or behind his back. But who could ever laugh up his sleeve? It just does not make sense.

Yet what now seems so meaningless an expression was quite intelligible (and possible) in days gone by. To laugh up one's sleeve, indeed, is part of the history of man's dress and its peculiar evolution.

The fact is that while costumes changed in shape and dimensions, language lagged behind and was slow to adapt itself. It carried outmoded notions and references to long discarded fashions. Man's sleeves were once not as tight-fitting as they are today. Nor did they extend only to the wrist. They were wide and exceedingly long, so much so that at times they had to be carried over the arm or knotted so as not to drag along the ground. Ingenious tailors even put holes in the sleeves which enabled the wearer to put his hands and arms through them much higher up — without having to reach down all the way.

In some circles the length of the sleeve indicated the owner's importance. This is a tradition which is preserved, like those wide, hanging sleeves themselves, in academic gowns. At Oxford University, for example, an undergraduate's gown lacks sleeves altogether. But those worn by a Master of Arts reach down almost to the ground.

In the days when the phrase was coined, it was quite simple to hide one's smile by lifting and holding the long sleeve in front of the face. It served as a screen and no one could see or guess what one was actually doing behind it.

THE DIFFERENT WAY OF BUTTONING FOR MEN AND WOMEN

How to secure one's dress has been a problem ever since man has worn clothes, which means from the beginning of human existence. Even Adam and Eve must have wondered at first how to fasten their fig leaves!

The bulk of early clothing used merely to hang down from the shoulders, but later the folds were secured by laces and braces. A later development was the button.

This was adopted as early as the 13th century, about which

time it first appeared on man's dress either hidden, visible or
conspicuous. Man used buttons either practically, decoratively
or rather shamefacedly, as in the case of man's fly, introduced
into the breeches in the days of King Charles I.

It might be thought that even though men and women wore
different types of garment at least they would share the same
method of fastening it. But, as everyone knows, this is not so.

Men button their clothes from pyjamas to everyday jackets
from left to right, while women do exactly the opposite.

The origin of this peculiar fashion and its variation in the
case of women is not due, as cynics have sometimes suggested,
to a woman's stubbornness and her traditional way of being just
contrary — but to the fact that most men and women are
righthanded.

It was practical, but now forgotten and obsolete, considerations that led to this little-noticed but nevertheless marked distinction in buttoning a garment.

Men were always independent. At least, in their manner of
dressing, which they did themselves and mostly without any
assistance. But women, and noble ladies especially, were dressed
by their maids.

Therefore, in the case of women, it was a convenient process
to reverse the sides of the garment on which the buttons were
secured because the maid, who faced her mistress during
dressing operations, used her right hand and so found it easier
to button the garment from right to left.

Another possible reason is that medieval man always had to be
prepared for a fight and, therefore, walked about armed. So that
he could readily grasp and effectively use his sword, it was essential for him to have his right hand ready for combat and not
stiff from cold. To ensure this he thrust it into his coat to keep
it warm. But to be able to do so, his coat had to open from left
to right.

In the early days men also wore a loose cloak which they
grasped with their left hand, throwing the left side over the
right so as to keep the right hand free. This, too, contributed to
the introduction of overlapping from left to right for men's
clothes.

Women had to carry a baby, usually supporting it with their

left arm. When it became necessary to breast-feed a child in public — and it quite often did, among the masses, anyway — the left breast was used as being most convenient.

To shelter the infant from wind and cold while it was feeding, they covered it with the right side of the dress or coat and thus designers of those days made women's clothes so that they would button-up from right to left.

All these motives no longer apply. Yet habits do not die easily, and men and women still carry on the now apparently senseless fashion of buttoning-up their garments in opposite ways.

THE SLIT IN THE LAPEL

Today the slit in the lapel of a man's jacket is only decorative. That is why its size and shape may differ according to taste and fashion. However, it was not consideration of comeliness that first introduced the "cut". Its origin can be accounted for in two different ways: one rather sentimental and even sorrowful, the other practical and rational.

The ancient Hebrews, as a sign of mourning at the death of a loved one, made a tear in their coat. In the case of parents they never sewed this up again; it served as a permanent reminder of their loss. Actually this custom is merely the last token of an even more ancient habit in which the garment was rent altogether at the moment of bereavement. Perhaps it was the manifestation of a psychological mechanism, helping people to overcome their grief by externalizing it.

No matter what the reason, the fact is that the "mournful" tear in one's coat became a wide-spread custom all over the world and is still being kept by observant Orthodox Jews of our time. Somehow their Christian neighbours adopted the slit in the lapel and an original mourning rite was continued even at moments of greatest joy. Without knowing it, men began to walk about all the time wearing what is really a gesture of sorrow.

Yet much more likely is a second explanation. This claims that not sentimental but practical considerations introduced the slit. In olden days collars were very large, mainly because in wintry cold they could serve as a natural shield. Men just turned them up to protect and keep warm their throat and neck. So that the collar could remain flat when turned down in normal weather, it became essential to insert a slit, which has endured to this day.

THE HANDKERCHIEF

Poets and dramatists have used the handkerchief both as a beautiful metaphor and a target of vitriolic attack. Bernard Shaw decried it as a vicious harbourer of bacteria, whilst Walt Whitman called grass "the handkerchief of God".

Today a handkerchief seems a very ordinary item of dress. But it has had an eventful history. It is full of contradictions and contains an Oriental past and a French corruption. Most disappointing of all, it got its *hand* only at the very end, though now this appears as its prefix.

Originally, the handkerchief had no connection at all with man's hand. It was a simple cloth used in the East to protect the head from the burning rays of the sun. Probably sailors introduced it from there into France, where it soon became fashionable. And quite logically the French called this new kind of garment (which it then was) "a covering for the head" — *couvrir chef*.

The cloth crossed the Channel and the British adopted it and its French name, but in the process they corrupted the word simply to kerchief.

It did not take long, however, to become apparent that such a light covering was inadequate in the cold English climate to protect the head. And without doing away completely with the new attire, people removed it from their head, and carried it (often very conspicuously) in their hand! They found the kerchief useful for blowing their noses and wiping away perspiration from the face.

They duly acknowledged the new way of carrying the cloth instead of wearing it by adding the *hand* to its name and thereby creating the monstrous and contradictory word of a hand-head-covering or, in its English hybrid form, hand-ker-chief!

A further development took place to add to the confusion. Men began to put into their pockets this piece of cloth they had carried in their hands which originally had covered their heads!

The Romans anticipated our modern handkerchief by napkins

carried by the upper class. This custom completely disappeared for more than a thousand years with the fall of the Roman Empire. Anglo-Saxons, too, had their "sweat cloth", which still survives, though for a different purpose, in one of the ecclesiastical vestments of the Church.

We know for certain that even in the late Middle Ages the handkerchief was still unknown by the fact that priests were then reprimanded by their superiors for using their sacred garments for the blowing of their noses. It was indeed only in the 16th century that the handkerchief (just as the word) came into use, though at first only among the aristocracy. Hygiene has led some of us today to replace the original cloth by soft paper substitutes. The handkerchief itself has quite largely resumed the role of a decorative accessory.

WIGS

Wigs have come into their own again. Yet they have been used for thousands of years. Mummified bodies, found in Egyptian graves, wore wigs. Men and women alike have used them. They did so for various reasons.

Wigs are rooted in superstitious fear and magic make-believe. Hair was considered a source and a symbol of strength and in earliest times people regarded their hair as a seat of the vital spirit of life. The more there was of it, the stronger they imagined themselves (or others) to be. Warriors, especially, let it grow long, lest they lost their vigour and invited defeat, as illustrated by the story of Samson.

For this reason primitive races refrained from cutting their children's hair for at least the first year of their lives. Otherwise, they were convinced, the infants' future strength and health would be impaired.

People tried not only to protect what hair they had but to add to it by every possible means. For that purpose, first and primarily, wigs were invented. It was thought that — magically — they increased vigour and that the abundance of hair frightened off enemies, real and imaginary. The wig deceived evil forces and threatening foes by emphasizing or simulating towering strength.

A beautiful crown of hair has always been treasured. It made people so much more attractive and has been found sexually exciting. A wig, most certainly, could add to the lure of both male and female. Thus it became a significant accessory and weapon in the battle of love. It enhanced a man's (and woman's) appearance by framing the head with dark, blond or white hair.

Sparse hair or, worse still, baldness made impossible the natural wish of men and women to be just like other people. The mere fact of looking so different caused disdain, suspicion and ridicule. Therefore wigs were also devised to hide baldness.

Wigs served, too, as a useful disguise. They could conceal the wearers' identity and were therefore chosen by spies, fugitives and actors. The Greek theatre was fond of coloured wigs. Their shade indicated the character represented. A black wig was the sign of a tyrant. Heroes wore blond curls. Red was the colour of the comic servant.

As wigs are distinctive and can accentuate social status, they became part of man's professional attire. They were worn to proclaim a dignitary's special standing, as they still continue to do in British courts and in Parliament.

The fashion of wigs, just as their shapes and sizes, has waxed and waned through the centuries. Like the ancient Egyptians and Assyrians, the Romans and Greeks favoured false hair.

In the days of Tacitus even primitive German tribes welcomed its use. They did so, however, not for the sake of adornment but for commercial reasons. They exported bales of their own blond hair to Rome. Yet the early Church frowned on wigs and denounced them as evil.

It was only in the 17th century that wigs became firmly established in Europe. A royal example, born of necessity, set the fashion. Louis XIII of France became bald prematurely. He first used a few artificial strands to supplement his own sparse growth but as his baldness increased, he had to don a complete covering wig.

Possibly out of courtesy, if not sympathy, and to make the king's new hair-style less conspicuous, the courtiers followed suit. Soon the "common" people, always anxious to ape nobility, copied the *perruque*, as the French called it. It was this word which gave the English language its *periwig*, eventually to be shortened to our present-day wig.

Another French king reinforced the custom. When Louis XIV

was a child, everyone admired his lovely locks which fell to the shoulders. Those who surrounded and served the prince tried to emulate him, at least in the growth of his hair. They did so by donning a wig. Imitation has always been the sincerest flattery. Many years later, the king adopted the fashion he had created as a boy!

From France, the wig spread all over Europe. It arrived in England during the second half of the 17th century. In no time it was thought to be "the proper thing", though its form changed frequently. Some people wore the "natural" or full-bottomed wig. Others adorned themselves with one of huge dimensions, towering above the forehead in two huge peaks and falling around, and far below, the shoulders.

The many variations became known by such descriptive names as "the staircase", "the spinach seed", "the artichoke", "the comet", "the pigeon's wing" and "the wild boar's back". By the middle of the 18th century there were almost 40 different types.

It was from those early days of the wig in Britain that we retain it as an accessory of ceremonial costume. As a survival of that general fashion it is still worn by the Speaker of the House of Commons, the Lord Chamberlain and all judges and barristers in the British Commonwealth.

Suddenly, the trade in wigs experienced a slump. To meet the cost of the French wars, the government introduced a tax on powder, so essential for wig-wearers. Wig-makers felt the pinch so much that they petitioned King George III to help them, as (so they wrote) their business had grown so small "by the present mode of all men in all stations wearing their own hair!".

When wigs became fashionable again, not a few men, probably on the score of expense, cleverly dressed their own hair so that it appeared like a wig. Still, the vogue of wigs continued. Some grew to such heights that caricatures showed barbers attending their charges while standing on ladders.

Immediately before the French Revolution, head-dress reached up to 3 ft. and more. Blond became the most stylish colour, though Madame Tallien, of Paris, preferred black. Some women owned 30 wigs in different tints.

Paradoxes and intriguing features are associated with the custom of the wig. Jewish ecclesiastical authorities made its wearing obligatory for a married woman! Her own hair was considered too seductive to be seen by any man but her husband. Therefore she had to cover it with the artificial creation, meant to render her unattractive, if not ugly. But women soon took their revenge and began to use wigs of the latest colour and shape.

Even in the Age of Reason, men of enlightened education continued to wear wigs and did not mind their artificiality. They did not think it strange at all to shave off their own hair and then to don that of others. Pepys went so far as to wear his own hair as a wig. According to him, to do so was more hygienic!

Others chose the hair of their wives or of children, who had to be guarded from robber-haircutters, trying to deprive them of their rich curly growth. Poor people soon discovered in the fashion a welcome means of livelihood. They sold their hair to the highest bidder. Even corpses were a source of material.

Wigs have been made of all kinds of stuff: wool, fur, horsehair, straw, wire and nylon. What a wealth of material men's wigs thus present. Ostentation, vanity and husbands' fear of losing their wives to other men: they all participated in making the wig a distinctive feature — coming and going in the course of civilization.

THE FAN

Fans were the earliest — man-propelled — air-conditioners. The first fan was probably a huge palm leaf, or some other naturally grown device (such as a bird's feathers), swayed by slaves. The artificially created breeze appeared to cool the air, and the movement kept away irritating insects. Ancient Egyptian hosts employed special servants to stand behind their guests and fan them with big fans of papyrus.

Though thus completely utilitarian in origin, it did not take long for the fan to assume other significant functions.

Only the rich and noble could be concerned with their comfort or afford extra servants to carry and sway the then sizeable fans. Therefore almost inevitably these became a symbol of the "upper class", of dignity and position. The fan came to indicate superiority and importance, and thus was used for state and religious purposes, as it is today among Oriental potentates and in Papal processions.

The original, naturally grown, fan eventually gave place to new gadgets, cleverly constructed to fold in a small compass and, when expanded, to take the form of a section of a circle. Because of their new small size, servants were no longer needed to carry or sway them. The fan had become an accessory for all people, but especially so for women.

Feminine ingenuity soon discovered yet a further and quite unexpected value of the fan: it could rouse passions. Women of primitive races had learned the usefulness of a sham-flight from the men, to be pursued all the more fervently. Now their modern sisters discovered that by just sitting still behind their fan, in an assumed retreat of modesty, with their eyes peering over its top from time to time, they could lure their prey all the more easily and in comfort. The fan had become a potent weapon in the war of the sexes, with the woman's dignity well preserved.

Charming is a Chinese tradition as to how the fan was first invented. It was one of the pleasant chance-discoveries of daily life. A royal princess, participating in the Feast of Lanterns, had her face covered with a mask, which was proper for a person of her rank. But the heat and the pressure of the mask became too much and she lifted it slightly. Then, to cool her brow but at the same time still to conceal her features, she moved the mask quickly to and fro in front of her face. Others, similarly distressed, followed her example. The fan had made its entry.

THE UMBRELLA

Originally, the umbrella served only as a sunshade. Its name is a reminder of this fact. *Umbra* is the Latin word for shade.

Umbrellas were introduced in the East thousands of years ago. They were known in Mesopotamia, Egypt and China as early as the 12th century B.C.. They were then a mark of nobility. The audience chamber of the king of Siam was furnished with three umbrellas — and nothing else.

Few people could afford an umbrella. No wonder that kings prided themselves to own one or, luckier still, several, such as the ruler of Ava who signed himself as "The King of the White Elephants and Lord of 24 Umbrellas".

Umbrellas were not only costly, but heavy, and special servants, mostly slaves, carried them. Ancient pictorial representation shows dignitaries, kings and priests, being accompanied by
their umbrella-carriers, whose only duty it was to shelter their
master from the sun. Inevitably, the open umbrella, like its rolled
descendant in English society thousands of years later, became
a status symbol.

Europe eventually adopted the umbrella, though for a considerable period it remained a guard against the sun only and was
reserved for the rich and noble. That is how Papal Rome came to
use it, and even horsemen in the Italy of the Renaissance.

.Technical advance and the invention of cheaper material in
the 17th century made the umbrella available to everybody. The
traditional leather was replaced by lighter cloths, of which silk
became most popular. Whalebone was used for the ribs and the
umbrella became so light that the owner could carry it himself.
Yet another occupation of man had been made redundant by the
progress of science.

Only then did people begin to appreciate the umbrella's usefulness as a protection against rain. The logical French wisely
differentiated between its dual functions and, ever since, have
continued to speak of the para*sol* — in the case of the *sun* — and
the para*pluie* — in reference to the *rain*.

Yet the umbrella was still not generally adopted. Opposition
arose from various quarters. Men considered it effeminate. Snob-
bishness, too, made people avoid its use. It was reasoned that
only those who could not afford a carriage needed umbrellas.
Thus, to carry one immediately stamped its owner as a man of
little means. The umbrella, once the precious property of wealthy
potentates, had thus deteriorated into a cheap substitute for a
carriage, appropriate only for the impecunious.

Jonas Hanway (1712-1786) made Britain umbrella-conscious.
The claim, commonly held, that he actually introduced it there,
is a slight exaggeration. However, he was the first to display it
conspicuously. Because of it, he had to suffer ridicule and almost
assault. The general population, always suspicious of new-
fangled gadgets, jeered at him whenever they saw him walking
about so suitably fortified against the inclement English climate.

Worse still, he angered sedan-chair men and hackney coach-men, who deemed it their monopoly to protect people from rain. They saw a threat to their livelihood in the new contraption. But in spite of all their abuse Hanway continued to carry his "guard from chilly showers".

Only when his example was followed by one of Britain's famous dandies, popularly known as Beau Macdonald, did the umbrella at last catch on. Though he, too, at first was subjected to ig-nominy. His own sister refused to be seen with him in public.

Improvements reduced the umbrella's weight and added to the efficiency of its mechanism. Metal replaced the whalebone and a new frame first constructed in the 1850s gave the umbrella even less weight and more strength and Samuel Fox, its inventor, large profits.

Of course, people continued to use the umbrella as a sunshade as well. To protect the skin from sunburn was then presumed to be essential for health and a pale face was looked upon as digni-fied and attractive. Then, soon after World War I, people chang-ed their opinion. Sunshine was now taken to be health-giving and a sun-tanned face beautiful and desirable. As a protection against rain, the umbrella resumed its initial role of a status symbol, "the acknowledged index of social position". To carry it over one's arm, neatly rolled, came to symbolize the English gentleman.

The umbrella has played a part in many spheres. It has formed the object of affection and inspiration, been an instrument in the psychological interpretation of dreams and even, at a moment of grave crisis, it has led one of our modern dictators to draw wrong conclusions.

One woman became so attached to her umbrella that she left instructions in her will that it was to be enclosed with her in the coffin. Sigmund Freud's vivid imagination saw in the appearance of an umbrella in dreams, an indication of their sexual content. It was a symbol of the phallus.

Chamberlain's umbrella at Munich has become almost prover-bial. The story is told that when Hitler, at that crucial hour of history, saw Britain's Prime Minister alight from his plane forti-fied with an umbrella, he sneered loudly. A nation whose leader was so much concerned with protecting himself from rain at a time when the existence of whole countries was in the balance must lack power of resistance, he reasoned—so wrongly, as he had to find out in the deluge that was to follow.

THE HATBAND

The colour and width of the band around a man's hat may vary according to fashion. But the band itself today is considered as something without which a hat would be incomplete. Its purpose is accepted as merely ornamental, to add a little "colour" to an otherwise rather dull male attire.

Yet the origin of the band leads back to man's earliest head-dress. It served then an indispensable practical function. Indeed, it could be said that the band itself was man's first hat. Egyptians, for instance, when travelling, secured their hair (not cut as short as ours) with a band around the head.

However people did not just think of keeping their hair tidy. They were much more concerned with their health. They knew that to walk about bare-headed at times was perilous and could impair their well-being. They had to take notice of the vagaries of the weather and protect the head both from the sun and cold.

A simple piece of cloth was an obvious device. It is still retained, almost in its original form, in the *Kephiyeh*, worn mainly by desert tribes of the Middle East. Here again, a band, or cord or, first of all strands of camel hair, were essential to keep the "hat" on. It was tied around the crown of the head.

Early examples of the modern type of hat, which supplanted the primitive cloth, were not made to measure. They fitted loosely and a gust of wind or sudden movement could dislodge them. Again, the band was utilized. Tied under the chin, it fastened the hat properly and kept it on. When the sun went down and a head-covering was no longer required, there was no need to take it off and carry it. All that was necessary was to loosen the band and let the hat hang down the back. It was a simple and sensible method of wearing and carrying it and yet keeping one's hands free.

The making of hats improved and use of new materials and methods at last enabled hatters to take note of individual taste and measurements. Suddenly, the band had outlived its usefulness. If logic ruled our life, the band, having thus become obsolete in its original function, could have been discarded forthwith. But people soon forgot its initial purpose. They retained it, considering it a "must"for those who wished to be properly dressed.

The streamers which hang down at the back of the Scottish cap and children's sailor hats are vestiges of the original hat band. They are just its loose ends.

THE MAD HATTER

Only in recent times have we learned to regard insanity as a sickness. For thousands of years the mentally sick were decried as people possessed by the Devil or harmfully affected by the rays of the moon, and therefore called lunatics.

To describe a person unbalanced in mind as being "as mad as a hatter" added insult to injury and slandered a respectable occupation. The two completely different explanations which exist for this unfortunate phrase reveal the wretched effect of ignorance.

The observation has nothing to do with hatters. It refers to atters, which is Anglo-Saxon for an adder or viper. The word mad formally was used in a quite different sense. It described something as harmful or poisonous. Hence, the phrase originally spoke of a person being "as venomous as an adder".

The second version asserts that the words really meant what they said, and that the saying is the result of an early occupational hazard of those who, before the industrial revolution, made hats for a living.

Hats were then mostly manufactured from the fur of animals such as the beaver and rabbit. Mercury, more commonly known as quicksilver, was used in the processing. Its harmful qualities were then not realized and hatters, through frequent handling of the dangerous metal, slowly absorbed it into the system and poisoned their body. The first symptoms of sickness appeared as "the shakes". These were soon followed by mental aberrations.

Of course, at the time no one even guessed the cause of the illness, and it was not to defame hatters, but merely to acknowledge an unfortunate phenomenon, that people began to compare anyone unbalanced in mind with hatters.

That is how the saying first entered English phraseology. It was popularized by William Thackeray and, most of all, Lewis Carroll, in their writings.

TO RUN THE GAUNTLET

The word gauntlet is of French origin and refers to a glove. It was worn as part of medieval armour, being made usually of leather, covered with plates of light steel or chain mail.

But when speaking of "running the gauntlet", to describe a passing through a critical ordeal or being attacked from all sides, that kind of gauntlet has nothing to do with wearing apparel. Its place there is only because of mistaken identities.

In this phrase gauntlet is derived from a combination of two Swedish words: *gata,* meaning "a passage" (which actually created the English word gate) and *lopp,* meaning "to run" (responsible for our leap). And this explains the expression.

The passage referred to consisted of a double row of soldiers, who faced each other. Through it an offender, stripped to his waist, had to run as a form of punishment.

Each of the soldiers was provided with either a knotted cord, the end of a rope or a stick, with which he had to hit hard the passing delinquent. It goes without saying that the latter did not amble through this double row of soldiers but ran as quickly as possible in great leaps to avoid as many blows as he could.

The description dates back to the Thirty Years' War when military authorities first introduced this kind of punishment. Later, it was adopted by American courts of law, the first reference to it being made in 1676.

Indians made use of it also, subjecting their captives, red or white, to the ordeal. Scottish regiments applied the same treatment to minor offenders, mostly in order to keep good discipline.

Another, but less likely, explanation is that the phrase comes not from the Swedish but from the Flemings. It is said that the gaunt in gauntlet is a corruption of the city of Ghent in Flanders, where the punishment is believed to have been invented.

SPECTACLES

Ancient Nineveh knew spectacles of a kind. They were magnifying lenses which were made, not of glass but of crystal.

However, it was not until the 13th century A.D. that the first real spectacles appeared. It is now assumed that Roger Bacon was one of the first to make them. The credit for inventing them has been given to an Italian, the Florentine Salvina Armato, who died in 1317.

These early spectacles were used by short-sighted monks to read manuscripts. At first, they held the lenses in front of their eyes and the two "glasses" were joined by some kind of hinge. Eventually, this was made stiff enough to keep them, though very precariously, on the nose.

A long period of trial and error followed during which all kinds of methods of fixing the spectacles to the head were tried out. Long strips of metal were used, leading from the bridge of the nose over the centre of the head and down to the neck. It was a complicated and cumbersome way and not very successful.

Further experiments employed chains with little weights at their end. Straps, not very different from present-day motor-cycle goggles, were another attempt to solve the problem. Some people even attached their spectacles to the hat. This was not pleasant for indoor studies nor for the citizens obliged to greet superiors in the street.

After many years — the precise date is unknown — someone hit on the idea of fastening the glasses to the ears with side pieces or "legs".

By the end of the 14th century spectacles were in common use. They then frequently appeared on paintings and, as they were considered a precious possession, were specially mentioned in inventories. Records show that in 1520 Pope Leo X went hunting wearing spectacles.

Bifocals are not as recent an invention as people imagine. They were known by the end of the 18th century. Benjamin Franklin had a pair made so that on his trips he could enjoy both the beautiful scenery and his treasured books. Contact lenses were first applied in France in 1888 for medical reasons. Certain diseases of the eye impaired the vision in such a way that it could not be improved by the use of ordinary glasses. An example at hand is conical cornea.

CHAPTER IX

BEAUTY CULTURE

AMONG the many treasures exhibited by the British Museum in London is the mummified body of an Egyptian woman, at least 5000 years old. Conspicuously it displays an astonishing feature. It shows that her finger and toe nails had been painted dark red.

Women have used make-up as long as it can be remembered. None of our so-called modern cosmetics is new. They were applied in like manner in ancient Egypt, Babylonia and China.

Actually, women today are still lagging behind and have either forgotten or not yet taken up other old-established beauty aids. Apart from shaving off unwanted hair, using rouge, beautifying their eyes and colouring the lips, women of antiquity stained the soles of the feet with henna and touched up the nipples of the breasts with a purple dye.

Make-up has been used on all kinds of occasions. Queen Jezebel of Israel painted her face before throwing herself out of the window, so that she would die attractively. Pepys proudly wrote in his diary of the black patches worn on her face by his wife.

Throughout history men have tried repeatedly, but with little success, to stop women using cosmetics. Apart from moral or religious reasons, they have done so in self-defence. Clement of Alexandria in the 2nd century A.D. thus encouraged the proclamation of a law to prevent women from tricking husbands into marriage by means of cosmetics. Some 200 years later, John Chrysostomos wrote: "If anyone were painting the ideal body to house the soul of an ideal woman, he would not dream of show-ing a face that had bloody lips like the mouth of a bear, or sooty eyebrows that look as though they came from a dirty kitchen pot".

In 1770 a Bill was introduced into the British Parliament (but subsequently defeated) which demanded:

> "That all women of whatever age, rank, degree or profession, whether virgins, maids or widows, who shall from and after such an act impose upon, seduce or betray into matrimony any of His Majesty's subjects, by the scents, paints, cosmetic washes, artificial teeth, false hair, Spanish wool, iron stays, hoops, high-heeled shoes, bolstered hips, shall incur the penalty of the law in force against witchcraft and like mis-demeanours, and that the marriage, upon conviction, shall stand null and void."

A century later a disappointed husband sued his father-in-law for the depreciation in his wife's looks after her make-up had been removed. He claimed "compensation suitable to her real, and not her assumed, countenance". He pointed out that he had never realized, until the morning after the wedding, what a hag he had chosen to be his spouse.

Millions of pounds are being spent annually on cosmetics. Fortunately, their ingredients no longer include such obnoxious elements as dog's urine, once used by Italian nobility as a tincture against thinning of hair.

Next to the beautifying benefit of cosmetics is their psycho-logical effect. Dry skin, dull eyes and pale lips have depressed many a woman and given her feelings of inferiority. To remedy them, and also any suggestion of ageing, make-up proved a wonderful medicine. Its application led to a cheerful mind, a happy disposition and a sense of well-being. In hospitals the use of the lipstick has proved itself a tonic.

Cosmetics have had a place even in the fostering of democracy and the removal of class distinctions. They gave every girl a fair chance to shine and be equal.

Make-up thus covers an enormous field. Its range extends to economics, psychology and social living. Women have always found it useful to hide blemishes and to improve natural beauty.

They applied it for the attraction of the masculine sex and the envy of their own. Yet originally cosmetics were a necessity.

PERFUME

The sense of smell is one of man's most precious possessions. Certain odours immediately recall to mind certain people and places. Doctors identify some diseases by their odour. Even the like or dislike of food is closely linked not so much with its taste as with its smell.

Smell can cause both nausea and euphoria. Human beings have their individual smell, a fact of which dogs are well aware. African natives asserted that white men reeked of dead meat whilst Europeans, in turn, found "non-whites" to exude an unpleasant odour.

The history of perfume extends over a period of 5000 years. It has been known to the most ancient races and has penetrated into almost every aspect of living. When, in 1922, the tomb of Tutankhamen was opened in Egypt, it contained several vases of perfume which had not yet lost its fragrance, though dating from 1350 B.C..

Aesthetically scent is beautiful. Psychologically, it gives women a feeling of well-being and superiority. Erotically, it can excite the senses. In the realm of religion, it has served as a deodorant, a gift to the gods and a stimulant to the faithful, in whom it produced a state of ecstasy. Sorcery and witchcraft employed it because of its "compelling power". Medicine has applied perfume as a curative and a prophylactic. No wonder that the ancient Greeks believed that perfume was created by the gods themselves and called it accordingly "the scent of divinity".

Egyptians were convinced that perfume gave perfection to all parts of man's body and that, after his death, his soul was wafted to heaven by the smoke of incense. Holy Scripture, similarly, knew that "ointment and perfume rejoice the heart", and supplied numerous recipes for the making of aromatics.

Mohammed admitted that the three things he enjoyed most in this world were women, children and perfume. Not inappropriately, therefore, Islam promised its faithful believers a Paradise that was permeated with the finest of scents to arouse their desires and passion. A regulation of the Zoroastrian faith commanded that five times every day man must burn sweet savour on an altar.

The humorous definition of perfume as "any smell which is used to drown a worse one" is not as far-fetched as some people might think. That was, in fact, its first purpose.

Perfume originated at sacred shrines. It belonged to religious cults and was the concern of priests, not, as in later times, of beauticians.

Early in history man believed that the best way to serve God was to serve Him with meals. These consisted of the burnt carcasses of slaughtered beasts. Animal-sacrifice, so man imagined, was a welcome food for the gods and gained their favour. Altars became the very pivot of worship.

But the burning of beasts was far from pleasant, especially because of the stench it created. To cover this up, perfume was introduced, and it became an essential ingredient of divine sacrificial service. It still survives in the form of incense in some churches. This early use of perfume is recalled in its name which, derived from the Latin, literally means *through the smoke* (in this case of the burnt offerings).

Almost immediately, a natural development took place. People came to believe that the odour itself, thus added to the offering for man's sake, actually pleased the gods. When Noah, grateful for his survival from the Flood, burnt animal-sacrifices as a thanksgiving to God, the Bible records that "the Lord smelled the sweet odour" and promised never to repeat such calamitous punishment.

Associated with this earliest religious use of perfume was a belief that it also was a potent agent against evil forces. These were allergic to it and immediately took their leave. Perfume was even considered a means to exorcise the demon of disease. That is how medicine came to apply it. Greek doctors recommended its health-giving properties, specifically so in the prevention of respiratory ills.

People experienced the stimulating effects of perfume. They imagined that its fragrance cleansed the body and cleared the head, not least after their brain had been fuddled by too much drink.

Man's body contains more than two million sweat glands and the unpleasant smell of their secretion has been a frequent cause of embarrassment. Perfume was an ever-ready aid to remedy this.

Women realized its sexually-exciting qualities. Just as flowers by their scent attracted bees, women, too, could draw near a mate with perfume. Indeed, the choice of the right kind of scent became as much part of a woman's attraction as her voice, her smile and her hair. Rudyard Kipling went even so far as to say that "scents are surer than sounds or sights to make your heart-strings crack".

THE LIPSTICK

No one can deny that the features of the mouth can reveal character. We speak of sensuous lips. Easily we can recognize the cupid's bow and the tightly-closed mouth and, again, protruding lips. Look at a person's lips and you may find there affirmations of generosity, self-control and intelligence or of bad temper, hardness and selfishness.

One purpose in painting the lips was thus fear— of giving oneself away. Lipsticks were a perfect instrument to accentuate a woman's good points and to disguise her bad ones.

Fear and sex are two of man's strongest instincts. They aim at self-preservation of both the individual and the race. It was those two forces which most of all were responsible for the painting of the lips.

One of man's most dangerous zones was thought to be his mouth. It was an invitation to mischievous spirits to enter the body and take possession of it. Red has been universally a protective colour. It has been used from time immemorial to stop evil forces. Thus, people began to paint their lips red. Even in the ancient Babylonian Epic of Creation it is told that the god Marduk smeared red ochre on his lips before engaging in deadly battle against the dragon Tiamat.

Paradoxes abound in life. The same streak of colour that was used to repel and frighten demons came to serve also as a force to allure man and to arouse his passion.

Nature demands the survival of man. Anything that aids him in this has been judged right. From the most distant past, women have found a colourful mouth a powerful bait and when the modern girl paints her lips, she does so exactly as her ancestors did, 4000 years earlier. She knows that it helps not only to remedy defects and to enhance her beauty but, most of all, to ensnare man.

THE SHAPING OF EYEBROWS

Eyes do not only see but are seen as well. They reveal their owner's thoughts and feelings perhaps more clearly than any other part of the body. A mere glance can convey a message of love or hatred, scorn or encouragement. At times some people look daggers, others shoot arrows of love; and we all know the person who cannot look one "straight in the eye".

Sight is one of man's most precious gifts. Its mystery has fascinated the human mind from earliest days. To preserve and protect the eye, therefore, has always been a natural instinct. This was once reinforced by the ancient belief that the soul of man rests in his eye.

That is how paint and razor were first applied as a supernatural device. A certain shape of the eyebrow and a definite colour, so people believed, would ward off evil. And when, in the course of the evolution of civilization, paint and razor were no longer used magically, they were employed for medical purposes. The make-up of the eye was considered efficacious against disease and blindness. People assumed that eye-paint was a defence against flies and infection. It was described as good for sight and a means to stop bleeding.

Only third in importance and chronological order were reasons of beauty. Eventually these outweighed all other considerations. Women realized that the eye could draw near and bewitch the male. It dominated the face and, in no small measure, could render it ugly or enticing. Thus, anything that would enhance its beauty was good and right.

Tastes differ and continuously change. What is fashionable and refined to one generation is decried as cheap and unseemly by the next. However, modes of make-up have repeated themselves time and again.

Eyes have been called the signature of character and it was even believed that fate was written there for those who were able to decipher it. The appearance of the eyes much depends on the shape of the brows. No wonder, therefore, that these were given special attention. High, eminent and unconcealed, they showed part of the mind within. Soon this was thought to be their only function!

Eyebrows that touched each other, for instance, were once viewed with admiration or fear. Goethe described them as an expression of sensuality. Others saw in them an indication of arrogance and pride. In medieval times, a man whose brows touched each other was marked as a *Werewolf* or vampire, or fated to die a bachelor.

Not surprisingly, women refused to accept their natural brows as final. They examined them and manipulated the shape with razors, tweezers and pencil, in search of the character they wished to show. A little adjustment, paint and powder, they found, could work wonders.

To shave eyebrows off altogether served an important purpose — it prevented recognition. No one could now see a woman's true thoughts. But then, and not least, it also gave her a sphinx-like appearance, producing an expressionless mask. The very enigma of the face so created, served as a magnet to men who, thus baffled, were anxious to penetrate the screen of inscrutability.

One's eyes express individuality. Even if only slightly so, they make women look different. But we live in an age of mass production and a love of crowds. Individuals count little. To be just like our neighbour is a commonly held ideal, greatly fostered by commercial concerns. To shave off one's eyebrows and replace them with the latest and last general shape, half-moon or straight, thin or tapering, serves well in mass producing the common woman. This, too, is an expression of character: not only of a person but of an age.

THE PAINTING OF NAILS

Women have painted their finger-nails for thousands of years. In ancient Egypt, all women followed the practice. Cleopatra used stain on her nails.

In Europe women did likewise. To enamel their nails belonged to their daily beauty culture. It had become a custom so prevalent in Cromwell's days that he denounced and banned it. But women eventually won their way and, with the Restoration, painted finger-nails also were restored. Only when, centuries later, Queen Victoria was "not amused" by the habit, did women's nails lose their colour again. But not for long.

Originally, women thought that the conspicuous colour of their nails repelled evil spirits. Then women used the paint to make themselves more attractive and arouse passion in the male breast.

The painting of nails helped equally to cover up small imperfections. The protective cover of varnish, so it was claimed, improved the health of the nails and made them less brittle.

But other significant considerations reinforced the custom in countries as far removed as China, Spain and the United States.

Chinese Mandarins gilded their nails to indicate their high rank. It was part of their insignia of nobility: not worn, in the form of pips and stripes, on a uniform, but painted in distinct colour on a conspicuous part of their body. So to speak, look at a person's nails and you will know who she is, her position and rank.

It is an unfortunate fact of historical experience that certain races have considered themselves superior to others. They were possessed with the wish to preserve the purity of their blood. Thus anything darker than white was frowned upon. Anyone showing the slightest stain—of "impurity"—was socially ostracized.

But often nature was stronger than convention, and miscegenation took place in numerous cases. All laws of segregation were not able to prevent the mixing of the white and the coloured, socially and sexually. The inevitable results were children who bore the mark of their parents' mixed blood.

Sometimes they were lucky and took on almost completely the features and colour of their white parent and, apparently, did not give away the (to them) unfortunate secret of their dark (prenatal) past. And yet, there was one slight but most visible indication. This existed in the pigmentation of their nails. Therefore to cover them up and to give them the right kind of colour became a necessity.

This applied equally to Spaniards with Moorish blood in their veins as to American citizens, one of whose parents had not quite

withdrawn from the line of segregation. They needed the camouflage. Indeed, it was as if the wheel had come full circle. Once
again, as in savage days, the paint on their nails was not a matter
of beauty culture, but a weapon of defence. It was used to ward
off misfortune, though this time of a different and more tangible
kind.

All this is now mostly a matter of the regrettable past. Women
once again have extended the painting of nails from their fingers
to their toes. But they are doing so for no other reason than that
all other women do likewise.

SOAP

None of the many industries serving the modern way of life
has had as complex and contradictory a past as soap-making.
Though soap can be traced into far-distant times, it was not used
or known for its real qualities for thousands of years.

The Hittites cleaned their hands with plant ashes, dissolved in
water, and the early Sumerians in Ur boiled oil with alkali. Possibly first discovered in ancient Egypt, soap was brought by
Phoenician seafarers to Southern France in 600 B.C.. From there
it found its way into Germany.

The Bible, at least in its Authorized Version, mentions soap.
But in spite of this often-quoted evidence, the prophet Jeremiah
refers to it only as a cleansing agency for clothes. The passage
speaks of washing-soda and potash. True soap was unknown to
ancient Palestine.

Similarly, when excavations at Pompeii seemed to have unearthed the oldest soap factory in the world, this, too, was soon
proved to be incorrect. Chemical analysis showed that the product found there was Fuller's earth, used for washing clothes
but not the body.

Greeks and Romans loved cleanliness. But they never used
soap. After gymnastic exercises they took hot baths and removed
the sweat and dirt by beating their bodies with twigs or scraping
themselves with an instrument, known as a strigil.

Soap is now considered a mark of cultured living. Yet it was
unknown to ancient civilizations as a means of cleaning the body.

It was invented as such by a "barbarian" people, and it took millennia for it to be adopted as an everyday necessity.

Actually, the first mention of real soap occurs in the writings of Pliny the Elder. He refers to it explicitly as an invention of the barbarian Gauls. They made it from goat's tallow and beech ashes, which were the ancient equivalent of modern palm oil and caustic. They used it not for washing but as a pomade to give extra sheen to the hair.

When, in the following century, soap at last was used in the bath, it was for medical and not hygienic reasons. Indeed, a Greek doctor in 160 A.D. recommended the use of soap for the treatment of elephantiasis, and a physician in 385 A.D. as good for shampooing.

It was only during the later Middle Ages that, very slowly, soap was accepted for washing the body. As such it was in general use in the 16th century. But even then only the aristocracy applied it (or could afford to do so). After all, we must remember that Queen Elizabeth I had but one monthly bath, whilst lesser folk indulged in this kind of ablution even less, if at all.

For centuries, washing oneself with soap continued to be considered not a necessity but a luxury. Thus it is not surprising that the British used soap — and very effectively — to raise revenue. Soap was taxed (from 1712 onward) for almost 150 years and it was only through public pressure that Gladstone, in 1853, was forced to abolish this tax on cleanliness. Then he condemned soap as "most injurious both to the comfort and health of the people". Probably to make up for the substantial loss, he introduced in the same budget death duties. They and soap are still very much with us.

THE BARBER'S POLE

The barber's pole with its red and white stripes originated in England, and is a relic from the early days when barbers not only cut hair and trimmed beards, but were also surgeons. Actually, until 1745, they were members of the Barbers' and Surgeons' Company. They practised blood-letting, tooth-pulling and many other kinds of rough and ready surgery.

During the process of blood-letting, which was considered most beneficial, it was customary for the patient to hold a pole tightly in his hand, so that the veins would swell and the blood flow freely. It was inevitable that the pole became blood-stained, which did not encourage squeamish patients. Therefore barbers soon painted it bright red.

When not in use, the pole was hung outside the shop and the barber wound around it one of the bandages used for tying up the arm. Eventually, one brainy member of the fraternity hit on the idea of replacing the real pole and bandage with a dummy one, painted red with white stripes. This then became a fixture and the barber's trade mark.

The gilt knob at the end of the pole represents the brass basin used for the dual purpose of catching the blood and the lather.

THE BEARD

Nature has provided men and women with hair, first of all, as a means of protection. It can soften blows and, as a non-conductor, insulate the part of the body on which it grows against changes of temperature.

Eye-lashes screen the eyes from dust and foreign matter, as well as from too much sun. The eyebrows, at least partially, prevent perspiration from running down the face, while the hair in the nose acts as a filter.

Hair is one of man's distinctive features and has given him many problems and opportunities. Undoubtedly, it has been a significant factor in the growth of civilization. There was something dangerous about the hair, so people believed in almost every part of the world in early days.

To grow a beard was the natural thing to do. But to cut or shave it off was abnormal. No wonder that, early on, the beard became an object of man's anxious concern.

Men first cherished a beard for religious reasons. Primitive races were convinced that as hair grew out of man's body, it was saturated with his personality. Hence it had to be carefully guarded from possible foes.

It was firmly believed that a sympathetic link existed between a man and every part of his body, and that this continued even after the physical connection was broken. Thus, the man himself

would suffer from any harm done to the clippings of his hair
(or the parings of his nails, or his severed foreskin). This accounts
for the centuries-old custom of burning cut hair (and nails),
thereby preventing them from falling into the hands of an enemy
who could use them for nefarious purposes.

The best course was not to cut the hair at all which was soon
looked upon as actually sacred and the seat of a god's spirit. If
the hair was shorn, he would lose his abode and seek revenge.
This explains why priests especially, and those dedicated to gods,
never cut their hair. The sanctity of the hair made people swear
by their beard as we do now by the Bible.

Primitive man considered that even more sacred than his hair
was his head. Merely to touch it was dangerous. Hence, the cutting of hair was a most perilous operation. It might incon-
venience, if not injure, the in-dwelling spirit which, once its
anger was roused, could do untold harm.

Thus man's earliest beard was faith-conditioned. But there
were other aspects which further increased its importance and
value. Women could not grow a beard (if they did, they were
reckoned witches). Consequently, the beard was regarded as the
special sign, privilege and ornament of manhood. Indeed, it was
explained as God's gift to man to distinguish him from woman.

Ancient Egyptian and Babylonian monuments display men
with full, well-groomed beards. The men tended these with
meticulous care, using tongs, curling-irons and dyes. On festive
occasions, they added scented, yellow starch and sprinkled it
with gold dust to give the beard a golden sheen.

Shaving was then looked upon as perverted — it was against
nature. If the gods had created man to sprout a beard, surely, to
cut it off was against their will. To do so would not only antago-
nize them, but deprive the man of his dignity and male beauty.

That is why the cutting-off of beards was reserved for the defeated enemy, the dangerously sick and the bereaved. In the
treatment of the foe, it was a sign of disgrace — he was thus
branded. In the case of a leper, it called public attention to his
dreaded disease and kept others away from infection. The
mourner who shaved his hair originally did so to sacrifice it,
as a vital and sacred part of himself, to the dead.

The growth of civilization soon restricted and regulated the beard's length. A long beard, and not a knighthood, was used to distinguish members of the aristocracy. That is why in early Hebrew, for instance, an elder was called "the bearded one". To grasp a man by the beard showed intimate friendship. In the second millennium B.C., beards more than crowns were the sign of royalty, and for that reason kings (and queens!) wore false beards. These were made of metal and held in place by ribbons or chin-straps.

Continuously growing hair was regarded also, like the blood, as an expression of vitality. The beard certainly was an indication of mature manhood.

Eunuchs and young boys were beardless. It was therefore inevitable that primitive man further reasoned that a beard was not only an indication of virility, but its very source. It was actually the seat of man's strength. That is why a Samson (and others like him in the mythology of many races) once bereft of his hair lost all his vigour. It was for that reason (and not later considerations of vanity) that men cherished the beard and lavished the greatest care on it.

"May God pluck your beard!" is still one of the most fearsome curses among some primitive Bedouin tribes.

Apart from these earliest superstitions and concepts that lent special meaning and value to a man's beard, its fate often depended on particular circumstances of time and place, and its history is marked by the vanities and vicissitudes of human life.

Pagans used to round the hair of the head ceremoniously to dedicate its clippings to the gods. It was to combat this idolatrous practice that Hebrew Scripture proscribed the cutting of "the corners of the beard". Eventually, a beardless man was thought to offend good taste and the Creator.

Alexander the Great, on the other hand, ordered his soldiers to shave off their beards because they presented convenient handles by which their enemies could grasp them.

In the time of Queen Elizabeth I, the English discovered a welcome source of revenue in beards. Anyone sprouting a beard of more than a fortnight's growth was taxed. The assessment was graded according to the man's social standing. The lowest rate was 3/4d. a beard per annum. This must certainly have prompted many a man to start shaving.

Frenchmen changed the fashion almost periodically. They did so not haphazardly, but out of respect to various kings. They grew beards under Francis I because he did so — in his case to hide an ugly scar on the chin. A hundred years later, they considered it proper to go around clean-shaven, as Louis XIII was beardless. Eighteenth-century Spaniards did not wear a beard because of their king's inability to grow one.

Beards became most popular among troops fighting in the Crimean War. They felt that a beard guarded against cold and neuralgia. In a book published in 1860 by one "Theologos" and entitled "Shaving a breach of the Sabbath and a hindrance to the spread of the Gospels" it was stated that "the beard was a divinely provided chest-protector". Its lack certainly was an impediment for young 19th century doctors, as a beard was then viewed as the trade-mark of an experienced physician. Without a beard, a doctor was without patients.

THE PARTING OF THE HAIR

There are reasons for the various partings of hair. Women, in particular, realize that the choice of the "right" place for the parting can influence their hair style and, with it, their facial expression. The place chosen often depends on the shape of the face and the head. A centre parting, for instance, is only advisable in those rare cases where a woman has perfectly symmetrical features.

However, parting of the hair on one side or the other is not primarily due to considerations of beauty and appearance.

People have often wondered why it is that men part their hair mostly on the left. For once, superstition has played no part in this selection of sides. It is the result of purely physiological conditions. The explanation is that for right-handed men it is easiest to part the hair on the left.

Most of all, however, the place of parting is the outcome of the growth of hair. It depends almost entirely on the position of the whirl (or crown), which divides the hair naturally.

Mostly, the crown is on the left side, hence the parting is on the left. In exceptional cases (fiction claims among the most intelligent people) nature has provided two whirls. The fortunate person with two crowns can part his hair either way.

HAIR STANDING ON END

An obsolete defence mechanism, inherited from the animal kingdom, and a gruesome relic of American-Indian warfare account for all that is "hair-raising" in our speech.

At the first scent of fight, cats and dogs bristle. Their raised hair is meant to frighten the foe, to soften his blows, and to resist his bites. A porcupine's use of its quills is perhaps an even better illustration.

Man, descended from the beast, has retained its protective instinct, though in his "civilized" way of fighting, this now serves no purpose. Nevertheless, on sudden fright, his hair still stands on end. It is this immediate reaction to danger by a built-in defence mechanism which, by contracting the scalp to erect the hair, creates the sensation of gooseflesh and "tingling of the scalp".

The microscope enabled man to detect the muscular tissue attached to the hair that caused it to rise. The only function now left to the *arrector pili*, as it is called, is to keep the shaft of hair in its place.

The scalping of enemies by Red Indians at first horrified early American soldiers and pioneers. But, unfortunately, people mostly assimilate downwards and adopt the worst features of those whom they fight or with whom they mix. They imagine that they must fight fire with fire.

That is how the white man retaliated in like manner and, imitating the worst, began to bring home as trophies the scalps of slain Indians. Indeed, soon he learnt to cash in by their possession, as some authorities paid special bounties, according to the number of scalps presented.

At that time, it is claimed, Indians began to refer to scalping as "lifting the hair" and "hair-raising". The vivid expression stuck to the language.

CHAPTER X

animals in our language

ANIMALS are among man's best friends. Once worshipped and considered sacred, they have fulfilled a significant task in his daily life for thousands of years.

Even where technological advance has supplanted animals, we remember them as faithful servants who have left their mark in civilization and culture. That is why, for instance, we still reckon the force of our cars in horse-power. No wonder, therefore, that our language is rich in references to animals, used as similes and analogies. Many superstitions attach also to the animal kingdom. The origins of these phrases and beliefs are sometimes much more complex than they appear on the surface.

Animals have the habit of creeping into many places. But no creature excelled in this more than the cat. And perhaps not without reason. After all, it is renowned for its curiosity; we all know of the nosey cat.

The cat has found its way even into the loom of language and left its traces there in most diverse ways, to discover which is almost a game of "cat and mouse". Everyone likes to be thought the cat's whiskers, and lucky are those able to indulge in a catnap. Though we must beware of cat-burglars and of being used as a cat's paw.

It is also good for us to appreciate that often we have been misled. There are cases when what appears as (part of) an animal is only something else in disguise. Catgut comes from horses or sheep, and the cat o'nine tails is a frightening instrument of flogging, far removed from our purring friend. A dog-

141

watch has nothing to do with the canine species. Elephants do not have a good memory, and bees are not as busy as we may think. They spend most of their time doing nothing.

Man prides himself in having tamed wild beasts and having taught animals many a lesson. He forgets, however, that he himself could learn from his dumb friends, who excel him in numerous ways.

An owl's eyes, for instance, are sensitive to infra-red radiation. A bat in flight has been using its own system of radar for thousands of years. Dogs pick up sound waves of a frequency up to 100,000 vibrations a second, as compared with man's limit of a mere 30,000.

Animals, indeed, have been sacrificed numberless times to serve man, for better or worse, on altars, on menus and for the sake of medicine and civilization.

All this should make man humble if not ashamed. "Why was man created only on the sixth day and as the very last of all creatures?", an ancient sage asked. He himself gave the answer, which is still valid. He said: "To be able to tell man, whenever he becomes overbearing or is swollen with pride, 'Even a flea preceded you in creation!'".

THE WHITE ELEPHANT

A white elephant nowadays describes something whose up-keep costs much more than it is worth.

Albinos among elephants are rare and it is little wonder that early generations considered them holy. While ordinary elephants worked hard, the albinos were worshipped and nourished, and lived in idleness. Ownership of a white elephant contributed to the sanctity of the home but it added considerably to running expenses, so much so that in not a few cases it caused bankruptcy.

The story is told that the ancient rulers of Siam welcomed this tradition regarding albino elephants. When the king was anxious to get rid of a courtier, who had lost his favour or had become too influential or powerful, far from actually dismissing him and thereby gaining his open hostility, he treated him as his best friend. He presented him with the most sacred and precious gift — a white elephant.

The courtier had to accept it. He would not dare to refuse the holy beast, or dispose of it later. That would imply an insult to His Majesty as much as to divinity. The upkeep of the albino elephant was so costly that in the end it would bleed the nobleman white—which was exactly what the king intended to happen.

The albino's exceptional colour (or lack of it) is sufficient reason to account for its early deification. However, an ancient Chinese legend gave its own explanation, associating the animal's high status with a dream incident in the life of Moyë, a mythical mother figure.

The story goes that one day Moyë was walking along a river bank when a rainbow encircled her with the result that, 12 years later, she gave birth to the hero Fo-Hi. During the sacred time of pregnancy she dreamt that the child in her womb was not of a human figure but of that of a white elephant. That is why, the legend says, white elephants ever since have been venerated and honoured, addressed as "Lord", and attended by a minister of high rank. "King of the White Elephant" became the most treasured title of Siamese royalty.

It is interesting to note that so-called white elephants found in the East are not white at all. They are distinguished merely by a small patch of colour on some part of their anatomy, slightly paler than the rest.

A RED RAG TO A BULL

Wide-spread and general is the belief that a red rag infuriates a bull. Therefore to enter a paddock with anything red where there is a bull would be foolish and dangerous.

The idea is so deeply ingrained in common thought and speech, that we describe anything that makes us get really angry and excites our rage to be "like a red rag to a bull".

Equally well-known and accepted is the explanation that the phrase stems from the experience of Spanish bull-fighters. To attract their four-legged adversary's attention and rouse it into an angry charge, it is said, they flourished their red cloak in front of the bull's face.

It is certainly true that, from the earliest days of this Spanish pastime, the torero employed a red cloak. Yet that the bull's anger was roused by its colour is completely fallacious.

A bull is not affected by any colour. Like most animals, it is colour-blind. It is the motion of the cloth, not its hue, that annoys the bull. A waving white cape would make it just as angry. Red was chosen only as a spectacular çolour.

An ancient but now discontinued presentation in the bull-ring supports this explanation. In early days a man would stand on a pedestal in the arena and keep absolutely still. When the bull rushed towards him, he had to hold even his breath. For a while, the beast would gaze and sometimes even sniff at the human statue. Because it lacked all motion, the animal would walk away. But let the frozen figure move ever so slightly and the docile bull would change into a ferocious fighter.

Thus the colourful phrase lacks all foundation in fact and proves once again how some of our most cherished expressions are based on fiction.

TO PUT A FLEA IN ONE'S EAR

The flea is Anglo-Saxon, at least in the origin of its name. Very descriptively this recalls one of the insect's outstanding gifts: its ability to "jump". Feeding on the blood of man and beast, it can leap thirty times its own height. This fact was first established in Greek days by Socrates, the philosopher.

Others have discovered a close affinity between the *flea* and *fleeing,* as this lively creature always seems to be able to get away.

Usually, a flea — like its bite — points to something trifling, a thing of really no importance. And yet, to put a flea in one's ear can assume tremendous proportions. It becomes most annoying and can drive a man almost mad.

Commonly the phrase has been explained as the result of watching a dog with a flea in its ear. It makes him so restless that sometimes he flees in terror.

However, man himself has long been a flea-victim. As far back as 700 A.D., Saxon nobles complained bitterly of its bites, though only a few of the over 500 different species of fleas choose man as their host.

Fleas became especially aggravating at the time of the medieval Knights. In mail from head to foot, those valiant men soon discovered that almost more worrying than the adversary they had to face outside was that small glutton which had invaded the inside of their suit of armour which now shielded the flea as much as its wearer.

At first the flea enjoyed a good feed, truly having a field day. Jumping about freely without the Knight being able to hinder its progress, it went and bit where it pleased. No one could stop it from sucking the man's blood.

Sooner or later the flea felt it had enough of the gentleman. Trying to leave its dark prison, it just could not find a way out. In its search for an escape route, it eventually got into the Knight's ear.

There it settled — sometimes for hours — intermittently biting and jumping. This caused the helpless Knight unending frustration, aggravation, and even torture. That is how, when we speak of putting a flea in one's ear, we recall — unknowingly — those former days of chivalry, when Knights in shining armour experienced alarm and distress through those wingless insects which, unwantingly, had become their prisoners.

TO GO THE WHOLE HOG

Not all hogs are swine. In the late 13th century a hog referred also to a young sheep that was as yet unshorn.

Wool has always been a precious commodity. When there was plenty of supply elsewhere, those early "hogs" were left alone. Their fleece was so short that to shear it was quite difficult, and not really worth the trouble. Therefore most farmers used to clip their hogs only superficially, haphazardly and without much care. But there were some who felt that a lot of a little makes much and therefore they "went the whole hog", shearing the lamb closely and all over.

It was this practice by economical herdsmen — changing a hog into a sheep — that eventually was applied, in everyday speech to anything we do thoroughly, without compromise or reservation, going all the way, seeing a thing through to the very end.

THE MAD MARCH HARE

Hares have had rather a sad role in man's folk history. It was considered unlucky, for instance, if a hare crossed one's way.

Witches were said, at some time or other, to transform themselves
into the shape of that innocent creature.

Medieval "science" described the hare as a beast that suffered
from bouts of depression and tried to cure itself by feeding on
special plants. People who ate hare, it was thought, would catch
the disease and themselves become melancholy.

It is thus not surprising that in man's manner of speech "mad
as a March hare" became a common phrase. But why the selection of March?

March was the hare's mating season. People imagined — and
perhaps not without reason — that during this month for the
benefit of its love-making, the animal displayed itself in peculiar
ways and seemed "off balance".

It has been suggested, too, that the so-called madness of hares
has no connection either with the month of March or the animal's
sex life, and that the phrase was the result of an error. Originally,
it did not speak of March but referred to a marsh. Hares living
in marshes were unable to hide themselves because of the lack of
bushes and trees and, driven to desperation, in the face of foes,
went insane.

TO LET THE CAT OUT OF THE BAG

Were we to hear the phrase "to let the cat out of the bag" for
the first time, we would imagine that, obviously, it gave account
of a rescuing act. After all, cats love their freedom and would
loathe being imprisoned in a sack.

But, of course, the words are used in a completely different
sense. They show no concern whatsoever for the cat's fate, its
likes and frights. Rather strangely, they tell of a secret coming
out, quite suddenly, just as a cat, kept prisoner, would jump out
of a bag.

For the origin of the phrase we have to look at marketing
methods at the country fairs of old England. There, sucking-pigs
were frequently sold ready wrapped in a sack.

Tricksters bent on taking advantage of a trusting customer,
would hand over a sack containing, not a piglet, but a cat, and
the deception would not be discovered until the purchaser
opened the bag at home.

The wary buyer who insisted on opening the bag at the fair to examine the non-existent pig, let the cat out of the bag and exposed the cheat!

Naval circles suggest another origin of the phrase. It referred, they say, not to an animal but to the whip known as the cat o'nine tails. This cruel instrument of punishment was kept in a sack and to "let the cat out of the bag" meant to take out the whip for a flogging. The action certainly left the sailors in no doubt as to their captain's intention.

TO HAVE KITTENS

For anyone to confess "nearly to have had kittens" is a dramatic way of admitting how anxious and scared he had been. For us it is just a metaphor, and no one would dream of taking it literally. Yet the phrase itself goes back to times when women were really worried that, instead of giving birth to a child, they would bring forth kittens.

It was an age when people believed in witches and the mysterious influence of cats, which extended even to their sex life. A black cat, for example, that turned up at a wedding was taken as an omen of good luck and of a fruitful union.

A superstition, once prevalent among Scottish people, may be directly responsible for the phrase. This assumed that a woman would conceive kittens, if — unknowingly — she ate any food on which cats had ejected their semen.

In medieval times women, suffering agonizing pain in pregnancy, were assured by witches that its cause was not the growing child but kittens inside their womb, and that only a magical potion could destroy the brood and thereby alleviate their suffering. As late as 1654, a woman tried in a Scottish court for attempting to procure an abortion, pleaded in excuse that she had done so because she had "cats in her bellie . . ."

The association of cats with man's reproductive power can be traced to ancient Egyptian days, when the cat was considered not only divine but to have an occult influence on the fertility of both the earth and human beings. It was known as a passionate creature whose couplings and conceptions abounded especially at periods of the full moon. No wonder that it was thus linked with both Osiris and Bast — the lunar deities.

Apart from its sexual propensities, a cat was equally renowned as a good mother. It was not difficult for people, aware of the animal's strong sexual and maternal instincts, to believe that the cat truly dominated man and ruled his sex life.

RAINING CATS AND DOGS

A combination of cats and dogs in itself appears most unnatural. It becomes even more puzzling and extraordinary, if people speak of its raining cats and dogs. Of course, they mean to say that it is pouring with rain or, colloquially speaking, "bucketing".

Why, in order to picture such a phenomenal cloud-burst, did people couple the names of their canine and feline friends, whose mutual dislike is so well known and who, on most other occasions, strictly adhere to a policy of Apartheid?

Greek scholars believe that the mystery can be solved easily. In its original meaning the phrase had nothing to do with cats or dogs. Their presence in the downpour of rain was truly "fantastic", in the literal sense of the word. Human fantasy put them there and not nature.

Catadupa is the Greek (and also obsolete French) word for a waterfall. According to the historian Pliny, it was the actual name of a cascade of water on the Nile, at a point in Ethiopa where the stream rushed down with a mighty roar. To compare heavy rain with such a waterfall was natural — but eventually people who lacked sufficient geographical knowledge and were not conversant with the Greek tongue imagined that they heard in the sound of the Greek (word for) waterfall — *catadupa* — cats and dogs.

There is more than one school of thought on the origin of this phrase. An alternative interpretation steers clear of the Nile and its rushing waters and links the saying with ancient Norse mythology and early meteorological misconceptions. Weather prophets of old believed that rain storms were caused by the nefarious influence of both cats and dogs. Indeed, sometimes sailors said that an exceptionally frisky cat had "a gale of wind in its tail". Again, witches which rode upon the storm were believed to assume the form of a cat.

Dogs, on the other hand, in Nordic myth were the associates of Odin, god of storms. Old German pictures thus frequently show the wind in the form of a dog with a blast issuing from its head. As the cat symbolized rain, a combination of those two animals therefore seemed to be an appropriate figure of speech to express lashing rain.

Much more realistic is a third view. This goes back to 17th century England, where numerous cats and dogs ran wild. After a cloud-burst, many of them were found drowned, their corpses floating in the filthy torrents that rushed down the streets. People seeing the dead animals, and unaware of their unfortunate fate, imagined that they had actually come down from the sky with the shower and that — believe it or not — it had rained cats and dogs.

THE CAT'S NINE LIVES

The first reference to a domestic cat stems from the year 2100 B.C. and, naturally, from Egyptian lands, where also, soon afterwards, the mother of a Pharaoh's courtier was nicknamed "Pussy".

The tradition that a cat has nine lives goes back equally far into the distant past and to the river Nile. It is linked with both mystical thoughts and very realistic observations.

A cat is strong, hardy and a good fighter. No wonder, therefore, that the legend arose about Kilkenny cats which — very Irish — fought until nothing was left of them except their tails.

A cat always seems to fall on its feet, whose paws are well-padded and shock-absorbing, a feature which protects the body from injury.

The cat is one of the most tenacious of creatures, taking good care to guard itself. Suspicious in nature and taught to be cautious, the cat watches its steps and looks out before leaping. It takes no risks and approaches unidentified objects and persons gingerly and with great deliberation. Whilst an expert in catching mice and rats, it certainly knows how to look after itself and to avoid being caught by others.

All these many and varied facts, physiological and psychological in nature, have combined to preserve and lengthen the cat's life. But to express its longevity and tenacity by assuming that a cat lived not just once but nine times has its source in ancient religious belief.

Nine is a mystical number. It is composed of three threes, a trinity of trinities. Thought to possess supernatural power and to work as a charm, this figure has featured prominently in the myths and traditions of many parts of the world.

Egyptian astronomers taught the existence of nine spheres. The Greek lunar year counted not 12 but 9 months, and the river Styx was thought to encircle (the Greek) hell nine-fold. Odin, the Teutonic god, gave power to Freya, the goddess of love, over nine worlds. Even Christianity followed this numerical tradition; according to the Gospels, Christ died in the ninth hour.

It is not surprising, therefore, that to express the cat's mystical power of life, use was made of that very figure as well. Bast, the cat-headed goddess of Egypt, where our feline friends were divine, was said to possess nine lives, and this no doubt is an important factor in the legend of cats' longevity.

As it were, to add further protection to our cats, lest the full span of nine lives be diminished, humans have been warned (no one knows by whom first) that they should never attempt to take even one of its lives. If they did so — from the beyond — the cat would haunt them and devise a particularly nasty revenge. It is one of the most useful cat superstitions — to the cat.

NO ROOM TO SWING A CAT

There are all kinds and types of cats: Siamese, Persian and Manx; black, ginger, tabby, white and tortoise-shell. No matter what their origin, colour or habitat, they all share definite features and characteristics. They are independent individualists and cannot be bribed. They have a mind and will of their own, either accepting or rejecting us, and no saucer of cream will change their opinion. Perhaps they remember that once they were considered sacred and were worshipped, which would account for their looking so dignified and self-possessed.

We have grown accustomed to find cats in all places and at all times. A cat may even look at a king, as the saying goes. But, as if in a topsy-turvy, dream world, there are some occasions when we merely imagine that we see a cat. In reality, it is not there at all. When we look closely for it — it just disappears.

Therefore, it is not surprising at all that the very phrase "there's not enough room to swing a cat" most probably does not refer to cats either. Who, after all, could be so cruel as even to try to swing a cat. Though, at some time, it is said, this was a strange kind of amusement, practised among so-called sportsmen. To inflict pain on cats was then considered by the ignorant and superstitious almost a meritorious act. They believed that cats were the companion, if not the incarnation, of witches and evil.

Actually, the expression leads back to naval days that knew harsh punishment for recalcitrant sailors. The "cat" mentioned is the cat o'nine tails, the thonged instrument used in the British army and navy for disciplinary thrashings.

Its link with the cat was forged by the fact that the marks left on the flesh of the unfortunate victim looked much like deep scratches inflicted by a cat's claws.

Sailors to be flogged were usually taken up on to the deck as in the confined space below there was no room to swing "the cat" (o'nine tails) for a proper whipping.

To those worshippers of cats who are loath to see their pet associate — even only "conversationally" — with cruelty of any kind, another, yet less likely, explanation offers itself. This makes the cat a kind of sleeping partner, still within naval circles — though only in a corrupt way!

Sailors used to sleep in swinging hammocks which they called "cots". Ashore they usually dossed in cheap lodging houses, so crowded that they would say that there was no room to swing a cot. In time, through frequent usage and indistinct enunciation, the cot changed into a cat: at least so in its sound and spelling.

THE CHESHIRE CAT

Cheshire, one of England's old counties, was noted for its cheese and its independence. Out of these sprang one of the versions of the origin of the grinning Cheshire cat.

For almost 500 years after the Norman conquest of England, Cheshire kept politically independent. It prided itself on its own Parliament, courts of law and taxes. Judges, appointed by the

king of England, had no authority or jurisdiction over that part of
the land, whose ruling Count possessed royal privileges.

This distinction, so her people imagined, amused even their
cats and made them so proud that they grinned from ear to ear.
Even though the cat's grin was merely imaginary on the part of
its owner, he soon found a way to materialize it: if not on the
pet's own face but in the form of cheese!

Cheshire has always produced some of the finest of cheeses,
that staple food of high nutritional value. It was enjoyed far
beyond the county's borders. Cheshiremen thought: why not use
this product to tell the world of our proud tradition of freedom,
recognized and treasured alike by man and beast!

That is how, according to this tradition, the people of Cheshire
came to sell their cheese in the shape of a cat — with the cat
invariably grinning.

Another explanation sees in the smiling cat the remnant of a
feared man — one Caterling of Chester. The fact that Cheshire
was sparsely populated outside its few cities, and lacked England's power, attracted fugitives from justice. Soon the large
Delamere Forest became a haunt for highwaymen and other
criminals. The county itself just had neither means nor men
to enforce the law.

Things thus got out of hand until, under the reign of King
Richard III, Caterling became the Forest Warden of Cheshire,
determined to stamp out the evil.

His zeal knew no bounds and within three years of taking the
office he was responsible for the apprehension and hanging of
at least 100 offenders.

Proud of this achievement, Caterling attended himself each of
the executions, sadistically grinning from ear to ear. And it was
his sneer at the hangings that people remembered. In no time it
became proverbial all over England. And when people saw a
smirk on a face they could not but help immediately to be reminded of the Caterling sneer and accused their friend of
grinning "like the Cheshire Caterling".

As time went on, the identity of the man was forgotten and all
the horrible circumstances that had given rise to the phrase. And
as, after all, cats were so much more common than Caterlings,

eventually Mr. *Caterling's* grin was shortened into the much more pleasant (but non-existent) grin of a Cheshire cat.

All this certainly would not make Mr. Caterling a very nice sort of person, in spite of his desire to see justice done. Therefore, and if for nothing else, another story is so much more acceptable. This relates that Caterling himself took up the sword against the many brigands who were roaming his territory. And it was his terrifying facial contortions during the duels that became famous and were misinterpreted as a grin.

There is a third view, given by Eric Partridge in his "Dictionary of Slang and Unconventional English". This recalls that a cat, very fond of cheese, was called a "cheeser cat". Hence, when speaking of the grin of a Cheshire cat, people tried to say that they were as pleased as a cheeser cat that had just eaten cheese.

CHAPTER XI

the story
of man's dwelling

ARCHITECTURE is the reflection of man, the spirit of his age, the preoccupations of his mind, his hopes and frustrations.

When Heinrich Heine, the great German poet, was asked how it was that people no longer were able to build the awe-inspiring cathedrals of medieval times, he replied: "Men in those days had convictions. We moderns have only opinions. And it requires something more than opinions to build a Gothic cathedral".

Buildings, like human beings, can be honest or deceptive. Some are mainly "facade", whilst others, almost to a frightening degree, are completely functional.

Though much of ancient Egypt's culture has been preserved, hardly any of its homes survived. This was not accidental; Egyptians built their dwellings of perishable material. All that mattered to them was life *after* death and thus the home of the dead was their chief concern. The Greeks laughed at the Egyptians' strangely constructed tombs, calling them "wheaten cakes", which gave us the word "pyramid"!

South Africans used to build their banks in the style of the Greek temples. Many a modern church is shaped like a supermarket. On the other hand, the United Nations Centre in New York has been likened by critics to a king-sized tombstone.

It is told of the famous American architect, Frank Lloyd Wright, that he used to sleep all night on the ground under a tree to get the feel of a client's property, before even starting his design. The story emphasizes that building a home means more than putting together bricks and mortar or glass and steel.

Churchill, on the occasion of the reconstruction of the House of Commons in 1944, remarked that first "we shape our dwellings and afterwards our dwellings shape us".

Architecture can be most confusing. It stresses the diversity of man; his frequent changes of mind, taste and values. Americans have turned flats into apartments and lifts into elevators; they have heightened the traditional ground floor into their first floor.

The exploration of the foundations of everyday architectural terms is fascinating. *Bungalow* is built around a Hindustani word and records the fact that it comes "from Bengal". *Residence* goes back, through French, to Latin. It is a place where we "sit back". Disappointingly, the noble-sounding *Mansion* is most humble in origin. All it means is an abode "one lives in".

THE PALACE

Geography has contributed numerous words and expressions to the vocabulary. In most cases these plainly reveal their place of origin. Turkey has given its name to a bird. The province of Burgundy in France is recalled both by a wine and a colour. However, some words are so common that their "geographical" connotation is completely forgotten. This applies especially to the description of the most notable of all homes, the palace.

Palace now designates the official residence of a sovereign ruler. Its dimensions and costly ornamentation made it the most distinguished dwelling place anywhere. The Roman Emperor Nero is said to have built the first palace. Actually, we owe its name to Rome. It is derived from the proper name of one of her seven hills, the *Palatine* Hill.

Originally this was the main part of the ancient city. It was indeed the cradle of Roman civilization. There, so tradition has it, Romulus traced the first furrow, and around it he built the first wall. When the city spread, the Palatine Hill became the most fashionable district.

When the Roman Empire was established, it was a foregone conclusion that Augustus, its first ruler, having been born on the Palatine Hill, would choose it as the place for his official home. His example was followed by nearly all his successors who erected a series of splendid and substantial dwellings there.

Many years passed and Roman dominion was accepted and feared all over the world. Emperor Nero, in his lust for power and unsurpassed vanity, was not satisfied to share the Palatine with others, no matter how noble or aristocratic they were. He wished to have it for himself alone. He issued orders that all other private homes situated there should be razed.

When that had been done, he gave instructions to his architect for the erection of a building of unprecedented magnificence. The edifice, the sole residence on Palatine Hill, soon was identified with that name and became known as *the palace*. That is how, ever since and all over the world, a royal abode, as well as its cheap imitations, is called by this name.

THE DRAWING-ROOM

A drawing-room has nothing to do with lines, designs or art. It is a shortened form of the original *withdrawing*-room which traces back to the 16th century. It was attached then to public rooms to give persons of high station an opportunity of finding some privacy away from the crowds.

Two hundred years later the room's function had changed. It was reserved for women. They withdrew to it after a dinner party, leaving their menfolk to talk freely and enjoy their port.

This new association gave the withdrawing-room its elegant meaning which it retained even when, still later on, it was again opened up to both sexes and no longer used for purposes of privacy. Time withered away the word's first syllable and shortened the room, if not in its architectural dimensions, but in the length of its verbal description.

THE ATTIC

The attic comes from Athens. Though now at the top of our homes, its meaning has come down to an all-time low. We now use the attic, if we use it at all, for menial purposes. For centuries, the poorest of people alone chose this part of the house for their living quarters. Situated immediately under the roof, and sometimes within its framework, it could be reached, in most cases, only through a narrow manhole.

Yet originally an attic spelled neither poverty nor neglect but an elegant style. In architecture it referred to a specific Athenian way of decorating a building and giving it symmetry and refinement. This was achieved mostly by the use of a certain type of facade enriched by columns and placed above another storey of greater height.

When 18th century England revived the ancient classical mode of construction, architects ornamented the top floor of a house in exactly that way. They faced it with the Athenian — "Attic" — kind of pilasters. Hence people came to refer to the top storey by its conspicuous classical style and called it briefly the "attic". Even when styles changed again and the room under the roof had lost all its Athenian splendour and pillars, the name remained.

THE LUMBER-ROOM

The lumber-room has come a long way. Its name dates back more than 2000 years to the Teutonic Lombards. Caesar is said to have named them so on one of his campaigns, because of their long beards *(longobardi)*. In 568 A.D. they invaded Italy and settled there in the North-central part of the Po Valley, which was eventually called after them.

They specialized in lending money and did so in large amounts on terms and for a security. Gradually their occupation became synonymous with their name. Some of the Lombards migrated to England in the Middle Ages and continued their original trade there. In fact, they became London's first bankers and resided in the street which to this day is called after them.

Until the reign of Queen Elizabeth I the Lombards held a monopoly for pawnbroking. The many and miscellaneous pledges they received were kept in a separate part of their establishment. This was soon known as the Lombard Room. As with most foreign words, it did not take long for it to become corrupted and Anglicized into Lumber Room. Though nowadays this no longer stores pledges, it is still reserved for all sorts of odds and ends.

THE "W.C."

Many taboos have surrounded man's bodily functions. To leave evidence of them was once regarded as dangerous. It was a source of defilement and had to be carefully removed and hidden away. Worst of all, one's enemy could use it for nefarious, magical purposes. Though the origins of sanitation thus stem from primitive man's superstitious fears, it might well be that a healthy instinct also played a part.

Those early dreads were responsible for later feelings of shame, and the mere mention of excretion became taboo, though the Bible itself does not shun referring to it, even in relationship to a king. Whilst pursuing David, King Saul felt the need to "cover his feet", as the Hebrew Bible discreetly put it. However, its later official Latin translation, the Vulgate, bluntly rendered that passage by the words, "to void his belly". Young David duly took advantage of the situation and, to show the king later how easily he could have killed him, "cut off the skirt of Saul's robe privily".

Society was most reluctant to call "the smallest room" in the house by its "proper" name. It invented numerous euphemisms to refer to it. Medieval monasteries had their "necessaries" and castles their "garderobes" (literally "to keep the robes"), a forerunner of the modern cloak-room.

Toilet is derived from the French for "little cloth", possibly a towel used to wipe the hands. Lavatories suggested the action of "washing" (from the Latin). Latrine is simply the contraction of its original Latin root. Privy emphasized isolation. So, too, did *retirade*, in Dutch-speaking countries.

This multiplicity of words used to speak of the toilet is a record of man's continuous endeavour to circumvent in speech the room's real function. To mention it in so many words was viewed to be improper, if not obscene. And yet, all attempts to do that proved futile. No matter which innocuous word was chosen, after some time, it became soiled by its association. Even the English "water closet", whose abbreviation "W.C." was internationally adopted, suffered the fate of devaluation.

Nowadays men ask where they can wash their hands, women where they can powder their nose, and pupils to be excused. Men and women travellers diffidently inquire for the comfort station or rest room. No doubt, these latest terms invented in search of a "bathroom" that does not soil one's speech, will lose their respectability, become unmentionable and thus, in their turn, be in need of replacement.

The toilet dates back to ancient civilizations, which could pride themselves on most modern standards of sanitation. Excavations in Mesopotamia, Crete, Egypt and India have brought to light examples of elaborately constructed and carefully designed water closets and sewerage systems.

Brick-built seat-closets of 2000 B.C. were discovered in the Indus Valley. They were situated on the ground and first floors of private homes. Sloping channels joined them either with a receptacle outside, or a sewer. In the 14th century B.C., Cretans in their island's capital, Knossos, had closets built over a conduit of running water. The palace of their famous king Minos, which was unearthed by Sir Arthur Evans, contained most up-to-date toilets. The pans were constructed so as to hold water. They were flushed either by rainwater or, if that was not available, by water drawn from a cistern. Residents of Pompeii in Italy, which was destroyed by a volcanic eruption of Mount Vesuvius in 79 A.D., used water-supplied closets hidden in a niche next to the kitchen.

Yet those curiously modern conveniences of ancient days vanished from the daily life of medieval society, which reverted in that part of its habits to almost primitive days. There was no drainage system. Privies were commonly placed over large pits. Worse still, people frequently threw all their refuse, including human excrements, out of the window into the open street where a gutter served as a sewer.

This is one of the explanations of the British custom of a man always having the lady walk "inside" along the footpath — away from the road. The upper storey of houses once jutted out and this protected anyone walking underneath from slops emptied from windows.

In 1596, during the Elizabethan era, Sir John Harington, a poet and the Queen's godson, invented the first modern water closet. He called it "a privy in perfection" and installed one in his home near Bath. Its design included a high water-tower on top of the house, a hand-operated tap that controlled the flow of water into the pan, and a valve that could be opened and closed to release sewage into a cesspool near-by.

Though the Queen had the closet copied in her palace at Richmond, the general public cold-shouldered it and regarded it as a joke. They continued their usual filthy habits.

Nothing further of a permanent nature happened to sanitation for almost 200 years. Then, in 1775, Alexander Cumming, a mathematician and watchmaker, took out the first patent for "a water closet upon a New Construction". This certainly was an improvement on Harington's design. It differed in one significant aspect which, though small in itself, was revolutionary and most beneficial. It has been applied ever since. The soil pipe immediately below the pan was bent so as "constantly to retain a quantity of water to cut off all communication of smell from below". At long last, the nauseating feature of the toilet had been eliminated. All that followed were merely refinements and comparatively minor advances.

WINDOWS

Man's housing problem has always existed. Yet it continuously changed according to the level of civilization, people's peculiar way of life, as well as climatic and geographical circumstances. From earliest times, man showed great ingenuity in devising his dwelling.

A simple wind-break of trees and branches was the most primitive house. And, as is obvious by its very name, the *wind*ow, too, is linked with the wind. When glass was unknown, windows were mere holes in a wall, covered by shutters or some kind of curtain. The hole served a two-fold purpose. Like an *eye*, it enabled people inside the house to look out. It also helped to ventilate the interior. Thus window, a combination of Anglo-Saxon words, means "wind's eye".

GOTHIC

The name Gothic suggests an architectural style of great splendour and beauty. But it is a complete misnomer.

The Goths themselves never employed it. They were a Teutonic tribe (of the 3rd to 5th century), and have long since vanished. With the Vandals, they destroyed Roman civilization and large parts of Southern Europe. Therefore they were looked upon as barbarians, insensitive to beauty and culture. The story of their misdeeds lived on in peoples' memory, to whom their name became synonymous with all things that were uncouth and lacking in refinement.

When the generation of the Renaissance revived the classical style, it sneered at the "modern" manner of building, as being crude and ugly — "Gothic". That is how the name came first into being: to throw scorn on an architecture that was misunderstood and abhorred.

Yet in this case, too, a description intended to be abusive, because of the inherent value of Gothic art, assumed the contrary meaning, and Gothic changed into a term descriptive of priceless, awe-inspiring beauty. Paradoxically thus the name, derived from a barbarian, pagan people, was identified with the loftiest style of Christian architecture — "the most beautiful of all, and by far the most in harmony with the mysteries of religion". A Gothic Cathedral therefore was no longer a contradiction in terms.

Apart from constructional and ornamental considerations, it was religious fervour which, in the 12th century, really called Gothic architecture into being. Its soaring style, typified by the pointed arch, expressed in stone man's yearning for the divine. Dissatisfied with the old way of building, which seemed so heavy and gloomy, the new shapes reflected the people's lofty ideals and sacred aspirations. As it were, like their own souls, their churches and cathedrals flung themselves heavenwards.

JERRY-BUILT

Anything that is jerry-built does not last. But the word itself, describing impermanent and faulty construction, has been built very well. It has lasted for at least 80-odd years now. Its foundations have proved exceedingly strong, though the material used is still unidentified, and various theories exist as to the origin of the jerry-builder.

Some authorities suggest that it perpetuates the name of a builder renowned for the poor quality of his work. Nothing he ever built stood the test of time, and consequently his customers were dissatisfied. That is how Mr. Jerry's name became proverbial, a by-word of faulty construction. And on any occasion that people wish to stress the frailty of things or ideas, they compare them with Jerry's work, saying that they were jerry-built!

Others have assumed that the word originated not on firm land but on the high seas and as long ago as the 17th century. Sailing vessels then had to meet many a trial, worst among them high winds and storms. Masts often snapped, and crews had to rig up a temporary pole to enable the ship to reach the nearest port.

The make-shift mast, used for the emergency and not expected to outlast the trip to the sheltering harbour, was referred to as *jury*-built. It may be that the fact that a jury served on a panel only for a restricted term was responsible for the choice of word. Soon common usage and the slurring of speech changed the jury into jerry. From the sailors, land-dwellers eventually adopted the word, and the jury-built mast became the father of anything jerry-built.

According to yet another theory, "jerry" is the Anglicized form of *jour,* the French word for "day". Cheaply-built houses certainly were so unsubstantial that they were said to last merely for a — French — day.

Some people like to find in the Bible the answer for everything. Jerry-builders definitely have some claim, and on two counts. It has been suggested, first of all, that jerry is an abbreviation of Jeremiah, that prophet of doom. He foretold so much destruction, of whole people and nations, that his name was most apt to describe all things destined to speedy decay and ruin, and so of impermanence.

But then, others found in Jericho's walls the origin of the expression. They fell down at the mere shouting of people, and collapsed at the blast of trumpets. Jerry-built thus may stand for *Jericho*-built. A house constructed in a hurry and with cheap material will be like Jericho's walls, unable to withstand even the sound of people shouting.

CHAPTER XII

MAGIC

MAN has always been fascinated by the mysterious. Anything that is strange, weird and unknown attracts and challenges him: doors to which he finds no key and veils through which he cannot see. Myths are the early dreams of people and nations. They express their philosophy of life. Ancient legends, however fantastic, have some background of realism. They grew out of many strands of experience and belief.

Here are the stories of four mysterious and legendary traditions that have assumed a world-wide significance: the spell of Abracadabra, the witch's broom and the magic carpet, and the message of the Three Wise Monkeys.

ABRACADABRA

Abracadabra is a charm against sickness, which was first mentioned by a physician who lived in the days of the Roman Emperor Caracalla, in the 2nd century A.D. It was considered a special cure for inflammation, ague, fever and toothache.

There are several explanations of the magic formula. It is said to be Hebrew or Aramaic. According to one tradition, it is a combination of the initials of the Hebrew words for FATHER, SON and HOLY GHOST. Another version sees it as a corruption of the Hebrew words for "blessing" — *bracha* — and "word" — *dabar*.

Probably, however, it is the name of an ancient demon whose identity is no longer known. In early days people believed that once they knew the name of a supernatural being, they also possessed its power for good or evil and thus, by merely applying its name, could perform miraculous deeds.

That is why the use of Abracadabra's name bestowed the power to heal sickness. Eventually it became a magic formula. This had to be written in a special way on parchment, to be worn by the sufferer around the neck on a linen thread.

The prescription demanded that first the whole word had to be written on the top line; then, on each subsequent line, the word had to be repeated but with one letter less, till finally — at the very bottom — only one letter was left. The whole script thus formed a triangle.

```
A B R A C A D A B R A
  A B R A C A D A B R
   A B R A C A D A B
    A B R A C A D A
     A B R A C A D
      A B R A C A
       A B R A C
        A B R A
         A B R
          A B
           A
```

It was believed that, just as the word lost a letter with each line, so this amulet forced the spirit of sickness to relinquish its hold gradually on the patient, till at last he was completely free from it and again a healthy man.

Another interpretation joins Abracadabra with an ancient Persian cult which demanded the worship of 365 different gods. The believer, anxious to enlist their aid, had to recite their names. This was a most arduous and lengthy procedure, fraught with many pitfalls. Should one name be omitted or mispronounced, his whole effort was futile. To minimize the task, priests devised a magic charm which replaced the 365 names by Greek letters which added up to their numerical value and were put down in the shape of an inverted cone. Simplifying matters (and worship) even further, later generations adopted the magic triangle's first line, using this for the whole, and that is how the word Abra-cadabra, so meaningless in itself, came into existence.

THE MAGIC CARPET

The legend of the magic flying carpet belongs to the Orient and is found there in numerous miraculous tales.

In their simplest form, these tell of a carpet that to all appearances is quite ordinary. But once a man is sitting on it, his wish to be transported to any other place, no matter how distant, comes true.

The story became so famous and wide-spread because it is based on Mohammedan sacred legend and the Koran, the holy scripture of Islam. There the carpet belongs to King Solomon.

But it was not the carpet itself that was responsible for the unusual kind of transportation. This was due solely to Solomon's power over the forces of nature. The king commanded the wind to carry the carpet wherever he wished it to go.

According to Moslem tradition, this carpet was woven of green threads. It was so huge that it could carry all the king's forces. Like our modern aircraft, the carpet was permitted to take off only when its load was rightly balanced. Solomon himself supervised the proper placing of cargo and men, grouping them around his throne, which always travelled in the centre of the carpet. Men and women had to take their places on the king's right and the spirits on the left. To protect the company from the sun, he had birds fly in formation over the carpet, forming a canopy with their wings.

THE WITCH'S BROOM

That witches were flying about on broomsticks is a tradition based not just on fairy tales and legends but on arguments, once seriously presented at courts of law, as a matter of life and death for some unfortunate woman. Frequently, the accusation was supported by the "witch's" own confession and observers' reports, given under oath.

The fact that people used to believe in flying witches need not surprise us, who have grown accustomed to hearing of flying saucers. Hysteria, mass-hypnosis and hallucinations may account for their "conviction". Indeed, there are records that endorse such explanations.

In 1560, for instance, a woman promised a certain Mr. Porta to bring information from a far-off city. She shut herself into her room, as she said, to depart from there. Porta was anxious to know what really happened and, therefore, watched her through a chink.

He saw her undressing and then rubbing her body with an ointment, whereupon she fell into a trance. Porta now forced his way into the room and tried to rouse the woman. But he did not succeed. He beat her up so cruelly that, when eventually she came to, her body was covered with black and blue bruises.

But she still insisted that she had travelled far and fast and had visited, as promised, the distant place. Even her unmistakable bruises she explained away as the result of the hazards of flying. Nothing could convince her of the spuriousness of her claim.

No doubt, vivid dreams and illusions of this kind caused gullible people, even judges and juries, to believe in the actual existence of flying witches. But their appearance was only the culmination of a long evolution of queer and weird traditions.

Flying demons are a commonplace in the ancient mythologies of countries as far apart as Scandinavia and Persia, and this deep-rooted belief contributed to the picture that was eventually built up of a witch riding through the air on her broomstick.

Originally, witches were not air-borne at all. They moved so quickly that it merely seemed as if they were flying. It did not take long, however, for human imagination to bestow on them the gift of flight and a fantasy was accepted as fact. A legend and myth thus became responsible for the prosecution and burning of numerous women.

Still the question remained, what gave them the power of propulsion. Some said it was mere demonic force. Others claimed that they were riding on certain beasts, such as goats, black rams and wolves. Finally, those early conveyances were dropped and, of all things, a broomstick took their place.

Several reasons present themselves for this curious metamorphosis. It may be that it was the result of a freak of language. Cats were the usual company of old women and, especially so, of those weird witches who were said to keep them for the express purpose of using their eyes for the preparation of evil potions. An early word meaning "stick" sounded exactly like "a cat", and it was by the confusion of those two terms that the cat changed into a stick!

But perhaps the cause is even more simple. For many centuries, the broomstick served as the symbol for a woman, just as the pitchfork did for a man. By an old custom, housewives used to place a broomstick outside the front door whenever leaving their home. It was a sign of their absence.

A much more likely explanation traces the broomstick back to a simple pole, which women (like our modern boy scouts) used to cross streams and other obstacles that obstructed their way. The fact that the witch put the rod between her legs gave rise to the belief that this in reality was the Devil's phallus.

But the story does not end with the broomstick. This was the mere vehicle, like our aircraft of today. The witch needed fuel, without which she could not get off the ground. This was presented to her at her initiation in the form of a Flying Ointment, with which she had to grease herself and the stick each time before flying.

The chimney was her usual runway, first mentioned as such in 1460. As in our modern days, take-off and touch-down were the most dangerous moments. Once air-borne, the witch had little to fear — except from church bells, which could ground the broom. But this was a hazard she could overcome by increasing her speed.

THE THREE WISE MONKEYS

It is a fallacy that the Three Wise Monkeys, who hear no evil, see no evil and speak no evil, are indigenously Japanese. It is true that they have had their domicile there for many centuries. But originally they came from China and were introduced into Japan by a Buddhist monk of the Tendai sect, probably in the 8th century A.D.

The monkeys were at first always associated with the blue-faced deity Vadjra, a fearsome god with three eyes and numerous hands. Their characteristic gestures of covering their ears, eyes and mouths with their paws were a dramatic pictorial way of conveying the command of the god. This shows an early realization of the psychological fact that a striking picture is more impressive and lasting than a spoken message.

Nevertheless, the story has been told in various traditions in prose and poetry. It dates back at least to the 7th century and is part of the teaching of the Vadjra cult that if we do not hear, see or talk evil, we ourselves shall be spared all evil.

In folk etymology and by a play on words the very names of the monkeys — Mizaru, Kikazaru and Iwazaru — express their three gestures and thus anyone by merely referring to them immediately proclaims their message.

CHAPTER XIII

meдicine

THERE IS romance in medical terms. A doctor means "someone who instructs"; a nurse "nourishes" and a hospital is a "guest house". But a patient is called so because he "suffers".

Endless in its application and interest is the art of healing. According to biblical writings, the first operation ever performed was the excision of Adam's rib by God. Even then surgery was done under an anaesthetic. God first of all "caused a deep sleep to fall upon the man".

The Sumerians called their doctors "those who know water"—an early recognition of the diagnostic value of urine. The ancient Romans already realized the power of man's mind over the body. "It is part of the cure to wish to be cured," wrote Seneca almost 2000 years ago.

Even as objective a craft as that of healing has not remained unstained by national prejudice. A telling example concerns syphilis and the way it has been described by different people. Early English writers used to call it "French pox". The French, in turn, spoke of it as "the Italian disease", whilst Japanese doctors linked it with the Portuguese.

Napoleon liked neither doctors nor medicines. He preferred by far fresh air, water and cleanliness. And yet, a physician is man's best friend. The Chinese were wise when they used to pay their doctors for keeping them well but stopped the fee at once, when they became sick.

All this is indicative of medicine's long standing. There is further and perhaps more interesting evidence in the terms and symbols that have been connected with medicine from earliest times.

THE DOCTOR'S RED LAMP

The red lamp which indicates a doctor's surgery also recalls the early practice of blood letting, so popular in former days as an imagined, and apparently effective, cure of many ills.

We need little imagination to see in the red globe evidence of a flourishing practice. The sign represents a vessel brimful with patients' blood. "Here is the place where you can get relief!", was the unspoken but once unmistakable message.

The red lamp was introduced in 1745, the very year when the Barbers' and Surgeons' Company was dissolved and surgery became an independent profession, practised by "specialists" — properly qualified doctors. There was need for them, too, now to display their presence, in spite of all later adverse opinions on advertising. They wanted people to know where they could be found. The obvious choice was the bloody globe.

That the red colour is easily seen from a distance and is therefore a good guide for the distressed added to the importance of the doctor's red lamp.

Perhaps an ancient survival of the belief in the curative power of the actual colour may also be responsible subconsciously for its retention. Centuries ago, for instance, people suffering from smallpox were treated not merely with drugs but with the colour red. When John, one of the sons of King Edward II, was treated for the disease, his bed was surrounded with red drapings, his body was covered with red blankets and he was prescribed a gargle of red mulberry wine and a diet of the red juice of pomegranates.

Times have changed. Ancient cures are outdated and patients and doctors alike frown on the primitive method of letting blood. Yet the red globe remains. It is a symbol of the advance of medicine, a monument to the birth of an independent medical profession and, at the same time, another vivid example of the conservatism of our customs which linger on even when their original, and then logical, meaning and reason no longer apply.

THE EMBLEM OF STAFF AND SERPENT

The staff and serpent, a doctor's symbol all over the world, leads back to Greek mythology and Aesculapius, god of healing and father of physicians. In his most famous statues he is represented with his hand resting on a staff around which a serpent is coiled.

The staff itself might have been merely a support, though it is much more likely that it symbolized the tree of life. A further tradition saw in it an early emblem of solar divinity, which could act like a magic wand.

Homer described such a rod of gold which alternately "charmed the eyes of men and called them from their slumber". It could lure the dead to Hades but equally was able to bring them back to the light of day.

As for the serpent, various and even contradictory explanations may account for its association with Aesculapius, who was born the son of the divine Apollo and a mortal woman, and whose art of healing roused Jupiter's anger so much that he had Aesculapius killed.

The serpent has always figured as an emblem of all that was evil and harmful. This was the inevitable result of man's frequent experience of the deadliness of a snake's bite.

The fact that Aesculapius is shown with his right hand so near the serpent's head implied either that he knew all the antidotes to cure its bite or that, because of his supernatural power, even the worst of poisons became ineffective. The staff and serpent thus told of the doctor's ability to combat sickness and to help preserve life.

The serpent also became the symbol of renewal and regeneration. A person restored to health, as it were, has shed his body of sickness and taken on a garment of new life. The image of a snake was the most appropriate picture of such a change. Did not the serpent itself, once every year, cast off its skin and thereby acquire a new existence?

There is yet another tradition, equally old but completely different. This held that the serpent was the most cunning of creatures; not the incarnation of evil but of wisdom. It had magical powers of prophecy, dreams and healing. For that reason sacred serpents were kept in the many temples dedicated to Aesculapius all over Greece and beyond.

More than coincidental is the fact that even the Bible contains a reference to the healing qualities of a rod and a snake. When the Israelites were bitten by poisonous snakes while on their desert trek, Moses instructed them to have a copper snake made and held high above their heads on a pole. And "everyone that was bitten, when he looked upon it, was healed".

SURGEONS ADDRESSED AS "Mr."

Today, all surgeons are doctors. But as at first they had been just barbers, they maintain their original form of address and go on being called "Mister". A present-day courtesy thus leads back to humble beginnings and shows how "titles do not reflect honour on men, but rather men on their titles".

THE "CAESAREAN"

The delivery of a child by cutting through the walls of the abdomen is generally known as a Caesarean section. First-century Roman author Pliny was one of the earliest writers to refer to it by that name, listing "those (children) who have been cut out of the womb".

It is one of the oldest operations known and is mentioned in the mythology of the ancient Romans, Indians and Persians.

The first legendary "Caesarean" section was Apollo's removal of the babe Asklepios (the Greek rendering of Aesculapius) from the womb of the dead Koronis.

Bacchus, the Romans' god of wine and fertility, also is said to have been brought into the world in this manner.

Persian tradition tells of the lovely, moon-faced wife of King Sal. Being with child, her womb had grown to such enormous dimensions that she almost died. Then a Zoroastrian priest gave her a hypnotic drug so that she fell into a deep sleep. He cut open her body "to deliver a great, lusty son" — Rustam — who was to become the Persian Hercules. When the operation was over, the priest tidily sewed up the incision, which soon healed.

Oldest Roman law required that all women dying in an advanced stage of pregnancy should be cut open to save the child. Numa Pompilius, first ruler of Rome, had thus decreed (in the 8th century B.C.) that "if any woman died while she was pregnant, the child was to be cut out of her womb". It was one of the few operations which was whole-heartedly supported by the early Church.

Originally (and for almost 2000 years), all Caesarean sections were performed on the mother's dead body. That is why the usual explanation — first introduced by Pliny — that we speak of a Caesarean because Julius Caesar himself was "from his mother's womb utimely ripp'd", is unhistorical and incorrect. We know through Caesar's own letters to his mother Aurelia that she must have survived his birth by many years.

Much more likely is the suggestion that the term was first coined simply because, in the Latin way of speaking, it was an exact description of what was being done. The Latin word for "to cut out" is *caedere*. And because the earliest member of Caesar's family, Scipio Africanus, was born by excising him from his dead mother's body, he was given the name *Caesar*. To celebrate and commemorate his miraculous, unnatural way of birth his father called him "the cut out one" — Caesar.

The first printed illustration of a Caesarean operation appeared not in a medical but in a biographical work, "The Lives of the First 12 Caesars", by Suetonius. Written in the 2nd century A.D., its first printed edition appeared in 1506 and included a drawing of the actual surgical delivery. This was used as the frontispiece of the book in its second printing.

The first account of a Caesarean operation which the mother survived is dramatic. It was performed (about 1500 A.D.) not by a doctor or midwife but by a husband, to save his wife's life. He was Jacob Nufer of Sigershaufen. In great distress he watched his wife's labour going from bad to worse, without her being able to deliver the child. He knew nothing about obstetrics but he was an efficient sow-gelder. On the spur of the moment he took a razor and with it cut out the child.

Where 13 midwives had failed, he succeeded. In later years his wife gave birth to six other children. The "Caesarean boy" lived to the age of 77.

"NOT TO BE SNEEZED AT"

Some of the sayings popular today started long ago and in totally different circumstances. A case in point is the phrase "not to be sneezed at". We, who have become so germ-conscious, might immediately jump to the conclusion that the words originated as a commendable precaution to avoid catching other people's colds, as "coughs and sneezes spread diseases". But far from it.

People in older times imagined that a sneeze cleared the mind. It certainly gave them a feeling of exhilaration. Suddenly, 17th century Europe caught a craze for sneezing. It was considered the right thing to do in good society. Indeed, the more you sneezed, the more you proved yourself a member of the privileged class.

To build up this new status symbol, all kinds of devices were used. It was soon realized that snuff caused sneezing. Therefore everyone who was someone carried with him a little box, containing a mixture of sneeze-producing herbs or tobacco. By drawing an ample pinch of it into the nostrils, a hearty sneeze resulted in no time.

Of course, only the rich and idle had time to sneeze or could afford snuff. Hence the self-induced sneeze became synonymous with aristocratic living. If you were able to sneeze "on call", you showed audibly your status in society.

But one matter had still to be decided. Just to sneeze haphazardly was not good enough. There had to be a special occasion. Soon sneezing became part of men's conversation. You indulged in it whenever you wanted to show your disapproval of anything said or, even more so, your lack of interest in the matter discussed. A sneeze was an unmistakable way of saying politely "you bore me".

Consequently and logically, anything "not to be sneezed at" was something really worthwhile.

THE QUARANTINE

Everyone now understands quarantine as a medical term. It refers to the isolation for a prescribed period of people or animals arriving by sea or air from abroad. The object is to prevent their carrying a contagious disease into the country.

Originally, however, quarantine was just a figure, meaning 40. It was used to describe any period of that duration, whether measured in hours, days, months or years. There are many examples.

In ancient legal tradition, for instance, a quarantine meant the 40 days during which a widow had the right to stay in the house of her deceased husband. The privilege of sanctuary, equally, extended to one quarantine — 40 days.

In a truce between England and Flanders there was a special stipulation that "if the Earl should depart from the Treaty and the parties could not be reconciled in *three quarantines* (i.e. 120 days), each of the hostages shall pay the sum of 100 Marks".

The choice of the figure 40 was not arbitrary or accidental. Once it was believed that there was magic in figures and the number 40 especially was thought to possess supernatural power. That is why Moses spent 40 days and nights on Mount Sinai to receive God's revelation, and the Israelites wandered through the desert for 40 years. Both Elijah on his journey to Horeb, and Christ during His temptation in the wilderness, fasted for 40 days. The period of Lent extends over exactly 40 days. This caused Italians to call it, simply and appropriately, by that figure — the *quarantena*.

A unit of 40, so it was imagined in early days, could shield man from all kinds of evil. For that reason, widows in primitive tribes had to mourn their husbands for 40 days. They did so not in sorrow but out of fear — to ward off any evil from the disembodied spirit of the deceased, effective for that period of time.

Plague was once considered to be brought on by demons. To fight them one needed magic — supplied by 40 days! Thus, sailors were first kept in "Quarantine" not out of medical wisdom but in magical superstition. Only 40 days exactly could achieve a cure or provide protection. To increase or to reduce that figure immediately broke the spell and subjected the men to the influence of evil forces.

In 1348, at the time of the Black Death, Venetians introduced the quarantine as a magical shield against the disease. England adopted the institution from them. That is how we still retain the word and the precaution. But we have forgotten how it first started — in the field of magic and through the mystical figure of 40.

CHAPTER XIV

SOURCES OF JUSTICE

MAN has always had a passion for justice. From the beginning of civilization he has felt the urge to see right prevail and wrong punished. At first, the execution of justice was part of religious faith, even in its most primitive forms. It is not accidental that the Five Books of Moses are known as "The Law". The priests were the earliest guardians of justice.

It is a well-known dictum that ignorance of the law is no excuse and it has been generally applied in every country. There should be no excuse either for being ignorant of the origins of the law, its colourful institutions and great variety of procedure. To delve into the past and see how it all started provides a wonderful insight both into the workings of the mind and the growth of civilization.

Research shows, for example, that the black cap worn by a judge when passing sentence of death is not a cap. It is a three-cornered piece of black silk, used as a sign of mourning.

Butchers were excluded from serving on juries in medieval times. Obviously, so it was thought, a man whose occupation was the killing of animals was so used to taking life that to him even the death of a human being would mean little.

An 18th century candidate for an important office in the City of London listed eight points as essential for winning a case. They were: a good cause, a good purse, an honest and skilful attorney, good evidence, able counsel, an upright judge, an intelligent jury and, last but not least, good luck.

"JUSTICE IS BLIND"

One of the most highly treasured possessions of Britain's democracy is the independence of her judges. They are guarded
jealously against even the slightest suspicion that their verdicts
might be influenced by any personal consideration, prejudice
or sympathy.

Perhaps one of the best-known statues in the world is the
figure of Justice over London's Central Criminal Court — the Old
Bailey. Traditionally she is blind-folded, so that she may not see
the scales she holds in her hand. This implies that there should be
no favouritism and that a judge should be completely impartial,
neither intimidated by the mighty and rich nor influenced by
pity for the weak and poor. Nothing but the evidence and its
right interpretation must guide him in the trial of an action.

That Justice should be blind is an ancient principle. It goes
back to the old Egyptians, who applied it literally. Their Courts
of Law met in a darkened chamber. This made it impossible for
a judge to see and recognize the accuser, defendant and
witnesses.

THE ORDEAL

When we speak today of an ordeal we refer to anything that
severely tests character or endurance. Use of the term dates back
thousands of years to the time when an ordeal was not just a
character test but an actual trial of suspects. The outcome of the
trial determined the charged person's innocence or guilt and thus
his life or death.

The word ordeal is Anglo-Saxon, meaning "judgment". That is
exactly what an ordeal was assumed to be — God's judgment.

"What is truth?", is a question which has puzzled man from
earliest times. But it has not always been possible to do like
Pilate: to put the question and then to walk away without even
waiting for an answer. In matters of right and wrong it is of vital
necessity to know whether a man is innocent or guilty. That
becomes the more difficult if sufficient evidence is lacking to
clear or condemn the accused.

Primitive man left the decision to the gods in a trial by ordeal.
The question of where truth lay was addressed not to a human

judge but to supernatural powers. It was always categorical and asked: "Is this man guilty or not?". A third possibility was disregarded — that the gods might not answer.

Trials by ordeal were held all over the world. They were known among early Aryan races and examples of them are found in the Old Testament. Surprisingly, this kind of judicial inquiry, where supernatural aid was invoked and relied on in place of evidence, did not disappear with antiquity. In the Middle Ages, ordeals were sanctioned and applied by both Church and State all over Europe, including Britain.

Ecclesiastical authorities devised special liturgical formulae to accompany the procedure, and Law Courts approved of several forms of the trial. All shared the principle that God would save the righteous and punish the evil-doer. If the accused succumbed to the ordeal, his guilt was proved. If he passed through it unscathed, God had declared him innocent. The individual choice of the ordeal depended on the standing of the accused.

In the *trial by battle,* the suspect was forced to fight the person who had charged him. It was believed that victory would go to the party who was in the right. The ordeal was not an appeal to force but to God, who would let the righteous win.

It is not difficult to discern that modern warfare among nations is based on this identical primitive misconception that not the force of arms but the justice of the cause determined the final outcome.

In the *trial by hot water,* the accused had to plunge his hand and arm — up to the elbow — into boiling water. The hand and arm were then bandaged. If after three days they showed any injury, this was taken as a divine indication that the man was guilty.

In the *trial by fire,* the suspect was forced to hold in his hand a red-hot iron or, blind-folded and with bare feet, to walk among nine red-hot ploughshares, placed haphazardly on the ground. If he passed through the ordeal unharmed, he was innocent. This type of trial was reserved for a person of high rank who could appoint a deputy on his behalf!

In the *trial by the morsel,* the accused person had to swallow — in one piece — either bread or cheese weighing 1 ounce. His innocence was considered proven if he could do so without effort. But should the "morsel" get stuck in his throat, God had pronounced him guilty.

In the *trial by water*, the suspect was thrown, with his hands and feet bound, into a river. If he sank it was an intimation by God that he was free of guilt. But if he floated, the opposite was the case.

At first sight and to the reasoning of our mind, such a decision seems rather paradoxical, and we should have expected it to have been the other way round. But the apparent contradiction resolves itself, if it is realized that water was considered the symbol of purity. It rejected the guilty — who therefore floated — but it did not object to receiving the innocent, who hence drowned!

It is one of the peculiar traits of human nature that once an institution or custom has been carried on for some time, it is taken for granted and never questioned. Even when eventually it has lost its usefulness or, worse still, has become harmful, people continue to observe it, accepting it as something right and proper. This applies especially to those features in human society which are closely associated with religion and said to be done in the name of God.

That is why the cruel and totally misleading *trial by ordeal* kept a hold on the people for so long. They had neither the courage nor the wisdom to rebel against it. But at last, in the second half of the 12th century, some enlightened men realized the total injustice of a system that, in the determination of a man's innocence or guilt, claimed to listen to the voice of God but in reality relied on pure chance.

Still, nothing was changed until the Church itself took matters in hand. In 1212 Pope Innocent III forbade the use of the ordeal when this was applied by the Bishop of Strasbourg against heretics.

The Lateran Council of 1215 decreed that henceforth no priest anywhere would be permitted to participate in a trial of that kind. As the presence of an ecclesiastic on such occasions was indispensable, trials by ordeals could no longer be held. It was one of the significant cases where religion proved itself not as a reactionary force but as a goad to progress.

The problem now facing the authorities was who should assume the function of the defunct ordeal in determining right and wrong. All agreed that a more rational form was needed. Wisely, the choice fell on the jury.

THE JURY

Juries had their beginnings in ancient Greek days and among Teutonic tribes. Many theories have been advanced as to their origin. Equally, there has been much controversy as to whence and how the jury-system found its way to England.

Trial by jury is now a proud part of the British judicial system. It is democracy at its best (at least in the opinion of many), as the people themselves are given an opportunity to determine the facts of a trial. Though, as is proper, questions of law and punishment are left to the judge.

Formerly, however, a jury served a completely different purpose. It was used not to foster democracy but to ensure the rights of the king and to enforce his rule.

It is now generally agreed that the jury system reached England by way of the Norman-French kings. Anxious to establish their power, they used to summon a body of neighbours — the original jury. These were compelled to "take an oath", which is the literal meaning of "jury", stemming from the French, that they would tell the truth and never mislead their royal master.

Through their appointment, the king was able to obtain all essential information for the administration of the district in which they resided.

When William I came to England he, too, was concerned, first of all, to establish the supremacy of the crown and therefore made equal use of a system of jurors. Summoned by the king's representative, the royal judge, they had to supply him with the correct facts concerning their county. They were obliged to do so by oath.

Later, a jury — to be known as a "Grand Jury"— assumed another significant role, although still completely divorced from its modern tasks. In 1166 a statute issued by Henry II ordained that 12 lawful men from each 100 should be sworn to accuse criminals, so that they might be presented for the ordeal. In 1215, as a direct result of the elimination of the ordeal, the jury itself was called upon to try the accused.

It was not until the 17th century that the present-day principle, that jurors are merely judges of fact, was firmly established. They no longer took part in the verdict nor could they act as witnesses.

TWELVE JURYMEN

Originally, juries consisted of a considerable number of men. Eventually this proved too cumbersome for practical purposes. What was needed was a convenient number of jurors, not too big to become unmanageable but still large enough to present a good cross-section of the public.

Why 12 men came to be chosen has been explained in various ways. Sources cited were the 12 tribes of Israel, the 12 officers appointed by King Solomon (as recorded in I Kings IV) and the 12 Apostles. However, the last claim is rather unfortunate. It would imply that there was a Judas on every jury.

Subconscious memories of the significance of the figure 12 may have contributed to its selection. Anglo-Saxons appear always to have had an abhorrence of the decimal system and therefore shunned the number 10. Eleven or 13, being indivisible, somehow did not seem right, either. But the dozen was favourably received. Just as the shilling had 12 pennies, "12 good men and true" were considered to make up the right value.

THE DERRICK

A whole gallery of men and women of all ages is hidden away in everyday talk and the dictionaries of all nations. Usage has so camouflaged many words that no one would expect to find behind them someone who, in some way, has enriched the language. This process was without design or intention. The mass of the people, impressed or revolted by a person's behaviour, ingenuity or mode of living, seized his or her name and retained it.

Thus, Amelia Bloomer's fashion, though shrunk to shorts, survives, the fourth Earl of Sandwich's hasty meal is still popular, and Adolphe Sax's name is heard whenever the *sax*ophone is played.

Similarly, Tsar recalls Caesar, the Count of Sade's sexual degeneration survives in sadism, and Quisling's name has become a byword. Shakespeare, once again, was so right when he said that "the evil that men do lives after them".

The ship's derrick owes its name to Thomas Derrick, of London, executioner during Queen Elizabeth's reign. His most renowned "case" was that of the Earl of Essex.

Derrick did not like the old-fashioned rope-method of hanging. He felt that there was much room for improvement. He certainly did not lack material on which to experiment. That is how, eventually, he developed his new "killing machine", the device which bears his name.

Not long after his death, a hoisting apparatus was introduced. Its appearance closely resembled Derrick's gallows, and inevitably people called it a derrick, as well.

That is how innocuously a hangman's name lives on. Once used to describe a gadget applied to transport men from this world to the next, it now identifies a much less gruesome machine, a crane, moving merely goods into and out of the holds of a vessel.

Derrick served in the Earl of Essex's expedition against Cadiz, where he was sentenced to death for rape. However, possibly aware of the man's usefulness in his peculiar trade, the Earl pardoned him and Derrick for a long time afterwards was able to continue his grim profession.

This would have been a suitable finish to any story. But unfortunately it did not end there. However grateful Derrick had cause to be to the Earl for saving his life, the day came when he was called upon to take the life of his own benefactor. When Essex committed treason and Queen Elizabeth condemned him to death, Derrick himself had to execute the sentence.

But the noble blood of the traitor excluded the usual method of hanging and beheading with an axe was considered more appropriate for his status. Derrick certainly did not like the job or the occasion. Politely he apologized to his former friend for what he was about to do: he was merely obeying orders. But then things went wrong. Inexperienced in this type of execution, Derrick had to apply the axe three times.

As a result, the huge crowd of the Earl's admirers who had come to witness his sad departure became enraged, seized Derrick, and would have killed him had not soldiers come to his rescue. Thus, for the second time, his life was preserved in order to end the lives of many others. He became notorious as "the hangman of Tyburn" and in people's minds his name became synonymous with the gallows. Thus are linked a man, a gibbet and a crane.

LYNCHING

At least four men named Lynch have been cited as the possible originator of the term describing mob-law. The word itself was first recorded only in 1817.

The Irish claim ownership of the original Lynch. His story was full of personal tragedy.

James Lynch Fitz-Stephen was the Mayor of Galway. About 1493, he sent his son to Spain to purchase a cargo of wine. But the young man lost his father's funds at gambling, bought the wine on credit and assured the merchant it would be paid for in due course. The Spaniard, anxious to see the debt paid and perhaps suspicious of the young man, sent his nephew with Lynch back to Ireland to collect the amount owing.

During the voyage, Lynch, to avoid discovery of his fraud, killed the nephew and threw his body into the sea. Lynch's father soon discovered the crime. As Mayor, he had to sit in judgment over his son and he duly pronounced the death sentence.

Everyone was shocked by the great tragedy that had befallen a citizen so well respected and loved. No one was prepared to carry out the sentence, but old Lynch was determined to see justice done, even though it meant the death of his own son. He hanged him from a window in their home.

Courts of Justice are most assiduous to establish the true facts of a case. But when popular feeling runs riot, the result can only be much confusion. This certainly applies to Lynch-law and the many attempts at explaining the origin of its name. Even the story of the Mayor of Galway has its two versions. The second tale, though still relating to the same year and the identical persons, differs in all other aspects.

According to this tradition, James Lynch Fitz-Stephen was anxious to improve trade relations between his own country and Spain. For this purpose he himself undertook the arduous journey to the then far-off country.

When he was ready to return home, he invited his host's son to sail with him to Ireland and stay as his guest. The invitation was accepted. In Galway, things went well and everyone seemed happy, till one day the Mayor's son became suspicious. He imagined (or perhaps it was not just fancy) that his father's guest was paying too much attention to his own sweetheart. Overcome with jealousy, he stabbed him.

The rest of the story — more or less — follows the pattern of the first. Lynch, as the head of the guard, seized the murderer and, as Mayor, passed sentence of death. But the Galway people wished to protect his son and a riotous mob tried to rescue him. However, Lynch forced his way through the crowd and when all others refused to execute the boy, himself hanged him. He then returned to his home and was never seen again.

Other claims to having originated the term Lynch-law belong to the American scene.

Charles Lynch (1736-96) was a Virginian planter and a Colonel in the army of General Greene. During the American Revolution, he was concerned to keep order in the Staunton River district, where he lived. He and two of his friends combined to protect the region from marauders, though some have suggested that this protective union was against political opponents.

Taking the law into their hands, Lynch and his associates punished all those breaking the peace of the realm (or not sharing their views!) by creating their own, extralegal, court. They punished lawlessness (or political disagreement?) either by flogging the offender or expelling him from the district. However, so different from what Lynch-law came to mean in later years, no one was ever killed.

Eventually — in 1782 — Lynch himself was apprehended and accused before the Virginian Assembly, for his unlawful execution of justice. But wisely the judges indemnified him.

Other authorities attribute this type of unauthorized tribunal and its name not to Charles but to his brother John Lynch, founder of Lynchburg in Virginia.

Early editions of Webster's Dictionary quote yet another American, James Lynch. He was a farmer at Piedmont in Virginia and highly respected. As the nearest court was a considerable distance away, neighbours elected him to try and pass sentence on accused persons at Piedmont.

Another tradition associates Lynch-law not with a person but a place. At Lynch Creek, in North Carolina, people set up their own tribunal to court-martial and execute the corpse of a Tory whom they had already hanged. They thus tried to legalize a death sentence posthumously.

Some authorities feel that neither a person nor a location but an old English dialect was responsible for the Lynch-law. People in the North of England used the word *linch*, meaning "to beat" or "maltreat". Could it be that, in spite of all those many stories, our Lynch-law simply goes back to this word?

BOYCOTT

Boycott as a word and policy was the result of the struggle between the Irish and the English and a landlord's refusal to take note of his tenants' poverty and distress.

In the late 70s of the last century, crop failures in Ireland were disastrous and there was a great famine. Thousands of farmers were unable to pay rent to absentee English landlords, and suggested paying as much as they could.

In many cases landlords reduced the rent. But not so Lord Erne, who owned big estates in the County of Mayo. He instructed Captain Charles Cunningham Boycott, his local agent, to use any measure he deemed essential to get the money. Some 3000 people were concerned, but Boycott showed them no mercy.

He had reckoned without the Irish temper and the people's determination to throw off the English yoke once and for all. Far from being intimidated, the farmers now refused to pay any rent. They stopped reaping the harvest, such as it was, and formed the Irish Land League. Thus organized, they decided to have no dealings of any kind with the agent, Boycott.

The campaign against the Captain gathered strength. Servants were forced to leave his employ. His mail was intercepted and attempts were made to cut off his food supply.

In retaliation, 50 Orangemen from the North of Ireland, under the protection of 900 soldiers, were sent to Mayo. There they harvested what remained of the crop and managed to rescue Boycott. He fled to England, where he died, 17 years later, in 1897. His name was quickly adopted everywhere as a new word describing the very treatment of which he had been a victim.

One of the vigorous young Irish members of Parliament, J. Dillon, with Boycott's fate still fresh in his mind, expounded to his countrymen the new policy as a bloodless safeguard against their rapacious and avaricious masters. In a speech, delivered to the Land League in 1881, he said:—

"One word as to the way in which a man should be boycotted. When any man has taken a farm from which a tenant has been evicted, or is a grabber, let everyone in the parish turn his back on him; have no communication with him; have no dealings with him. You need never say an unkind word to him; but never say anything at all to him. If you must meet him in fair, walk away from him silently. Do him no violence, but have no dealings with him. Let every man's door be closed against him; and make him feel himself a stranger and a castaway in his own neighbourhood."

THE GUILLOTINE

The French Revolution, with its thousands of executions, inherited from the monarchy a carefully graded system of death. Different methods were used, according to the condemned man's crime, and also to his position.

Under King Louis XVI, heretics were burnt, traitors quartered, and assassins and highwaymen broken on the wheel. Others who had committed any of 115 capital offences were treated with class distinction. If they were of the common people, their fate was hanging. But if they belonged to the aristocracy, they had the privilege of being beheaded, which was a method less cruel and not so prolonged in its agony.

Dr. Joseph Ignace Guillotin, a true son of the Revolution, did not question the actual putting to death. But he was horrified at the differentiation in the means of execution. He demanded that the new spirit of fraternity and equality should reach to the scaffold and that decapitation should be extended to the masses!

Therefore, on humane grounds and with a passion for equality, he took up his cause in the French Chamber. Eloquently he pleaded it, demanding a gadget which was more merciful. It should be applied to all and sundry, "whatever the rank and status of the guilty party".

The Press enthusiastically echoed his feelings and recommended "the humane sentiments which breathed in the Guillotin proposal". Commentators referred to the need for some machine which would be "worthy of the new order into which we are about to enter".

However, although Guillotin had urged the necessity of a device, he did not invent it himself. Another medical practitioner, a Dr. Louis, adapted earlier mechanisms of similar type and constructed the first modern beheading machine, which was soon introduced all over France. Because its adoption was due solely to Dr. Guillotin's indefatigable agitation, people gave it his name, and not that of Dr. Louis, and despite Guillotin's strong objection, his name stuck.

A story says that he himself died by means of his "invention". Actually, Guillotin died at the age of 76 from a carbuncle in a shoulder. After his death, his children petitioned the government, out of deference to their father and for their own sake, to change the name of the guillotine. Their request was rejected, but they were permitted to change their own name instead!

Psychologists have been at pains to explain why Guillotin devoted so much time to the question of humane execution. Some of them have felt that the reason was Guillotin's own premature birth. While she was pregnant with the future Joseph Ignace, his mother unexpectedly witnessed a criminal being tortured to death on a wheel. The experience so shocked her that she gave birth to her son prematurely. Thus the guillotine may have been envisaged through pre-natal influence.

THE SCAPEGOAT

Throughout history the goat appears to have been identified with fools and sin.

The Bible taught to separate the goats from the sheep. Though we no longer, like our medieval forebears, represent the Devil in the shape of a goat, we still rebuke people for "acting the goat".

Those blamed or punished for the sins of others are known as scapegoats. This description is based on an ancient sacred rite and, originally, was not a mere metaphor. Mosaic law decreed that on the holiest day of the Jewish year, the Day of Atonement, two he-goats had to be brought to the altar of the Tabernacle. They had to be without blemish. The High Priest, by casting lots, chose one of them to be sacrificed on the spot. The other was sent into the wilderness to *escape* there, symbolically carrying with it all the sins of the people.

The Book of Leviticus (Chapter XVI) describes the ritual in detailed form: "And Aaron shall lay both his hands upon the head of the live goat, and confess over him all the iniquities of the children of Israel, and all their transgressions, even all their sins. And he shall put them upon the head of the goat and shall send him away by the hand of an appointed man into the desert. And the goat shall bear upon him all their iniquities. And he shall let the goat *escape* into the wilderness . . ."

An early mysterious rite thus still survives in one of our common expressions. But the omission of a single letter, which once prefixed the word, hides its original meaning. The escaped goat became the scapegoat!

paRLiamentaRy pRoceδuRe anδ Royal ReGalia

PARLIAMENT is the very heart of democracy. Its growth in British lands reflects the maturing of a nation's desire to rule itself in the most effective and reliable manner. Every detail of Parliamentary tradition and procedure was evolved in the pursuit of that ideal. Added to this was a determination to stop any government from becoming an autocratic force.

Parliament goes back to 1258. In that year, in opposition to King Henry III, the Earl of Leicester convened an assembly at Oxford. He ordered two Knights from each shire and representatives from certain boroughs to meet selected Barons and members of the Clergy there and then. However, what has been called the Model Parliament dates back to 1295, when "Commoners" were first elected — and not just appointed — to represent the people.

Rules of courtesy permeate all Parliamentary procedure. A member must stand up to speak. He is expected to do so without reference to notes. Maiden speeches are treated with special consideration. Tradition demands that a member of the opposing party shall congratulate the speaker on his first effort.

Even in the heat of debate, everything that might hurt or insult a member must be avoided. No one in Parliament can be accused of having lied. That is why Churchill, when trying to point out how a member had made an untruthful statement, was unable to do so in so many words. Instead, in his ingenious way of coining new phrases, he suggested that the man had been guilty of "a terminological inexactitude".

Parliament has taught man that democracy means not: "I am
equal to you" but that "You are equal to me".

THE CHAMBER

A 14th century chapel, which was destroyed by fire in 1834,
was the earliest Chamber. It still is the prototype of British
Houses of Parliament throughout the world. They continue its
original rectangular shape, but the altar has been replaced by the
canopied Speaker's Chair. The ancient pews survive in the members' benches. This explains why, up to this day, those sitting in
Parliament do not occupy individual seats.

The comparative smallness of the Chamber gives all debates
dignity and intimacy. It also creates an atmosphere of friendship
even among opponents who, though far removed in political
views, sit close together. Furthermore, as was pointed out at the
rebuilding of the House of Commons in London in 1941, after
its destruction by enemy action, a crowded small Chamber is so
much more advantageous than a large one, depressing by its being
mostly half empty.

The arrangement of benches along two sides, following the
example of the ancient church, fostered the two-party system.
British tradition taught members to respect their opponents'
opinion. Thus the Opposition is officially known as "Her Majesty's
Opposition", with its implied suggestion that the "Opposition" is
as much a part of "Her Majesty" as is the Government. In re-
muneration its leader is not far behind the Prime Minister. To
pay someone to oppose you is a telling example of British
democracy.

THE SPEAKER

The Speaker is one of the most important persons in Parliament. His word is law and those who dare act against it are duly
punished. Presiding over the House, he controls its debates.

Tradition demands that he be nominated and selected by back-
benchers. This is done to stress his duty to protect minorities,
and to express his complete impartiality.

Invested with royal prerogatives, in Parliament itself, the
Speaker ranks superior to the Crown. Anyone who wishes to

approach or address him must pay due deference to his standing. Like a king, he is distinguished by regalia: the Mace is his sceptre, the Chair his throne, and the wig his crown.

Today a coveted position of the highest honour, the Speaker's office at first was least desired. Its duties, at times, were perilous and unrewarding. His very title preserves his original function. The Speaker spoke up on behalf of the Commons, expressing their majority view to the king.

This all goes back to the time when Parliament, in the literal sense of its name, "talked" (from the French *parler*) about matters of state to ascertain the wish and opinion of the greatest number of its members. At first these discussions were held in unofficial meetings behind closed doors. The only right of the "Commons" then was not to direct the king, but to address humble petitions to him. The man chosen to convey to the Crown the wish and desire of the House thus acted as their mouthpiece — their "Speaker".

It was an unenviable task, especially when the views of king and people clashed. Then the Speaker had to bear the brunt of the sovereign's wrath and, at times, to pay with his life. At least nine Speakers are known to have died a violent death.

Sir Peter de la Mare is said to have been one of the first to be called upon to act as the Speaker of the House, and his thankless mission illustrates the origin of the office.

Dame Alice Perrers was a "lady to the bedchamber" to Philippa, the Queen of Edward III. However, far from being satisfied with her appointed duties, she showed much greater interest in the king himself, who reciprocated her feelings. It was a most remunerative relationship for Alice. She amassed a truly royal fortune, which included a grant of land, jewellery worth hundreds of pounds, and the guardianship of wealthy orphans. When Queen Philippa died in 1373, her death further enriched Alice.

But her appetite grew all the time on what it was feeding on, whilst the king, certainly, was eating out of her hand. Wealth alone no longer satisfied her. She wished to wield power as well, and started to meddle in affairs of state.

Becoming ever more arrogant in her demeanour, Alice in 1376

dared to enter Westminster Hall and tried to instruct Parliament's presiding judge how he should act.

For a long time the Commons had watched with anxiety and exasperation Alice's mischievous influence on the king. But now she had gone to the very limit. Something had to be done and done quickly. Somebody had to be sent to the king, telling him how they felt and that, once and for all, he had to break up the affair and to put Alice into her place.

Sir Peter de la Mare was elected to go and *speak up* on their behalf. That is how he became the Commons' first Speaker, an office whose birth, at least according to this tradition, is due to a woman of doubtful morals and scandalous behaviour. However, the actual title of Speaker was bestowed first, in 1377, on Sir Thomas Hungerford, who was officially appointed to that office.

THE MACE

The Mace has come a long way. Now associated with the Speaker as his staff of authority, and symbolically representing the king, it stems from the Orient. Originally it was not a sign of sovereignty, but a most effective and feared weapon. It was used long before swords and consisted of a heavy, spiked, metal club hanging from a horseman's saddle. Its blows, though not capable of severing the adversary's head, could crack it and its spikes were able to pierce the heaviest armour.

The Mace was a weapon specially welcome in later years to hypocritical clergy who, in spite of their calling, were anxious to participate in battle. According to the Bible, they could not shed blood. But by adopting the Mace, they still could kill people — bloodlessly. It was a pitiable piece of casuistry on the part of ecclesiastics.

Even after the introduction of the sword, when the Mace became redundant as a weapon, it was not abolished altogether. Its antiquity gave it special value and it was thus retained by kings and noblemen. They carried it no longer for the purpose of individual combat but as a sign of their status and might.

The next step was obvious. For royalty to encumber themselves with a heavy iron ball was no longer considered the proper thing. Hence this office was delegated to a trusted Knight, the king's champion. He preceded his royal master on all state occasions, carrying the Mace on his behalf.

As the spikes no longer served any practical purpose, they were removed and the Mace, now silver and gilt, was richly ornamented and decorated with the crown. Ever since, it has been the symbol of the king. No longer protecting his person, it actually came to take his place. Wherever the Mace could be seen, people felt the sovereign's presence, though he might be miles away.

Thus the Mace found its way into Parliament as the visible sign of royalty. It is ceremoniously borne in front of the Speaker and, during debates, conspicuously displayed, resting on two hooks on the Table in front of the Speaker. In his absence, when the House "sits in committee" (which originally meant free from the king's supervision), the Mace is removed and concealed under the Table.

The word Mace has its roots in the ancient language of Sanskrit, but reached us through the Greek. It described an aromatic spice, once rare and highly prized. Bulb-like, it was similar in shape to the iron club which for that reason was named after it.

THE WHIPS

Each party elects its Whip whose duty it is to watch over the activities of members and enforce discipline whenever necessary. When divisions are about to take place, he rounds up all those belonging to his party to ensure they vote on a question and lest their absence may defeat a cause. Most of all, the Whip sees to it that members "toe the (party) line".

The Whip's power was illustrated by the traditional circular sent out before a motion in the House of Commons. This gave notice to the member that his presence was *earnestly* required. The number of lines — in red ink — under the word "earnestly" indicated the degree of urgency of the request. One line meant that he was *expected* to come; two lines that he *ought* to come, three lines that he *must* come and four lines that, if he stayed away, he did so *at his own peril*.

The Whip's manifold responsibilities and the power he wields prove the appropriateness of the choice of his name. Whip is an abbreviated form of the word Whipper-in. This was borrowed from the 18th century vocabulary of fox-hunters, who were mostly English Squires. The Whipper-in was a hunter's assistant and his task was to keep the hounds from straying by driving them back to the pack with a whip. The Parliamentary Whip lives up to the original meaning of his title. Though wielding his whip merely metaphorically, in the final result it is no less effective.

"HEAR! HEAR!"

The common way of applauding a speech or performance is to clap hands. This goes back to the Roman stage. Actors then did not take any chances. At the end of a play, they asked their audience to voice their gratitude and approval in "the usual manner". "Clap your hands!", they commanded. And, in most cases, the audience obliged.

This Roman custom of "giving a hand" spread all over the world and, from the theatre, to other occasions which demanded an audible sign of compliment and acclaim. Though others, and especially university students, devised a different way. Possibly to keep their hands free to take down notes uninterruptedly, they started to stamp their feet instead. Others again neither clap nor stamp but just rap the desk.

British Parliamentary institutions, however, created a totally different type of applause. This was not directed to the speaker himself, but to those who ought to listen to what he was saying. "Hear him! Hear him!" became the traditional call. It was meant to underline a statement, and to draw all members' attention (and especially that of those whose mind had wandered else-where) to a voiced opinion.

It was a procedure so much more dignified and appropriate in "the House". Altogether it was a logical way of showing acclaim. Eventually, possibly for the sake of brevity and so as not to interrupt the speech for too long, the "him" was dropped and "Hear! Hear!" became the traditional way of showing approbation.

Yet this method of voicing consent goes back to even earlier times, when to make oneself heard was not as easy as nowadays. Present-day rules require a proper decorum in Parliament, com-mensurate with the dignity of the nation's representative body. Technically a member must not leave his place or wander about in the Chamber while a debate is in progress. He is not permitted to read a book or newspaper or to carry on a private conversation.

Anyone who catches the Speaker's eye is not only given a chance to say his piece but, no less essential, to be heard as well. And if, at times, tempers run high and there is a commotion, it is the Speaker's duty to call the House to order and anyone disobeying can be removed.

Thus debates today usually take place in an atmosphere of respectful quiet. That has not always been the case. In former times, Parliament was a rowdy place with much noise and lack of attention. The voices of speakers frequently were drowned in uproar. Gladstone and Disraeli used even to write letters to the Queen while the House was in session and a member was making a speech.

Contemporaneous reports speak of "a sound of drone-like humming, having almost the sound of a distant hand-organ or bagpipes, coughing, sneezing and ingeniously extended yawning". If members considered a speaker boring or uninteresting, they made so much noise "that the speaker scarcely could distinguish his own words".

It was not surprising, therefore, that friends who wished people to listen to what he was saying, tried to stop the noise by calling out to others, "Hear him! Hear him!". As it was assumed that silence was demanded for a statement of special significance and value, this call soon came to be associated with actual applause. That, most likely, is how the call of "Hear! Hear!" became the Parliamentary type of applauding.

THE CORONATION STONE

A king is one of his kin (and kind) and therefore blood-related to the people he rules. The *Kaiser* and *Tzar* recall Julius *Caesar*.

The splendour of royal regalia and the solemnity of the ceremonial of coronation are rooted in most ancient and sacred traditions, going back to pre-Christian days and the rim of a hat, the branch of a tree, a magical potion and a stone, said to have been used as a pillow.

Stones have played a significant part in the history of religion, not least those which seemed to have descended from heaven and which we now recognize as meteorites. These were held to be sacred and regarded as the abode of supernatural forces which could act as a safeguard from evil.

In his flight from Esau's wrath, Jacob "by chance" had chosen such a stone for a pillow. His subsequent dream of the ladder linking heaven and earth convinced him of the sanctity of the site and the stone, which he thus set up as a pillar and anointed with oil. There is no doubt that it became the most sacred object in the later Sanctuary. If not divine itself, the stone was "the House of God", or, as the original Hebrew has it, a *Beth El.*

Had not the stone proved itself, as it were, to be heaven's gate, admitting the divine here on earth as well? As a king was God's anointed, he, most of all, was in need of this stone, which could act as a special protector and continuous source of divine power.

That is how the Coronation Chair, made by order of King Edward I and still in use at Westminster Abbey, was specially designed to enclose this very stone, believed to be Jacob's pillow. The story of how the stone finally found its place in the chair is full of mystery and associated with strange legends that proliferated through the centuries.

When Nebuchadnezzar of Babylon had destroyed the ancient Temple in 586 B.C., Israelite refugees are said to have carried the stone with them to Ireland. Recognized as the Stone of Destiny, the Irish used it at the coronation of their chieftains, initially when one of them married an Israelite princess.

More than a thousand years later (about 850 A.D.) the stone reached Scotland. There, at Scone, two miles north of Perth, it was enclosed in a wooden chair which served at the coronation of Scottish kings.

Still, its destiny was not settled yet. Once again, in 1296, Jacob's (alleged) pillow was carried away, as the Stone of Scone, by Edward I. Ever since, it has formed part of the throne in England, though from time to time Scottish patriots have tried, either by force or an Act of Parliament, to remove it to what they consider its rightful place.

THE ANOINTMENT

Christ — from the Greek — means "the anointed" and is the literal translation of the Hebrew word, Messiah. It was an obvious choice of a name for Jesus by those who considered Him "The King", just as the Roman executioners superscribed His cross by the telling words, "Jesus, the *King* of the Jews".

From earliest days, anointment has been an essential feature of a coronation. At times, British monarchs themselves wondered what was the purpose of anointment, apart from its symbolism. In 1246, for instance, King Henry III, in a letter to the Bishop of Lincoln, asked for an explanation of the rite. He was told that the sacrament of unction conferred on a king the seven-fold gift of the Holy Spirit, the better to help him serve his people. The Bishop wrote:—

"To His Most Excellent Lord, Henry, by the grace of God, King of England, Lord of Ireland . . . His Devoted Robert, by Divine Mercy the humble servant of the Church of Lincoln, greeting: . . . As to that which you have commanded . . . , to wit, that we should inform you in what manner the SACRAMENT OF UNCTION increased the royal dignity; our modesty is unable to satisfy it, as there are many kings who are in no way adorned with the gift of unction. But of this we are not ignorant, that the ROYAL ANOINTING is the sign of the privilege of receiving the SEVENFOLD GIFT of the most HOLY SPIRIT, and by this sevenfold gift the anointed King is bound in more especial manner than those kings who are not anointed, to carefulness in all his royal actions and those of his government; that is to say, by the gift of FEAR he is not by ordinary means, but with vigour and courage, to restrain from all illegal acts, in the first instant himself, and secondly, those subject to his government. By the gift of true GODLINESS he must defend, help, and cause to be helped widows, orphans, and in general all who are distressed; by the gift of KNOWLEDGE he must make, observe, and cause to be observed, righteous laws made for the just government of his realm, and abolish those that are evil; by the gift of MIGHT he must repel all the attacks of the enemies of his country, and must not be fearful of death for the good of the State.

In addition to these duties, which he is specially to perform, he must be adorned with the spirit of COUNSEL by which the rational order of this world is taught with art and knowledge; also, with the spirit of UNDERSTANDING by which the order of the company of angels can be discerned; and lastly, by the gift of WISDOM by which we attain a clear knowledge of GOD, so that he may be a pattern to the order of the world and the order of the angels; and at last, following the eternal laws, written according to the eternal purpose of God, by which He rules the whole creation, may rule in order the State subject to him."

In reality, the anointment of a king was the result of several deeply rooted beliefs and practices which, by many years, anticipated even the anointment of Saul, the first Jewish king, by Samuel, the prophet, who took a "vial of oil and poured it upon his head, and kissed him and said, "Is it not that the Lord has anointed you to be prince over His inheritance".

The primary, motivating force in anointment can be traced to the tradition that kings were divine. The sacred unction ceremoniously bestowed on them not merely symbolically, but actually, that distinction.

Primitive races imagined that certain types of organic matter were charged with mystical power and divine spirit. Potency varied according to the substance.

It was believed that man, particularly the elect, could absorb this sacred essence into his body by actually eating (the flesh) or drinking (the blood), which thus became a sacramental rite.

More than anything else, fat was regarded as saturated with the divine. It was thought, also, to be the very seat of life. But fat was too holy, and hence too dangerous, to be eaten. Therefore it was externally applied. Because of its highly potent sanctity, mere contact was sufficient to transfer its gift of supernatural power. At first, the king's whole body was rubbed with fat. Subsequently, fat was replaced by oil, in which the king was bathed. Finally, oil was poured on his head only.

Among the famous Tell el-Amarna Letters (stemming from the 14th century B.C.) has been discovered a "note" that once accompanied the gift of "a flask of good oil", sent by the King of Cyprus to the King of Egypt, advising that the oil was "to pour on your head, now that you have ascended the throne of your kingdom".

It also was believed formerly that the sacred unguent permanently immunized the king from the influence of harmful spirits. It served as a magical, protective armour against any kind of evil forces. Hedging the king with an invisible fence of sanctity, it rendered him invulnerable in the execution of his so dangerous office.

Lastly, it must be remembered that anointment was practised generally by the noble and rich of ancient races, especially on festive occasions. It was part of their toilet and a mark of honour. It refreshed the body, creating a feeling of comfort and personal well-being. But, most of all, by the extra sheen it gave to the skin, it lent that air of distinction and shining presence to the anointed which is so fitting to the supreme moment of a monarch's enthronement.

THE CROWN

The crown has uppermost importance in a king's regalia. Its very name has become synonymous with the sovereign, and his investiture is referred to as his coronation. The crown, indeed, came to symbolize power, prosperity, victory and glory. It can be traced back in history more than 5000 years, when it was worn both by kings and gods.

The practice of displaying a man's special status in the community by a symbol belonged already to the psychology of primitive people. Persons of higher rank were distinguished by their headdress, especially at celebrations. Chiefs, priests and medicine men dressed their hair most elaborately and ornamented it with all kinds of material, such as feathers, teeth, bones, shells and leaves. To stop the hair falling into the face, a band or skin was wound around the head. This "rimless hat" became the first crown.

A king's authority implied superiority. This could be expressed most conspicuously by giving him greater height that was easily attained by his wearing a tall hat — the crown. This made the king stand out above all other people, who thus were constantly reminded of their royal leader.

Kings were looked upon as divine. They claimed direct descent from the gods and it was believed that the crown surrounded the head with the radiate nimbus of the sun-god. The crown was his aureole, and a living, powerful being itself. In ancient Egypt, the crown was identified with the god's burning eyes, a flame protecting the king, and Uraeus, a mystical serpent which spat fire at the monarch's foes.

It may well be that the crown was also an evolution of the garlands worn by victors and gods in early times. At first made of the flowers and leaves of sacred plants and trees, the crown was "great in magic". The king used it as an instrument of divination and people tried to propitiate its occult power by singing hymns to it.

Thus, the crowning of a king was at first a magical, ritual act. It set the king apart from all other men as a person singled out by divinity as the ruler of his people and, if not a god himself, as divinely anointed.

THE SCEPTRE

The sceptre has served as a sovereign's badge of office from most ancient days, though its shape has varied with time and place. It is frequently mentioned in biblical writings, was part of the regalia of Oriental monarchs, and appears in the representation of Greek gods.

Behind its present-day, merely symbolic use, a totally different past lies hidden. Though views still differ as to its original purpose, all agree that at first the staff provided a potent means of exerting authority both over nature and men.

In the sceptre, an ancient, magical wand survives. This, it was said, was a branch from a sacred tree, if not of the tree of life itself, which gave those wielding it supernatural power to control the world.

Thus, it has been suggested that the sceptre grew out of the *lituus,* which Roman augurs employed in their acts of divination. Similarly, priests engaged in the ritual of rain-making, used such a mystical branch from the sacred oak tree.

Others have seen in the sceptre the original shepherd's staff, indispensable to him for keeping his sheep together. Later, the staff proved itself as an all-purpose utensil which also could be used effectively as a weapon, a tool to help break the soil and, in the case of overseers, an instrument for the punishment of idle slaves. Small wonder that, eventually, the staff became a symbol of authority.

In primitive wars the victors were always anxious to appropriate the foe's weapons not only to disarm the enemy but magically to secure for themselves his former strength. They thus kept and carried with them captured weapons, especially spears, as a continuous source of extra power. Eventually, the spear became the badge of victory, a telling sign of the victor's invincibility.

The captured spear lost its usefulness as a weapon and gradually was transformed into a ruler's emblem. As such it was richly embellished and finally the camouflage was so complete that the last traces of the sceptre's original role — in war — were lost.

CHAPTER XVI

symbols of nationhood

A BARBARIAN, originally, from the Greek, meant a stammerer. It was a word used to describe (and decry) the foreigner, whose language could not be understood.

An idiot, on the other hand, was a person disinterested in politics and public affairs. Literally, he was someone "private", who shunned civic responsibility, living completely "on his own".

Service to the community and patriotism have been part of national life from earliest days. Flags and anthems not only expressed and fostered national feelings and differentiations but, in their origin, reveal a people's soul and fundamental beliefs.

THE FLAG

Opinions differ on how the flag originated. Many trace its beginnings to a carved pole carried by primitive races in battle or before chiefs. The pole displayed the tribal totem at the top.

The ancient Egyptians are said to have topped a staff or spear with the figure of the animal they held most sacred. The Greeks carried a pole on the end of which were pieces of armour or a single letter. American Indians had pikes bedecked with feathers from eagles' wings. The Vikings made use of a raven and the Saxons of a white horse. Romans had shafts ornamented with circles and discs and surmounted at first by holy beasts and then, from 100 B.C., by the figure of an eagle.

The purpose of this original kind of "flag" is explained by totemism, one of man's earliest forms of religion. The pole symbolized and, it was believed, actually carried into battle the people's ancestral spirit, their totem and god, just as the ancient Israelites had done with the Ark, the seat of their God. Its presence was a source of power and an aid to victory. It gave courage to the warriors who fought under it and put fear into the enemy. Therefore it was viewed with awe and considered sacred.

Held aloft, the staff identified the forces, marked the position of their leader and served as a rallying point. Gradually it developed into a banner or standard. But its role remained the same. It did so merely in a more elaborate manner, and colours were added to the totem figure.

Thus, when the Israelites had escaped from Egypt, each of their tribes identified itself by an ensign, as referred to in the Book of Numbers. Though the Bible does not give a detailed description, allusions suggest that, for instance, Judah's sign was sky-blue with the emblem of a lion, Zebulun's white with a ship, and Manasseh's jet-black with the figure of a unicorn.

Finally, streamers or tassels were tied to the banner. This was done, not as may be imagined, as an ornament but, fluttering in the wind, they were meant to indicate and enforce divine will in battle. It is thought that from this bunting the present-day flag developed.

The story of how a piece of coloured cloth came to represent a nation begins with the ancient belief in omens and magical practice. The wind mystified primitive man. Its power evaded his grasp in every sense. Those who dared the open sea in their light craft learned to fear its force which could either hasten their advance or spell disaster. Anxiously, therefore, man watched the wind and tried to detect in its direction an omen for good or evil.

But as the wind was invisible, this was an almost impossible task — until he realized that the smoke of fire could expose it to view.

Man began to observe the smoke with awe and to imagine that the way it moved indicated, and then actually effected, the will of the gods. If the smoke blew towards the foe, it was an augury of his imminent flight and defeat. Significantly, the Welsh word for a bonfire means "sure omens".

Some ingenious mind then realized that far superior to smoke was a piece of cloth, fluttering in the breeze from a pole, to show which way the wind was blowing. After a time, the cloth was regarded as a magical means of determining the outcome of a battle. Activated by the wind, it symbolized and could bring victory. For that reason it was carefully guarded and became the first target of attack. Its capture or fall caused confusion, if not defeat.

Flags in their present form were invented by the Chinese. It is known that the founder of the Chou dynasty in the 12th century B.C. had a white flag carried in front of him. Yet national flags did not appear in Europe till the 12th century A.D.. They were introduced by the Crusaders on their return from the Holy Land, where they probably had adopted them from their Saracen foes who, in turn, had copied them from the Indians. No doubt, these had appropriated them from China.

As one huge Christian army, the Crusaders found a banner most useful in identifying themselves from their heathen opponents. Fighting in the name of Christ, their choice of the cross as an emblem was a foregone conclusion. But coming from every country of Christendom, they also had need to distinguish themselves from each other. For that purpose the Knights employed the various forms of the cross, linked with their individual patron saint, and a combination of contrasting colours.

From the Knights who had fought in the Holy War, their countries took over and developed the flag as a national emblem.

THE UNION JACK

Britain's Union Flag — usually wrongly called the Union Jack — records in its name and fusion of three different emblems the growth of one kingdom out of the successive union of three crowns.

The original English flag was white and bore the plain red cross of St. George, the country's patron saint. He was a 3rd century Christian soldier who had preferred death by beheading to denouncing his faith. The red cross recalled his martyrdom by Roman hands at Lydda, in Palestine. When the English Knights joined in the Crusades, they identified themselves by the saint's symbol. On their return, the religious emblem eventually became the national flag.

The choice of St. George as a patron has been linked with the tradition that during the Crusades the saint's apparition rescued the English from the fury of their Moslem foes. His sudden appearance on the battlefield threw the Mohammedans into confusion and flight. Thus the English recognized and acknowledged him as their patron. King Edward III adopted his name as a battle cry, and his emblem became the English flag.

St. Andrew was one of the 12 Apostles. A simple fisherman, he, too, suffered martyrdom. The story is told that because he had converted a Roman Consul's wife to Christianity, her husband had him flogged and afterwards crucified. The cross used for the execution was shaped like the letter X, which explains how this became the saint's symbol and is still called St. Andrew's cross.

His association with Scotland dates back to the tradition that in 368 A.D. a monk transferred some of his relics from Constantinople to Scotland, to be buried there on the East coast, on the very spot where the city and cathedral of St. Andrew's now stand.

The story is further told that when the Picts and Scots were attacked by the Saxons, they called on St. Andrew for help. Looking upward, they noticed a strange formation of clouds. It seemed as if their white vapour had formed itself into the shape of a cross, backed by the blue sky. This appeared to the anxious watchers as an assurance of victory and a manifestation of the saint. Spurred on, they joined in battle and defeated the foe. After their victory, they adopted St. Andrew's cross as their emblem, with the specific colours of cloud and sky. It was the birth of the Scottish flag.

When James Stuart came from Scotland in 1603 to ascend the English throne as James I, the two kingdoms were united. The immediate problem was which flag to hoist on the king's ships. English sailors resented the Scottish colours and the Scots scorned the cross of St. George.

A compromise was the answer and it led to the creation of the first Union Flag. In 1606, a royal decree declared that the ships of the Kingdom of Great Britain "shall bear on their maintops the red cross, commonly called St. George's cross, and the white cross, commonly called St. Andrew's cross". In 1707, after the Act of Union of England and Scotland, Queen Anne sanctioned this combination.

The white border which surrounds St. George's cross is due not to aesthetic or decorative reasons. It expresses deference to both original flags. Even in their union, they were meant to remain distinct. The rules of heraldry demanded that two colours must never be placed on top of each other, or even touch each other. They must be separated by a strip, no matter how narrow.

Neither the year nor place of St. Patrick's birth is known. It was toward the end of the 4th century somewhere in Britain or Gaul. At 16, pirates captured him and sold him as a slave to Ireland. After serving there for six years, he managed to escape to France. However, a vision, so it is said, made him return to the island to rid it from snakes and convert its pagan people to the Christian faith. In pursuit of his task he miraculously overcame the magic and cunning opposition of the Druids.

Because he died an old man from natural causes, no cross was linked with his name at first. The red saltire on a white ground, which eventually became his emblem, dates only from the 12th century and was adopted from the heraldic device of an Irish family.

When the Parliament of Ireland was joined with that of Great Britain in 1801, what was then recognized as the cross of St. Patrick was duly incorporated in the Union Flag. Thus the Union Flag recollects in its distinctive markings and colours the inspiring story of three great saints and the traditions of three ancient races which, step by step, grew into one United Kingdom.

The popular but erroneous description of Britain's flag as the Union Jack can be traced back either to naval tradition or to the historic union of Scotland and England.

James I was the first common ruler of the two kingdoms. He signed his name the French way, Jacques, which, spelled phonetically in its English pronunciation, was Jack. Colloquially, people nick-named his new flag the Union "Jack". The term therefore perpetuates the name of a specific king and one of the great moments of British history.

Correctly, however, a Jack relates only to the sea. It is a small flag used by naval vessels for signalling. It received its name because it was hoisted on a mast known as the jack-staff. Thus, in the view of some, the Union Jack refers merely to a flag of comparatively small dimensions used at sea.

THE AUSTRALIAN FLAG

When the first navigators reached the Southern Hemisphere, they felt greatly bewildered. A completely different world seemed to encompass them. There were strange beasts and birds. Instead of the familiar stars, totally unknown constellations looked down on them. But among them they recognized a cross, with great rejoicing.

They were now convinced they were still sailing under the guidance of their faith, whose very symbol was watching over them. They had nothing to fear. A sign from Heaven had shown them that, however far they proceeded, they could never leave the realm of divine care. That is how the Southern Cross assumed a significance far beyond that of a new constellation. It stood for promise and assurance.

We often see what we are looking for. Perhaps it was not an accident either that those early pioneers, scanning the alien skies, came to recognize in them the sign of the cross.

From earliest times Australia was thus linked with a group of stars apparently proclaiming the Christian faith and it was a foregone conclusion that if Australians were to choose a national emblem, the Southern Cross would be part of it.

Moreover, was not Australia's very name coupled with the religion symbolized by the cross? When in 1606, in search of "another Indies", de Quiros thought he had sighted the country, he called it Tierra Australia del Espiritu Santo, the Southern (Australia) Land of the Holy Spirit. To select a cross for the flag of such territory, from this point of view also, was appropriate.

On several occasions, long before the need of a national flag, Australians made use of the Southern Cross to symbolize ideals for which they were fighting. It was included in the flag of the Anti-transportation League, which proudly displayed it for the first time in Hobart in July, 1851. Again, the cross was conspicuous in the crudely designed banner flown at the Eureka Stockade at the time of the miners' rising on the Ballarat goldfields in December, 1854.

When Cook landed at Botany Bay in 1770, he naturally raised

the British flag. The original penal settlement grew under its colours into a nation. But with the establishment of the Commonwealth of Australia, the need of a new, national flag was felt. A number of private firms, supported by the Federal Government, invited suggestions for its design.

Thirty thousand entries were received. They were displayed at a special exhibition in Melbourne in September, 1901. Five of them were considered of equal merit and, therefore, the first prize was shared by five people, among them three youths, living in Perth, Melbourne, Sydney and — Auckland, New Zealand. A huge flag, incorporating all the features suggested by the five winners, was hoisted over the Melbourne Exhibition Building on the day the awards were announced.

This was the birth of the Australian flag which, with slight adjustments, has remained the same ever since. As a symbol of a British settlement, it made use of the Union Jack, in the form of the British Blue Ensign. But most conspicuously it displayed the five stars of the Southern Cross! An additional large, white star was placed in the hoist. This corresponds to nothing in the sky. It is purely symbolic of the Australian Commonwealth, its seven points representing the six States and the Territories.

It is wrong therefore to say that Australia owes her flag to one individual. Like so much in her life, it is the result of a joint effort, of co-operative competition and, in no small measure, the work of young people who, in the years to come, were to play an ever greater part in the building up of the nation.

THE STARS AND STRIPES

Officially, the first flag of the United States was adopted by the American Continental Congress in Philadelphia on June 14th, 1777. It was based on the report of a special committee, submitted by John Adams. Congress then resolved:—

> "That the flag of the United States be 13 stripes, alternate red and white;
> That the Union be 13 stars, white in a blue field, representing a new constellation."

George Washington explained the flag's features to the people in stirring words. He said: "We take the stars from heaven, the red from our mother country, separating it by white stripes, thus showing that we have separated from her, and the white stripes shall go down to posterity representing liberty".

There are various views on the flag's beginnings and to whom the credit should go for its final design. Not even the names of members of the committee have been preserved. In spite of sworn affidavits as to the accuracy of one certain claim, this has now been accepted as a legend.

Probably several people were responsible for the new flag, although Francis Hopkinson, a delegate to Congress and signatory to the Declaration of Independence, considered himself entitled to a reward as the originator. His claim was rejected because, as was pointed out to him, he "was not the only person consulted".

The fact is that the American flag is the result of a long evolution and in each of its parts has its own story.

What was regarded as the first distinctly American flag was flown on Prospect Hill on January 1st, 1776, by the American forces besieging Boston. Unmistakably it was meant to proclaim by 13 red and white stripes the Union of that number of seceding colonies, yet paradoxically it still carried in the canton the British crosses of St. George and St. Andrew.

It was a strange combination. While the 13 stripes told the world of the colonies' united revolt against the mother country, the inclusion of the Union Jack reminded the people of their allegiance to Britain. Indeed, it took almost a whole year after the Declaration of Independence to remove any obvious likeness to the British flag. The two crosses in the canton were replaced by 13 stars.

Several theories have been brought forward as to the origin of the stars. They were preceded, so it is said, by the picture of a rattlesnake with 13 rattles and the motto, "Don't tread on me!". No one knows whether the stars were taken from the flag of Rhode Island or from the coat of arms of the Washington family.

The story is told that in June, 1776, George Washington with two other men called on Betsy Ross, a widowed seamstress renowned for her needlework, at her upholstery shop in Philadelphia. They showed her a rough draft of the suggested flag and inquired whether she could make one.

Betsy convinced her callers that it was advisable to use five-pointed stars instead of the proposed six-pointers because these could easily be made by a single clip of the scissors.

Washington is said to have suggested that the stars should be arranged in a circle, to emphasize the full equality of the states. Actually, there was no definite rule about the arrangement of the stars at first. Earliest samples show a circle of 12 stars, with the 13th occupying the centre.

After the preliminary discussion, a sketch of the new model, prepared by an artist, was duly submitted to Betsy, who in no time sewed America's first national flag.

No contemporaneous independent report supports the claim which was made only by Mrs. Ross herself to her family. Though her descendants repeated the assertion and even supplied sworn statements, many now regard the claim as only a legend. Nevertheless, the house of Betsy Ross at 239 Arch Street in Philadelphia has become a national shrine to her memory.

Originally it was intended to add a new stripe and star for each state joining the initial 13. By 1818, their number had grown to 20, and it became obvious that the method adopted was impractical. Consequently, Congress resolved to revert to the original 13 stripes, but to indicate the admission of new states by adding a star for each. That procedure has been followed ever since.

THE ISRAELI FLAG

Religious symbols make up the flag of the modern State of Israel. The Star of David, its centre piece, both leads back to Jewry's glorious past and points to a Messianic future.

The praying shawl, in which the pious Jew wraps himself during worship, suggested the flag's blue and white colours. In the synagogue, those hues reminded the faithful of a pure life and a God-centred existence. Blue, by its association with the sky, immediately suggested Heaven.

There was no difficulty in re-interpreting those colours for a national flag. The white was to be symbolic of the purity of the new life the Jewish people, when returned to their ancient homeland, were meant to lead — a life of social justice, unsullied by arrogant nationalism. The blue was to remind the new citizens, and those whom they chose as leaders, that their country should be based on God's law and be worthy of a people called into existence with one aim in mind — to serve God.

The Israeli flag was designed almost exactly half a century before the establishment of the State. In 1895, Theodor Herzl, Zionism's great dreamer who wrote the blue-print of the new State, already had felt the need for a flag. "We need one," he then wrote. "If we desire to lead men, we must raise a symbol above their heads." He claimed that with a piece of cloth as a banner, even if fixed to a mere broomstick, he would be able to lead the Jewish people back into the Holy Land.

In 1897, the first World Zionist Congress met at Basle. One of the 240 delegates, who came from many countries, was David Wolffsohn. He was responsible for the arrangements and it was he also who designed the first Jewish flag. "Let us take the praying shawl from its bag and unfold it before the eyes of Israel and the eyes of all nations," he said.

When the Conference met, it did so under the sign of the new banner. Quickly this captured the imagination of Jewish people everywhere and came to express their aspirations to return to the Holy Land.

When during World War II, in 1944, Nazi armies threatened the Middle East, a Jewish fighting force was created in Palestine as part of the British army. On the occasion, Winston Churchill suggested consulting the king, as "I cannot conceive that this martyred race, scattered about the world and suffering as no other race has done at this juncture, should be denied the satisfaction of having a flag".

Two months later, Churchill was able to announce to the British Parliament the formation of the Jewish Brigade Group. With it, for the first time in history, the Jewish flag gained official recognition.

When the State of Israel was born in 1948, as everyone had expected, the Zionist banner was proclaimed Israel's official flag.

THE RED FLAG

There were, of course, red flags long before Soviet Russia or Communism were thought of.

Red is the colour of blood and since time immemorial has been associated with danger and bloodshed. A red flag was thus the signal for battle among the ancient Romans — their call to arms and war. The distinctiveness of the colour, which made it visible from long distances, added further significance to its choice.

In the 18th century, the ancient red flag was adopted by modern revolutionaries as a symbol of defiance and rebellion. In France the struggle was not between nations, but classes. It was then that the red flag became a political badge. It meant to express the people's challenge, violent and bloody if need be, to the established order.

In 1792 the French National Assembly decreed that the Paris Municipal authorities were to show a red flag at the principal window of the Town Hall whenever there was a sign of riot. It is said that it was from that moment onward that the red flag became finally identified with Revolution. As such it was flown again on the barricades of a rebellious Europe in 1848.

It was almost inevitable that Communists would take over this revolutionary symbol. Another intriguing factor might have reinforced their choice and lent it special importance. Russians consider red the colour of beauty. And they do so not accidentally. It is not just the result of a peculiar national aesthetic sense but the effect of a linguistic connection between "red" and "beauty". The Russian word for red is *krasny* and for beauty — *krasivy*.

NATIONAL ANTHEMS

How is a National Anthem created? Is it decreed by Government order and given birth to in a Cabinet room? Should a referendum "sense" people's opinion, and a competition call for suggestions? Should a country adopt a popular song, so that the National Anthem truly arises out of the people, as Australians unofficially seemed to have done with "Waltzing Matilda"?

National Anthems — at least in their text if not the music — differ from country to country. And rightly so. After all, they are meant to express the character of a nation and to stir its soul.

The British pray for their monarch. Germans used to praise their country "above everything in the world", whilst Americans visualize their Star-Spangled Banner.

Few Anthems have been specially written or were the result of a poet laureate's appointed task. Most of them were born out of some particular event of war or revolution. Written then, on the spur of the moment, for that one occasion, they have survived ever since. And it was the people themselves who made them their own, whilst Governments only (sometimes after years) acknowledged tune and words as the authoritative National Anthem.

As most Anthems go far back in nations' histories, the origin is often difficult to trace.

"GOD SAVE THE QUEEN"

Mystery and romance surround Britain's National Anthem. It was never written or composed as such. It just grew out of the people. It is first mentioned in the 16th century. But its text (first in Latin) has frequently been changed and added to.

Britons express loyalty to their country not with an exciting marching song or a martial hymn but a humble prayer for the health, long life and prosperity of their King or Queen. No wonder that the National Anthem's most essential words stem from the Bible. Three times in Holy Scripture occurs the phrase "God save the King".

Nobody is certain who composed the Anthem and wrote its final words. By 1545 "God save the King" had become a watchword of the British navy, to be responded to by "Long to reign over us".

An old prayer, appointed by the Church for the anniversary of the Gun Powder Plot (November 5th, 1605), may well be the original source of part of its second verse. This ancient supplication contains the lines: "Scatter our enemies . . . assuage their malice and confound their devices."

No doubt, the Anthem is a combination of such loyal phrases brought together at a moment of grave national crisis — though which is still a matter of controversy.

Obviously, for the people to ask God to save their king implied that his life was endangered. That is why one tradition ascribes the origin of the hymn to 1688, "when the Prince of Orange was hovering over the coast", threatening the ruling dynasty. This claim says it was written as a Latin Chorus for the private

Catholic Chapel of James II. Concerned with their monarch's fate, soon people sang it in London's playhouses and the streets.

Various composers have been credited with its original tune. It belonged to a Christmas carol, for instance, first published in 1611.

Best-known (and least likely) claim to authorship of the British Anthem is that of the man who wrote the original "Sally in our Alley", Henry Carey, son of the Marquis of Halifax. This unfortunate man, who ended his life by his own hand, is said to have written and sung it first at a London tavern dinner-party he gave in 1740 to celebrate Admiral Vernon's victory at Portobello the year before.

Others attribute both words and music to a Dr. John Bull, once a choirboy at the Chapel Royal of Elizabeth I and later its organist. Indeed, his tune, still preserved in the early manuscript of a copyist dating back to 1619, is similar to our present "God save the Queen". It certainly would be a pleasing coincidence if a man whose name was to become a symbol of Britain would be the author of the nation's Anthem.

It seems we owe the modern "God save the Queen" to no one man or composer. Its music is the development of airs extant long before the actual song. It had become a popular folk tune by the 17th century.

Our first concrete record of its actual use belongs to the stage and 1745, when it was sung at two concerts in London's Drury Lane and Covent Garden theatres. Again it was in a national crisis.

Scotland had risen in favour of Bonnie Prince Charlie. Marshal Wade was in the North to put down the rebellion. "God save the King", appropriately expressed the English people's fervour, imploring divine help for their reigning monarch. A special verse, added and later discarded, went:—

> Lord, grant that Marshal Wade
> May by Thy mighty aid
> Victory bring.
> May he sedition crush
> And like a torrent rush
> Rebellious Scots to crush!
> God save the King.

From this emergency on, the Anthem became the nation's most patriotic song, whose simplicity and sincerity took it to people's hearts. Soon it was sung on all patriotic occasions.

It did not take long for other nations to appropriate the tune. This typical and original English air was used, at some time or other, by at least 12 other countries, including the United States and Germany. It is certainly the world's best-known melody.

The story is told that when, during World War I on the Western front, English Tommies, on the spur of the moment, sang the Anthem, American and German soldiers came out of their trenches and joined in with their own words. Each group recognized in it a hymn of their own: hailing the Kaiser in his "garland of victory" or "America".

Composers, too, admired the tune enough to incorporate it in their own works — in Haydn's "Emperor's Hymn" and Brahms' "Triumphal Song". Beethoven was so deeply moved by it that he published seven variations on its theme and wrote in his diary: "I must show the English what a blessing they have in 'God save the King'."

The song's cosmopolitan character led to some confusion at a concert at a European resort attended by many English visitors. In Weber's Jubilee Overture, they recognized the National Anthem, and many immediately stood up — to the bewilderment of their Continental hosts. As the tune wove in and out they bobbed up and sat down, puzzled and unsure of what to think and to do.

The mechanical reproduction of music, so popular in the later years of the 19th century, led to all kinds of peculiar gadgets. Queen Victoria was delighted, when, it is said, on her Jubilee in 1887, an ingenious inventor presented her with a bustle. It contained an automatic music box which played the National Anthem whenever the wearer sat down!

"WALTZING MATILDA"

"Waltzing Matilda", Australia's most popular song, is based on a poem of "Banjo" Paterson, whose ballads express so vividly the early bushman's spirit.

Though of such comparatively recent date, "Waltzing Matilda" already shares with Britain's National Anthem un-

certainty as to its real beginnings. Even its title has been a source
of bewilderment and of various interpretations.

The poem is now a well-known description of the humping of
a swag. Yet in the earliest known use of the phrase, this did not
speak of waltzing Matilda at all, but of walking Matilda. However, "waltzing" is American slang. Mark Twain used it in the
sense of a verb that meant to carry and to transport.

Matilda, obviously, is a woman's name. No one knows why it
was chosen to identify the swagman's bundle. This contained his
private belongings and perhaps therefore he called it endearingly
with a personal name. Some, with lots of imagination, recognized
in its outlines the shape of a woman. This fancy and the fact that
he used to sleep with his swag may jointly account for the eventual choice of Matilda as the name of his portable luggage and
sleeping companion.

Again, views differ as to what gave Paterson the inspiration to
write his famous piece.

He was staying at a friend's station near Winton in Central
Queensland when his host's daughter, Christine Macpherson, to
pass the time, was playing her auto-harp. Among the tunes was
a very catchy one, which immediately caught the "Banjo's"
attention.

She had heard it at a Victorian race meeting, though actually it
was an air with a long tradition. Once the melody of an old Scottish ballad, it had been adapted from a song, popular at the time
of Marlborough among Kentish soldiers. Its words had been
forgotten.

Paterson wanted to give the tune a new lease of life. All it
needed was the right kind of lyric, appropriate for the Australian scene.

In search for a theme, he recalled an incident of the early
1890s. With two mounted police and an Aborigine, he had surprised a swagman, camping under a Coolabah tree beside a water
hole. The man, who had killed a sheep and wasted much of its
carcass, was taken aback and feared arrest. Fully clad, he jumped
into the hole, trying to escape. But he was unable to swim across
and his water-soaked clothes dragged him down and he drowned.

Here was Paterson's opportunity to perpetuate the incident in
song. A chance remark by the station overseer, while "Banjo"

was contemplating the new verses, seemed to fit in. He told "Banjo" he had seen "a couple of men waltzing Matilda down at the billabong".

That is how the song, according to one tradition, took shape in Paterson's mind. It was first sung in public at the North Gregory Hotel at Winton, as a plaque there still commemorates. It quickly caught the people's imagination and "Waltzing Matilda" became a favourite number of many bush singers. In 1903 Paterson sold the poem with other ballads he contemptuously described as "a lot of junk" to the firm of Angus and Robertson, and its eventual publication made the song popular throughout Australia.

The fact that it was being sung by Australian soldiers during the two World Wars on almost every battle front gave it world fame. Soon people of many countries came to identify "Waltzing Matilda" as Australia's National Anthem!

Another account also associates the creation of the song with Paterson's visit to his old friend at Dagworth Station. It says they were driving into Winton with Macpherson's sister and a drover. On the way they passed a man carrying a swag. "That's what we call Waltzing Matilda in these parts," Macpherson explained. The phrase so intrigued the "Banjo" that, there and then, he jotted down his verses.

On their return to the property, Macpherson's sister, a musician, wrote the tune. And on that same night all of the company joined in the song which, ever since, has reverberated in the hearts of Australians.

THE STAR-SPANGLED BANNER

No mystery is attached to the origin of America's Anthem. Its words were written on September 14th, 1814, at sea by a young patriotic American, when the British navy bombarded — unsuccessfully — a United States fort. Its tune, however, was composed by an Englishman in London for a club of music lovers! Few people realize that only on March 3rd, 1931 — 117 years later — did an Act of Congress officially recognize the Star-spangled Banner as the nation's Anthem.

Its story began in August, 1814, when the British fleet was anchored off Baltimore with William Beanes, an old doctor of

Marlborough, Maryland, a prisoner in the flagship "Surprise", which was commanded by General Ross.

His friend Francis Scott Key, a young lawyer who felt it his duty to come to the doctor's rescue, reached the British fleet in a sloop and his passionate appeal for his friend did not fall on deaf ears.

General Ross himself acceded to his request. He could take Beanes home — but not yet. The British were about to shell Fort McHenry, hoping to reduce it in no time. Therefore for Mr. Key's party immediately to return to the mainland might jeopardize the action, as naturally they would give due warning to their people. They would have to stay under guard on the sloop till the fortress had been captured.

Thus they were compelled to witness from afar the terrific bombardment. Anxiously throughout the day they watched the "Stars and Stripes" flying on top of the fortress, sometimes obscured by mist, drizzle and smoke. During the night, they continued to look out for it, happy to recognize it, whenever lit up by the burst of shells or the flash of guns.

When at last dawn came, with grateful hearts they could see that the flag was still showing. Obviously, the attack had failed, in spite of the Englishman's previous boast.

Stirred to the very depth of his heart, it was then that Key composed the poem, writing down its words on the back of an envelope. When the Fleet was about to withdraw, Key and his party were allowed at long last to go ashore.

With him he took his new poem. No wonder that it was immediately read by his friends who, equally deeply moved, had it printed at once and distributed as a handbill. Baltimore's daily paper printed it in its first issue after the city's liberation.

Still, it was merely a poem and not a song. But when Key wrote it on that glorious morning after a fearful night, he must have anticipated its tune. He certainly chose the right metre, fitting for an air that was then most popular. It belonged to a song which had come from England, where it had been used for the opening hymn at meetings of music lovers, who had established clubs, known as Anacreontic Societies.

American soldiers celebrating their victory were joined in a city tavern by Francis Key who, exhilarated, read them his poem.

An actor who was present got up on a chair and, on the spur of the moment, led them in song, choosing the melody Key had envisaged.

Within four days all Baltimore was singing it. It spread throughout the land. The original manuscript of the poem was sold for $24,000 at an auction in New York in 1933.

THE ISRAELI HYMN

Israel is one of the youngest of modern nations. Yet its National Anthem preceded the new State by almost 70 years. It was written by an Austrian Jew who dedicated it — with other poems — to a Christian English friend. For many years the manuscript has been treasured in America's Yale University library.

Its theme is optimism. Its words express the eternal Jewish hope of the fulfilment of ancient prophecy: the return of a re-habilitated and rejuvenated Jewish people to their ancestors' land. That is why, appropriately, the very title of Israel's Anthem is called "The Hope".

The hymn was written by Naphtali Herz Imber, born in Galicia in 1856. At 14 he won a Government prize for a Hebrew poem on a patriotic Austrian theme. Four years later he migrated to Vienna. But he did not stay there for long. Always restive, he led the life of a wanderer. He travelled through Hungary, Roumania and all over the Balkans, finally reaching Constantinople.

There he met Laurence Oliphant, one of the most outstanding non-Jewish Zionists. Born of Scottish parents in South Africa, Oliphant became a member of the British House of Commons, a diplomat by profession and a successful novelist. But the idea that dominated his life was the wish to re-establish the Jewish people in the Holy Land.

Imber and Oliphant became intimate friends, fervently sharing the Zionist dream. Together — in 1878 — they went to Palestine. There Imber was greatly inspired by the early Jewish settlers who, in the midst of malaria-ridden swamps, had founded their first colonies, one called (from the prophet Hosea) "The Gate of Hope".

This name gave Imber the title and message for his poem. In nine stanzas he expressed the eternal longing of the Jewish heart:

to dwell once again in the city where David had put up his camp, to become "a free nation in Zion and Jerusalem".

A young pioneer in an adjacent colony set it to music and, in no time, it became the people's hymn. Its tune is that of both an old Spanish and Slav folk song, which can also be found in Smetana's tone-poem *"Die Moldau"*. Spanish and Portuguese Jews had used the melody for one of their ancient Hebrew prayers, a supplication for dew.

Imber did not stay in Palestine either. When, in 1888, Oliphant died, he went first to Britain and then to the United States. Associating with mystics there, he became now interested in the Theosophical movement.

However successful Imber was in his literary work, there was no real happiness in his personal life. Eventually he took to drink. Taverns became his haunt. He was rarely sober. Drink did not make him amiable but quarrelsome. Even his friends could not bear with him any longer, a fact which made him still more bitter and cynical.

Typical was the incident at a Zionist meeting from which Imber, obstreperously drunk, had to be forcibly removed. Outside the hall he heard, at the meeting's end, the crowd join in his song. The cast-out drunkard, with shaking but triumphant voice, remarked: "They may kick me out, but they must sing my song."

Lonely and embittered, he died in 1909, aged 53, in a New York hospital. He had a pauper's funeral, but the hymn did not die with him. It circled the world. First sung by the colonists in the Holy Land, it soon became the fervent expression of Jewish national aspiration in every country.

The fact that "Our Hope" was sung by the world delegates attending the Sixth Zionist Congress held at Basle, Switzerland, in 1903 gave the hymn official recognition. It was a foregone conclusion that, at the declaration of Independence of the State of Israel, 45 years later — in 1948 — this Zionist song, the hymn of hope, was to become the National Anthem.

THE PASSPORT

The very name of the passport explains its (at least initial) purpose. It was issued to facilitate a traveller's progress by helping him to *pass* safely through a *port* on his journey.

Passports go back to the most ancient civilizations. It has been suggested that even the Bible implied their existence in its story of Abraham, when he sent Eliezer, his servant, to Mesopotamia to find there a wife for Isaac, his son.

Originally a passport was not a written document but a precious ring with the ruler's seal. Its possession secured the traveller's protection. Thus the Pharaohs of Egypt likewise gave their messengers a cartouche, an oval figure engraved with their royal name in hieroglyphic script.

The document was first given as a "Letter of Confidence" to subjects travelling on behalf of the king. It was actually referred to by this name as testified in a Greco-Roman papyrus of the 2nd century B.C..

Roman Emperor Caesar Augustus is said to have furnished Potamon, a philosopher, with a certificate for safe conduct, which certainly did not mince its words. It read: "If there be anyone on land or sea hardy enough to molest Potamon, let him consider whether he be strong enough to wage war with Caesar." The wording thus anticipated by 2000 years our own modern text. Though couched in more diplomatic terms, it still serves the same purpose and requests and requires "all those whom it may concern to allow the bearer to PASS freely, without lack or hindrance, and to afford him (or her) every assistance and protection of which he (or she) may stand in need."

Rulers throughout the world (and as far back as in China over 1000 years ago) deemed it their duty to control and protect the movement of their subjects. They claimed, too, the right to exclude other nationals from their territory, when necessary.

Eleventh-century King Canute is said to have been the first potentate to have issued documents to pilgrims en route to the tombs of St. Peter and St. Paul in Rome, with the express purpose of securing their safe passage through the many countries they had to traverse before reaching their destination.

Copies of this early passport, still extant, are interesting. Typical is this text:—

"I *(the name of the person granting the passport)* to our holy and apostolic and venerable father in Christ, and to all Kings, bishops, abbots, priests, and clerks in every nation of

Christendom, who devote themselves to the service of the Creator, in monasteries, in cities, in villages, or in hamlets. Be it known to you that this our brother *(the name of the holder of the passport)* and your servant, has obtained permission from us to proceed on a pilgrimage to the Church of St. Peter, your father, and to other churches, to pray for his soul's sake, for yours and for ours.

Therefore do we address this to you, begging that you will, for the love of God and of St. Peter, give him hospitable treatment, aiding, consoling, and comforting him — affording him free ingress, egress and regress, so that he may in safety return to us. And for so doing, may a fitting reward be bestowed on you at the last day, by Him who lives and reigns forever!"

That by 1215 passports must have been generally adopted in Britain is obvious from a clause of the Magna Carta, which provided that certain categories of persons might leave the country without such a document. This plainly implied that all others could not do so.

This passport, a royal instrument, had, still in the days of Charles II, to be signed by the king himself. Yet eventually, and generally until World War I (excepting periods of unrest), passports were no longer needed for foreign travel. They were just helpful in establishing a man's identity and nationality. A Texan likened them to a pistol: "You didn't want it often, but when you did want it, you wanted it very badly."

But 1914 changed all that. Passports became compulsory for going abroad, and in that same year photographs were first added to the British version. And when war conditions had passed, passports remained an essential.

For centuries the passport was merely a thin sheet of paper, sometimes torn from a roll and still showing perforation marks at top and bottom. But in 1921 the League of Nations introduced a uniform document which was adopted by almost every country. The ancient ring had become a booklet of 32 pages.

CHAPTER XVII

naval customs

THE TRADITION of the sea has widely and deeply influenced the English way of life and nautical terms and customs abound in our everyday talk and habits.

People who try "to make both ends meet" most probably do not realize that they are speaking in nautical terms. Many centuries ago, some frugal owners of sailing vessels were unwilling to replace broken ropes. They had the torn ends pulled together and spliced. Thus, by making both (of their) ends meet, they saved money.

Many people wonder why a ship is referred to as a "she". The explanation is that it was customary in early days to dedicate a new ship to a goddess, under whose protection she sailed. The ship carried the deity's carved image on her bow not as a decoration, as later generations imagined, but as an aid to finding the way.

Many customs and phrases "sail under false colours". Beneath their present meaning they hide surprising facts. It is well, therefore, "to know the ropes" (once there were hundreds of them on board ship) and to "fathom" how it all started.

Consider the pilot. Navigating vessels safely into port, he received his name from the fact that he did so without use of the *peil-loth*, the lead-line.

THE CHRISTENING OF SHIPS

In spite of its apparent Christian association, the christening of a ship dates back to pre-Christian centuries and a pagan way of life. It is a relic of a rite of propitiation, when anxious sailors, afraid of the vagaries of the sea, tried to influence divine powers controlling the ocean, to protect their ship and keep them safe. To buy their good will, so to speak, the mariners bought the gods a drink. In ancient days when a ship was completed, she was garlanded with flowers and the sailors wore floral crowns. And then, accompanied by loud acclamation to the gods, a pagan priest officiated at a ceremony. Equipped with a lighted torch, an egg and brimstone, he poured wine and oil on an altar, erected on the ship, and dedicated her to the goddess whose carved image she was to carry.

We no longer believe in idols and divine figureheads have ceased to adorn and protect our ships, but we still carry on the ancient libations in the form of the christening ceremony. Some researchers have suggested that the modern way of shattering a bottle of champagne over the bows of a new ship has a link with the days when the Vikings and South Sea races invoked the protection of the sea gods on launching war galleys.

They did this by making a human sacrifice! Victims were bound to rollers over which the ship was launched, and blood from the broken bodies of the sacrificed sprinkled the ship. In civilized times, blood-red wine preceded champagne as the christening beverage.

Modern authorities have vehemently decried as obnoxious and offensive the custom to call the naming of a ship her christening. After all, to christen implied to make Christian, and the use of a bottle of wine for this purpose appeared like a parody of baptismal water.

TATTOOING

Fascinating is the manifold and often odd use made of tattoo marks. On occasion they can be gruesome. A man once had a dotted circle tattooed around his neck with the inscription, "Cut along the dotted line".

During World War I some Tommies expressed their aversion to the German Emperor by having his image tattooed on their buttocks. A wealthy businessman in the United States ordered a tattooist to imprint hinges on all his joints. A famous doctor had his skin tattooed solely because the vibration of the needles soothed his nerves!

Perhaps the most ghastly tattoos of recent times were those with which Nazis branded their victims in concentration camps.

Tattoo is one of the few Polynesian words that have become part of the English language. The explorer Captain Cook introduced it in 1796 from the Tahitian, in which it was used in the form of *tatau* to describe any kind of mark. It has nothing to do with a military tattoo. In that use the word is derived from the Dutch *taptoe*, meaning "to turn off the tap of a cask".

Tattooing by means of gashes or, in the modern technique, with small punctures filled with pigment, is an ancient and widespread custom. Fear of the unknown and of evil forces may have accounted for its first appearance.

Tattoo marks were a kind of magic to protect men both from the evil eye and sickness. Just as the ancient Britons painted their bodies with woad to strike fear into their foes, so tattoo marks were used to ward off intangible dangers.

However, many other and less frightening reasons were soon superimposed. They rendered the custom a permanent feature, continued even when man had outgrown his primitive superstitions and dreads.

Sex has dominated the human mind at all times. Therefore, it is no wonder that tattooing was soon believed to serve as a potent means to increase virility and sexual attraction.

Tattoos were used as well as tribal markings or professional emblems, as a sign of rank or caste and whether a man or woman was married or not. Sometimes tattoo marks served as badges of courage, reminding both viewer and wearer of the pains suffered at the hands of the tattooer. Again, some parents tattooed their children with the sign of a god to ensure his protection.

Man has always possessed an aesthetic sense. This urged him to add beauty (or what he considered as such) to life as he found it. Instead of looking for stones and trees to impose on them his artistic creations, did not his own body provide a readily available canvas?

Thus with some tattooing became a form of artistic expression, a favourite way of bodily decoration. Man's innate desire to show off and impress others further fostered the custom. To have his etchings and paintings on constant exhibition, with no difficulty of transportation or danger of deterioration, made the "art" all the more popular. This way a person could carry his masterpiece with him wherever he went — in fair weather and foul — and it was no burden at all!

But weighty utilitarian reasons were responsible, if not for the creation, for the retention of those early tattoo marks. They were a lasting identification in time of war, so frequent in the annals of history. By his tattoo marks a combatant could be easily recognized on the battlefield — whether dead or alive. They were the earliest type of uniform and surpass those of today in one respect at least — they never wore out. And even traitors and fugitives could not disguise their identity, as the marks labelled them permanently.

But going even further, the scars' special significance extended from this world to the next. The Hindus of Bengal, for instance, regarded tattoo marks in a vastly different light. They believed that a person without them would find it hard to enter Heaven.

Though biblical legislation expressly stated that "you shall not make any cuttings in your flesh for the dead, nor print any marks upon you", tattooing became fashionable among Christian nations, including their Sovereigns.

That sailors are fond of being tattooed (even King George V had himself tattooed as a young midshipman) has several reasons. Sailors are reputed for their superstitions and their love of ladies. They maintained the ancient belief that tattoo marks made them all the more desirable, and assisted them in their amorous adventures, especially so if their bodies depicted suitable subjects and legends.

Sailors first introduced the art of tattooing into the Western world, from China, Burma, India. It is not surprising, therefore, that they themselves preserved their new discovery. Finally, there was the constant but secret fear among mariners that one day they might be drowned and their bodies washed ashore beyond the possibility of recognition. Tattoo marks, which were always individualized, were a wise precaution to ensure identification in such unfortunate circumstances. The custom was fostered all the more by the additional superstition that the mere fact of being prepared for such ill luck would keep it away.

THE SAILOR'S BIB

Most parts of the sailors' uniforms have their interesting story. The blue-and-white colour has a romantic association. It was chosen as the result of a king's admiration for a pretty horse-woman whose riding habit was of those colours.

Contrary to popular belief, the three stripes of the sailor's collar (which itself served as a kind of antimacassar to keep his uniform from getting soiled by his tarred pigtail) are only decorative. They definitely were not to mark a trio of famous victories by Admiral Lord Nelson.

The sailor's bib has been linked with Queen Victoria, her aesthetic sense and human susceptibility. It is said that when she inspected the Fleet at Spithead for the first time, she was deeply impressed — and said so. However, in her own private circle she later confessed there had been one feature of the review which had rather upset her — the men's hairy chests. This criticism came to the ears of the Admiralty and when next she inspected the Fleet, the sailors' chests were covered by bibs. They have continued to be so ever since. The bib has become an essential part of naval uniform.

There is another and much more likely, though less colourful, explanation. Sailors were expected always to look spick and span. To have any part of their uniform sullied, carried a penalty. On the other hand, in more distant days, clothes could be washed aboard ship only at certain stated hours, and these were few and far between. To add to the sailors' hardship, the frequent drill with greasy rifles inevitably soiled the men's uniforms, and especially so their shirts.

Therefore, whatever they did they could not do right. If they washed their shirts outside laundry hours, they were guilty. But if they did not do so and were seen dirty, they were punished as well.

They solved the shirt washing problem by making a dicky. This was detachable from the rest of the uniform and could be washed, clandestinely, in a small basin.

It did not take officers long to detect the ruse. Wearing a dicky was made a punishable offence and some ships even introduced searches for dickies. If any were found, they were confiscated and subsequently destroyed.

Even in modern times, the Navy did not recognize the dicky as part of a sailor's correct uniform. Thus, a man going on shore leave and found to be wearing a bib was dismissed from the shore-going party and made to replace his dicky with a shirt.

THE BLUE PETER

The Blue Peter is a blue flag with a white central square. It is hoisted as a signal that a ship is about to sail.

Of the many and diverse explanations given as to its origin, only one — the most unlikely of all — assumes that Peter actually represents the name of a person.

This recalls that between 1793 and 1799 Admiral Sir *Peter* Parker was Chief of Command of the British Navy. Convoys used to sail from St. Helens. But they were not given the order to leave until the wind was fair. It was only then that, from Portsmouth, the Admiralty gave the signal. And as it was known that Sir Peter himself issued the command for the hoisting of the blue flag, his name was coupled with it and the sailors referred to it as the Blue Peter. And ever since his name has stuck to the flag.

Others, however, detect in the Blue Peter a corrupted French word and a telling example of how the British always assimilate foreign words to their own way of speaking. According to this tradition, Peter is not a name but the Anglicized form of the French *partir*, "to leave".

A further interpretation discovered in the flag a relic of the old English word for a cloak bag, portmanteau. The signal was hoisted to inform all naval personnel that, as the sailing of their ship was imminent, they should get aboard at once with all their baggage — their *portmanteaus.*

Slovenly speech among sailors is yet another reason cited for the creation (perhaps it should be said in this connection, malformation) of the Blue Peter. It did not refer to Admirals, ancient obsolete English words or mispronounced French expressions but was a commonly used good English phrase. The signal of departure, once it had been given by the Admiral, had to be *r*epeated by all the ships under sailing orders. Actually, this was a procedure which applied to every kind of naval signal. By swallowing just a small syllable, the Blue *R*epeater soon came to sound like Blue Peter.

The most likely explanation, however, belongs to the 1750s. On taking command, Admirals used to issue instructions for their captains, detailing the various signals and flags to be employed. A flag book published by Sir Edward Hawke in 1756 listed a blue flag with six white balls.

Practical experience soon showed that this was a very unsatisfactory arrangement. It was impossible to distinguish the six balls from a distance and Hawke had the flag replaced by one which he described as "blue *pierced* with white".

Once again, lack of clear enunciation on the part of the naval men, it was said, led to the corruption of the Blue Pierced into Blue Peter.

Some authorities assume there was an intermediate stage, when the Blue Pierced was briefly referred to as the Blue P. Some sailors, ignorant of the real identity of the letter P, imagined it stood for Peter, which they spelled out.

FATHOM

It was natural that when man began to take the measure of things, he used his own body for comparison. With his *foot* he could step out any distance. The *inch* simply referred to the *twelfth* part of his foot's length. A *cubit* equalled the distance between his elbow and the tip of his middle finger.

These units of measurement are factual and unexciting. It was left to the sailors to bring romance into the field of calculations.

The fathom is the nautical measure of depth, now ruled to be exactly 6 ft. The well-known term comes from the old-English *faethm*, meaning "to embrace". Since an embrace of his sweetheart involved the whole length of a sailor's arms, averaging 6 ft., an Act of Parliament decreed that this fathom should become the standard measure for gauging the depth of the ocean.

A further development took place. As the extension of "a swain's arms around the object of his affections" (the actual words of the early statute) was now used to assess the depth of the sea, "to fathom" came to express a desire to get to the bottom of things.

THE SHIP'S BELL

A ship's bell is looked upon with almost reverential awe and considered so precious that it is preserved even after the ship has been broken up. This suggests that the bell once had a purpose other than merely sounding the hour and calling sailors out of their bunks to duty.

This assumption is reinforced by the fact that, after all, the bell could not be heard in the bowels of a ship nor could it be imagined that sailors would wake up each time the bell was sounded, assiduously to count the number of its strokes, to ascertain whether their turn had come to go on watch. Actually, they are called on deck by word of mouth or — a whistle.

Originally the bell was used to repel the nefarious forces of the ocean which followed ships, according to popular belief, waiting for an opportunity to harm or destroy them. But they could not endure a loud, clanging noise. Hearing it, they would scatter far and wide.

Horsebells and those that once were attached to the hem of the High Priest's cloak initially served the same purpose — to scare away demons.

THE DOG WATCH

A sailor welcomes cats on board ship, as their diet of mice and rats suits both parties concerned. But dogs really have no place at sea. Yet we speak of a "dog watch".

However, there is nothing canine about the expression. The dog crept into it only by linguistic corruption.

Members of the crew were divided into two watches — the starboard and the port. They went on duty alternately for four hours each. But soon it was realized that this division of time and service was neither practical nor fair. It could easily happen that the same men had the identical four-hour period every day.

To avoid this, the watch from four to eight in the late afternoon and early evening was halved into two short watches of two hours each, one from four to six and the other from six to eight. Thus the number of daily watches was increased from six to seven, an uneven number, which ensured a just rotation of duties.

For men to be called upon to do the same duty at the same time on the following day was now impossible. And as each watch would *dodge* a watch, it was called the dodge watch. Somehow its original purpose and meaning were forgotten, and the men came to speak of it as the dog watch.

No one likes to be associated, even in a manner of speaking, with dodging work. Sailors on guard might have found an affinity, and not merely a play on words, between a watch dog, in which capacity they really served, and a dog watch.

CROSSING THE LINE

"Crossing the Line" offers the modern tourist plenty of fun. A (mock) baptism, unique of its kind, awaits those who cross the Equator for the first time. The ceremonial includes a Court, held by Neptune, the ruler of the seas, and the victim's lathering, shaving and ducking. When all is over a "baptismal certificate" records that the person in question has been duly initiated and, therefore, never again need undergo the ordeal.

Everything appertaining to the event is now part of the social programme, arranged on board ship to keep passengers busy and amused. And yet, it all started — centuries ago — as a most serious occasion.

Crossing the Line was an auspicious event, not for passengers but for the crew. The first description of the ceremony belongs to French sources and the year 1529, when the brothers Parmentier crossed the Equator in a French ship.

Many important factors contributed to the introduction of the ceremony and its paraphernalia.

Sailing was not safe at the time. Storm and calms alike were a constant threat to the lives and health of those manning ships. Sailing south of the Equator presented additional hazards caused by the tropical climate, scarcity of drinking water and stale food. It was a big event for any sailor who had never travelled so

far before. First of all, therefore, the occasion was marked by a
service. Solemnly the men asked for divine protection in those
insecure and still little-known regions. And then, at the conclusion of the voyage, they thanked God for having guarded them.

Though invisible in the ocean, the "line" was conspicuously
marked on all maps. Hence in the mind of a sailor it played an
important role, showing where he entered the Southern Hemisphere.

The fact that the Equator could not be seen in the water, but
was an imaginary line, gave the occasion of its crossing a
mysterious and mystical meaning. Superstition and fear, always
present in a sailor's life, soon attached themselves to the event.
Somehow the Equator's spirit had to be placated. To achieve
that, sailors were ready to suffer ignominy, ridicule and even
pain. They paid with them, as it were, for their safe passage.

Passing from the Northern to the Southern Hemisphere was
like entering a new world. Therefore, it was considered a sailor's
graduation and attainment of maturity. Small wonder that he
adopted a kind of initiation rite, practised in other trades and
crafts as well. The baptism, like the christening of a child, signified his being admitted into the company of fully qualified
seamen.

The rough and sometimes merciless play that accompanied the
baptism belonged to all initiation rites. It was a test. The young
and inexperienced sailor was "on trial" and had to prove his
power of endurance, his courage and his indifference to physical
and mental pain.

That is why, in early days, apart from the shaving and general
humiliation, the ritual also included corporal punishment and
the throwing of the sailor from the deck into the sea. Having
passed the ordeal, this test of manhood, he was presented with a
certificate, stating that "it gives the god of the ocean particular
pleasure to be able to say that during baptism he bore himself
as a brave tar should".

The initiation soon came to serve other purposes. Voyages
were protracted and could become boring, which did not exactly
improve the morale of the crew. The rites of the crossing offered
a welcome break from monotony and served, too, as a safety
valve for the sailors to let off steam.

Discipline was rigid. The cat o'nine tails was not just a figure of speech. It left its deep marks on many a sailor's body and mind. It was good, therefore, to create a temporary make-believe world where things were topsy-turvy and members of the crew could imagine for once that they were the masters and ruled the waves.

Paradoxically, the ceremony reinforced discipline. Every member of the crew had to conform. However ridiculous or meaningless the ritual appeared to him, he was not permitted to exclude himself from it. Whether he liked it or not, he could not break the tradition of the group to which he belonged.

Travellers entering a new country have to obey strict health regulations in order to keep out disease and infection. Before entering the Southern Hemisphere, sailors equally had to cross an — invisible — border, the Equator. But, first of all, they had to be cleansed of all impurities, both physical and spiritual, and from the dirt of the North. Only then were they allowed to proceed.

Even the shaving part of the ceremony originally was not meant to be hilarious. To remove all of one's hair has always been part of initiation rites, on land and at sea. But then there was another significant factor. A youth who started sprouting a beard, and therefore needed a shave, had "grown up", just as a sailor who had crossed the Line.

Neptune with his Trident (or a fishing spear) now belongs to the festive occasion. Yet actually he is a comparatively recent (English) newcomer. He was preceded by a French figure, whose duties he first shared and in later times appropriated.

Neptune was the ancient Roman god of the water, identified with the older Poseidon, the Greek deity of the sea. He was, therefore, a most fitting figure to participate in the event. Yet his first appearance was the result of man's need to personify the invisible line of the Equator. People just cannot live with an abstract idea. They need its symbolic expression in something tangible, such as a picture, an ikon or, as here, a figure of flesh and blood.

The presentation of a certificate, also, had a practical purpose. To undergo the whole treatment certainly was not pleasant. Once was enough. But how could anyone prove that he had been baptized before? He could do so only by producing documentary evidence. Hence sailors treasured and always carried with them their baptismal form. The document's frequent use wore out the paper and therefore only a few of the original copies have survived.

THE ALBATROSS

The albatross has been the companion of sailors on the high seas far back into history. When all other birds had left off following a ship, this largest of web-footed birds kept on circling it, now and then alighting on the ocean, perhaps dropping back for a while, but always reappearing. In a sense, it became part of a crew who regarded it with superstitious fondness.

Anxiously they looked out for its presence. This fact alone could explain the objection to killing it, such a steady and loyal friend, whose company helped to relieve the monotony of sailing.

Imagination runs high on the lonely watches at sea. We do not know who the sailor was who first began to fancy that there was something mysterious about the way the albatross clung to the company of a ship and showed such stupendous power, flying long distances against the wind, apparently without ever using its wings as a means of propulsion. From his musing there sprang the haunting legend that the bird embodied the soul of a drowned sailor, clinging close to his own kind.

Once that was accepted, it was only a logical step to believe that the killing of an albatross was unlucky.

Samuel Coleridge's great poem, "The Ancient Mariner", which tells the tragedy of a sailor who deliberately shoots down one of the great birds, reinforced the spread of the old superstition.

As late as 1959 the belief was the cause of a sit-down strike of some 50 sailors on board the cargo boat Calpean Star. After an unlucky voyage in the Antarctic she was tied up in the port of Liverpool, England, because of engine trouble.

The sailors had attributed all their misfortunes on the trip to the presence on board of an albatross, consigned to a German zoo. When, on the day after arrival in port, the bird was found dead in its cage even the sturdiest of the crew refused to continue the voyage.

Perhaps, after all, mere self-preservation could account for the superstition among sailors. The bird was so strong that tales soon were current that it had lifted up ship-wrecked sailors out of the sea and brought them to safety. To kill a potential rescuer was tantamount to suicide.

"TELL IT TO THE MARINES"

To express disbelief in a claim or a statement, we invite the informant to "tell it to the Marines". People have often wondered how it came that these valiant men, specially praised by Rudyard Kipling, should be considered so gullible.

Most probably it all started as a natural dislike of experienced sailors for newcomers — troops serving on board ship. These might excel on dry land but seemed completely out of their depth at sea.

Britain led the world in stationing groups of soldiers aboard ship. These were soon referred to as the Royal Marines. They represented a new and significant development in military strategy but sailors at first resented them.

Proud of their own tradition of service and their knowledge of the sea, they looked down on the marines as land lubbers. What did they know of the hazards of the ocean? You could tell them anything and, in their credulity and lack of experience, they would believe it. Naive in matters of sailing, they would swallow any tale.

That is how empty bottles were nicknamed "marines". To the sailor, often keen on his drink, they served no purpose. They only took up precious space.

Another explanation is much kinder, though equally old. It goes back to Samuel Pepys, the famous diarist, who also served under Charles II as Secretary of the Admiralty.

One day he told the king about a naval captain who had alleged that, on a cruise through the Red Sea, he had brought up with his anchor a wheel of one of Pharaoh's chariots sunk there in Moses's time. He also claimed that, while sailing the Southern seas, he had frequently met with shoals of fish "flying in the air".

The king laughed heartily. It was just unbelievable. Who had ever heard of flying fish?

It so happened that during this conversation between Charles and Pepys, an officer of the newly raised Maritime Regiment of Foot was standing near by. The king called him over, asking his opinion. "What do you say, Colonel, to a man who swears he has seen fishes fly in the air?", he inquired.

The sea-soldier was not at all surprised. His reply confirmed what the captain had said. "I should say, Sir," he answered, "the man has sailed in the Southern seas. For when Your Majesty's business carried me thither of late, I did frequently observe more flying fish in one hour than the hairs on my head in number."

Having listened to the Marine confirming the story, the king, now convinced that there were flying fish, addressed Pepys again. "From the very nature of their calling, no class of our subjects can have so wide a knowledge of seas and lands as the officers and men of our loyal Marine Regiment. Henceforth, ere ever we cast doubt upon a tale that lacketh likelihood, we will first *tell it to the Marines.*"

That is how, according to this version, the phrase was first introduced by none other than Charles II. Obviously, it was then meant not as a slur at all. On the contrary, the king intended to convey by it that if his Marines would believe a story, he could do so as well. After all, they had served in all parts of the world and observed there many strange sights, unknown to anyone else.

THE "SENIOR SERVICE"

The Royal Navy is known as the Senior Service. Most people imagine, wrongly, that the expression highlights the fact that the Navy preceded both the Army and the Air Force.

Actually, the term first became current in the 17th century during the rise of the East India Company. Many of the Company's trading ships not only were better than those of the Royal Navy, but offered much higher pay. As a result, a number of officers relinquished their commission in the Navy and joined East India Company vessels which for many years were the finest even among merchant ships.

Nevertheless, compared with the Royal Navy, the East India Company's fleet was a mere newcomer. It was in recognition of this fact that the Royal Navy was spoken of first as the "Senior Service".

CHAPTER XVIII

In the army

CHURCHILL said that "the story of the human race is war. Except for brief and precarious interludes, there has never been peace in the world".

As long as can be remembered, people have fought for their lives, property and country. The earliest monuments celebrate victories. History, to a large degree, is nothing but a record of innumerable battles, defeats and conquests.

Military traditions and customs are the pride of every army and country. They express and reinforce the spirit and discipline of a nation and have contributed in great measure to the whole pattern of life — to the vocabulary of man, his phrases, customs and even dress. However, in most cases the original influence was exerted so far away and so long ago that nowadays it is concealed in a perfect kind of camouflage.

Etymologically speaking, all *soldiers* are mercenary. Their name recalls the (Latin) "money" or, originally, "salt", paid them for their services. *Privates* owe their (verbal) existence to the ancient Romans as well. They were men "deprived" of rank or office.

The modern *tank* is camouflaged, even in its name, which was specially chosen in December 1915 during World War I to mislead the enemy and make him believe that the oblong monsters, then being manufactured and assembled, were innocuous water-containers.

The Chinese have a keen sense of humour. They invented gun powder and found its best use in making fire-crackers to celebrate their grandfathers' birthdays. Similarly, nitro-glycerine was introduced by a French chemist in 1847, not as an explosive but as a remedy for headache!

Nothing is too costly for war. The latest inventions are first applied for defence and attack. Yet in its *martial* aspect, modern war shows its primitive roots and its link with ancient superstitions, polytheism and astrology. The term martial itself is derived from Mars, the Roman god of war.

KHAKI

Khaki is a Hindustani word meaning "dust". Thus the very name of Britain's earliest camouflaged uniforms points to the scene of their origin. They were first used during the Indian Mutiny (1857-8). An irregular corps of Guides raised at Meerut adopted the colour and was appropriately referred to as "the Khaki (dust) Squadron".

To protect themselves against native snipers, who excelled as marksmen, the soldiers dyed their white drill with curry powder or the mud and dust *(khak)*, available in huge quantities at the site of action. However, it was soon realized that this primitive kind of "khaki" neither lasted nor resisted the sun and weather. In addition, it spoiled the gleaming white uniforms and wasted a lot of time, as the process of dyeing had to be repeated again and again. Officers felt the urgent need for ready-made battle dress in khaki colour.

In 1883, a Mr. Leeman, the representative of a Manchester cotton firm, went to India to sell cloth. He met a Colonel Kinlock who related to him his problems and worries and suggested, that if he could find a way to produce cotton cloth of khaki colour that was fade-proof and resistant to frequent washing and changing weather, he would both profit the army and himself.

On his return to England, Leeman and a Lancashire dyer, F. A. Gatty, began experiments. His own wife's kitchen served as their laboratory. Samples of khaki cloth were boiled in Mrs. Leeman's copper pans. But somehow none of them was successful. The colour was there alright, but when exposed to the sun for any length of time, it faded.

Chance eventually led to success. Mrs. Leeman was cooking

dinner and all the pots were in use. Not prepared to wait till at least one of them was available, the two men boiled a piece of the cloth in a rusty old pan. The dye they used, oxide of chromium, was fixed by the oxide of iron from the rusty pan. From then on khaki had come to stay.

On the spot, the friends formed the firm of F. A. Gatty and Co. which for more than 50 years enjoyed a monopoly in supplying British forces with their khaki battle dress. The cloth was no longer used in India only, but in many places throughout the Empire, wherever British soldiers were sent to keep the peace or to restore order. However, it was not until the Boer War in 1899 that the khaki battle dress was universally adopted.

THE BATON

Several traditions together account for the officer's baton. To-day, it is a symbol of authority but practical considerations were responsible for its use first of all.

The baton was an aid to the good manners expected in army leaders. Carrying the stick prevented the officer from putting his hands into his pockets. To point with the finger is impolite, especially for an officer. To do so with a stick was deemed more refined. In addition, grasping the baton prevented him from fidgeting with his hands — a habit common to most of us. Just as in some countries modern policemen may carry truncheons for use at close range, so the baton served also as a weapon of defence.

All these explanations are of comparatively recent date. The baton actually recalls much earlier times, when it was an ever-present means of enforcing discipline. A General Order of 1702 prescribed "swagger sticks" for the British officer. Equipped with the baton, he could administer on-the-spot punishment to any recalcitrant soldier. Up to 12 strokes were inflicted for minor offences, which included such violations of regulations as "giving officers a cross look", "sneezing in the ranks" or "scratching one's head".

Authorities agree that the baton itself developed from an ordinary bludgeon, carried by Teutonic races and that, going back even further, it is a survival of the sacrificial axe of prehistoric man.

THE DRUM-MAJOR'S STAFF

Bands have accompanied armies for many years. Their music meant to rouse the men's spirit and to make them march all the better and always in step.

Though music has been used from earliest times in the service of war and soldiers, it was only in the 17th and 18th centuries that military bands were properly organized. This was due most of all to the music-loving warriors King Louis XIV and Frederick the Great.

The drum-major's staff is an old institution. People have always admired the deft way it is whirled, tossed into the air and caught.

This ornate staff, too, goes back at least to the 18th century. Napoleon's drum-majors especially were renowned for spectacular use of it. No one would imagine, however, that it was employed merely to give a grandiose display to onlookers. It came into being for important, practical considerations.

The band had to be properly conducted, but to do so in the usual way was out of the question. On the march, the men had to see the conductor's directions. He certainly could not move along with them raised on a platform or march backwards in order to face the musicians. Thus the staff originated as a sort of extended baton, whose flights and air-acrobatics were essential to guide the band's playing.

Its travelling through the air was not haphazard but followed well thought-out courses. It controlled starts, halts and stops, and the rhythm and volume of the music.

But then, an even more significant purpose was responsible for the introduction of the staff. The loud music made it impossible for the men to hear any given command. A shouted "right wheel", for instance, would go unheard and unheeded. Therefore, the staff's second reason was to convey all marching orders visually.

THE BUSBY

A high fur cap of cylindrical shape, with a bag of coloured cloth hanging from the top and often coming down to the right shoulder, made up the original busby which is now reserved for purely military wear. Its early beginnings lead back to much less martial associations.

No one really knows the derivation of its name, which has been linked with various people and places.

A village in Yorkshire, England, is called Busby and people were led to assume that the famous hat was born there. On the other hand, a Dr. Richard Busby, Master at Westminster School from 1638-95, has been credited with the invention of the hat. Also, there was a family named Busby, renowned as hatters about the time the conspicuous headdress was first introduced.

Actually, the busby is Hungarian by birth. In Hungary it was originally a peasant's cap made almost exclusively of red cloth. Then, its only furry part was a band around the edge. In time the furry rim became wider and bigger, until it reached the height of the modern busby. Simultaneously, the cloth was forced to retreat, until there was no room left for it except as a covering of the top, a last reminder of the original busby.

The Hungarian army adopted the peasant's cap, but reserved it for its most illustrious forces. It became the badge of Hungary's cavalry regiments, known as the Hussars. From them the British took over the busby.

The little flap which hangs from it is not, as might appear, merely decorative. Formerly it was attached to the Hussar's right shoulder and padded with cotton. It was meant to act as an effective buffer against sword cuts.

MEDALS ON LEFT SIDE

With few exceptions, medals are worn on the left breast. To-day, this regulation aims, first, at uniformity and trimness.

Obviously the fact that this military tradition is observed by the armies of every nation, points to a common origin. This can be traced to the days of the Crusaders. They treasured the emblem of the Order in whose name they fought and, therefore, wore it nearest the heart.

Practical considerations also influenced the choice of position. The left arm carried the fighter's shield which thus guarded the heart and left the right arm free to wield a weapon. To protect the badge of honour, this was placed behind the shield — on the left side of the soldier.

THE WHITE FEATHER

White is not only a symbol of innocence and purity. It has also assumed the role of indicating and branding cowardice. During World War I, patriotic British women used to present white feathers to men who did not wear a uniform and whom they therefore considered to be shirking military duty. They did so to stigmatize them, and "to show the white feather" became a telling phrase.

Yet the most obvious explanation, coming first into one's mind, is wrong. This would suggest that the association of lack of colour with lack of courage stems from the fact that frightened people get pale, become "as white as a ghost" — because the blood drains out of their head.

Actually, the white feather as a badge of cowardice is a legacy from cock-fighting days, once a most popular sport.

There are all kinds of decorations, invented by the ingenuity of man. Most of them are artificial creations, well thought-out symbols and designs to distinguish bravery and merit. But the emblem of cowardice "grew naturally" and is the product of birds, made use of by imaginative people.

Cock-fighting was a cruel sport, enjoyed by callous men from the days of the ancient Greeks and Romans onward, and was introduced by the latter into Britain.

The plumage of a game cock was taken as evidence of its breeding. Pure-bred stock had only red and black feathers. The presence of even a single white feather in a cock's tail indicated a cross-bred bird. Experience showed that only the thorough-bred was good as a fighter. All other birds were "cowards". Therefore only birds of black or red plumage were taken into the cock-pit and "to show the white feather" came not only to imply a display of impure strain but also to describe cowards, both among cocks and men.

THE EMBLEM OF THE RISING SUN

It is an interesting fact that the Rising Sun, symbol of the Australian Forces, originally had nothing to do with either the rising or, as some disgruntled soldiers would have it, the setting sun. This eliminates the otherwise surprising paradox that Australians should have chosen as their military symbol a motif traditionally Japanese.

The customary interpretation that the badge was meant to represent the young nation as rising out of the Southern Seas, however beautiful and patriotic, is equally incorrect. In reality, the apparent rays of the sun are the blades of swords and bayonets, and the solar body originally was a stained piece of wood.

When the first Commonwealth contingent was about to be formed in 1902, for service in South Africa, the military commander, General Sir Edward Hutton, felt that a distinctive badge should be chosen for the battalion.

He invited his staff to submit ideas. Most of the suggestions made use of Australian flora and fauna. But Sir Edward deemed the proposed Emus and Kangaroos, Waratahs and Wattles unsuitable, as they lacked martial significance. Rejecting the designs, he pointed to a trophy of arms over the doorway of his office in Melbourne's Victoria Barracks. This consisted of a semicircular board of red, which carried a crown and half-circle of bayonets and swords. Something like that would be much better, he said.

His advice was regarded as an order and a Melbourne engraver was commissioned to design an emblem embodying the General's suggestion. This was duly delivered, approved by the military authorities, and produced in sufficient number for all the men of the First Battalion. The emblem has become a motif of Australian valour, though under an erroneous name.

THE DIGGER

It is surprising how the origin of even modern traditions and usages is sometimes doubtful and shrouded in mystery. That applies to the Australian term "digger".

It is commonly accepted that it first referred to the miner on the gold fields of the 50s of last century. English people then generally regarded all Australians as diggers for gold and rolling in wealth. But how did the word become the description of the Australian soldier?

Some date this custom back to the South African War, though no record confirms their claim. Much more feasible and widely accepted now is the claim by Charles Everitt of Birdgrove (N.S.W.), that he introduced the term in its modern connotation. But gold diggers were then furthest from his mind.

He was stationed with the 17th Battalion at Gundagai Post on the Sinai Peninsula. "All we did," he recalled, "was dig trenches." Drifting sand made the work almost futile and again and again they had to dig the same trenches. "We aren't soldiers, we're *diggers!*" he complained. Use of the term soon became common throughout the Middle East and the soldiers of the A.I.F. adopted it as the proud title now emblazoned in the annals of Australian history.

THE SLOUCH HAT

Uniforms were introduced as a means of identification. In the heat of battle they helped those fighting to distinguish between friend and foe. Psychologically, they created a sense of belonging and greatly assisted in the disciplining of an army. As time went on, further practical considerations were responsible for innovations and developments in the soldier's dress. The slouch hat and its peculiar way of being turned up on the left side owes its origin to that purpose.

Now a conspicuous part of the Australian uniform, "diggers" wore it previously in the South African War. It is said to have originated in Burma. The turned-up side is due not to any kind of affectation or the wish to appear smart. It dates back at least to the 1880s and the Victorian Mounted Rifles. Their headgear, however, was turned up on the right. To them, this was essential for effective combat.

The rifles then used — of the Martini-Henry type — were very cumbersome and when soldiers were shouldering arms, the muzzle usually caught the brim of the hat. To avoid this, the obvious thing to do was to wear it with that side turned up.

Rifles and muzzles today are streamlined. Yet the turned-up, slouch hat of the Australian soldier remains in service and recalls an early precaution in military drill.

ANZAC

ANZAC is one of Australia's most sacred words, expressing a spirit of heroic values and sacrifice. Yet few of the very men who landed on Gallipoli had ever heard the word, which their action was to immortalize. According to one claim, it was not even an Australian but an Englishman who coined it.

There was no emotional quality or military glory attached to the expression, when it was first introduced. It was born as a mere code-word to replace the cumbersome title of the *Australian and New Zealand Army Corps.*

Soon after the outbreak of World War I, Australia's special volunteer army for overseas service was formed and named by General Bridges the Australian Imperial Force. It is best known by its initials as the (First) A.I.F.

It was sent to Egypt where Poona-born General Birdwood was appointed to establish and command a joint Army Corps of Australian and New Zealand troops. He intended to call it the A.A.C., standing for Australian Army Corps, but then agreed, as was only fair, to include New Zealand's name. Thus the title Australian and New Zealand Army Corps came into existence.

Stationery headed *A. & N.Z. Army Corps* was printed. The new name became even more familiar to those who frequented headquarters at Cairo's famous Shepheard's Hotel, as numerous boxes stored outside the clerks' room carried the Corps' title.

Those in charge of communications soon realized how tedious it was to use the long string of words. To register correspondence, therefore, two sergeants cut out a rubber stamp bearing just the initials A. & N.Z.A.C. In no time the clerks started referring to it as their ANZAC stamp.

One morning Major Wagstaff called at the office and asked the men whether they could think of a suitable abbreviation for the extended title of the Corps. Sergeant K. M. Little, trying to recollect in later years what happened, asserted: "We all had a shot and *I* suggested ANZAC."

His claim was contradicted by Lt. A. T. White, a member of the English Army Service Corps. With equal sincerity he alleged that it was he, also a clerk in the office when Major Wagstaff made his request, who — with the rubber stamp in his mind — had called out: "How about ANZAC?".

No matter to whom the merit really belongs, New Zealander or Englishman, Sergeant or Lieutenant, the fact is that the Major immediately took a liking to the new word. He duly passed it on, in January 1915, to his superior, General Birdwood, who approved of its choice and ANZAC was thus adopted as the Corps' official code-name, though no one at the time could guess the part it was going to play in the destiny and history of the Australian people.

ANZAC DAY

To prolong the weekend period of rest and recreation, Australians have acquired the habit of moving most public holidays to a Monday. But not so Anzac Day. This always is celebrated on the day on which it falls — April 25th. And with good reason. The day commemorates the first great action of the A.I.F. — the Gallipoli landing — and has become symbolic of Australians and their way of life.

Anzac Day was celebrated for the first time in 1916, the first anniversary of the landing, and by those very troops, whose valour made Anzac Day a date not to be forgotten.

The celebration took place not in Australia but at Serapeum in the Suez Canal Defence Zone, where the forces, returned from Gallipoli, were still stationed. General (later Sir) John Monash himself participated in the organization of the festivities that marked the first Anzac Day.

The event had been looked forward to with much anticipation. Manning of the Canal's defences could not be neglected and there was much disappointment among units and officers whose duty it was to do this. All the rest of the troops, however, made it a real holiday.

Every man who had served on Gallipoli wore a blue ribbon on the right breast, and every man who had taken part in the historic landing wore a red ribbon as well. Writing home, Monash regretfully noted: "Alas, how few of us are left who are entitled to wear both."

A short, dignified service was followed by "The Dead March in Saul", played by massed bands, after which all buglers joined in the Last Post. The rest of the day was free and all work ceased.

The morning was spent at cricket or taking part in other amusements. In the afternoon the whole Division went down to the Canal to swim and participate in a great aquatic carnival. From the Serapeum pontoon bridge, both sloping banks of the Suez Canal for almost a whole mile were a teeming mass of naked humanity. At times, there were more than 15,000 men in the water.

Championship Events commenced at 1500 hours. A special programme for the occasion was printed in Cairo. This listed a race across the Canal (about 120 yards) followed by plunges and underwater swimming, as well as a competition on the greasy pole and relay races.

A fifth event was entitled "The Bellman". A man with a bell or whistle dived into the water. Competitors were blind-folded and had to swim after the sound of the bell or whistle. Whoever caught the bellman first won. If no one was able to get hold of him within 60 seconds, he himself received the prize. Late in the afternoon the Prince of Wales joined the soldiers and enjoyed the fun so much that he stayed for more than an hour.

Cables were sent to General Birdwood and the Anzacs in France. Concerts concluded the celebrations and wishes were exchanged that there would be other opportunities of "enjoying many happy returns of this famous day — OUR DAY".

This wish certainly came true. What took place in 1916 as almost a spontaneous commemoration, subsequently was given official standing. Eventually, April 25th was set aside as a public holiday and a solemn Day of Remembrance not only for those who fought and fell at Gallipoli, but for all who gave their lives in the two World Wars.

THREE VOLLEYS OVER THE GRAVE

Fear of haunting spirits originally led to the firing of volleys over a soldier's grave. People were afraid that an evil ghost might attach itself to the dead person. Only the loudest possible noise would frighten it away. There is the identical explanation for the tolling of a bell at funerals.

But martial virtues soon rationalized and militarized the ancient superstition. Soldiers were used to the sounds of battle. To fight for their country and hear the booming of guns represented to them the essence of life. To fall in battle was a glorious end. Thus the last volleys tried to recreate an atmosphere of war and to convey an impression that the dead soldier was going to a life beyond on an occasion of battle; that to the very end he was doing his duty.

Belief in the Holy Trinity is responsible for the actual number of volleys fired. Just as a child the soldier had been baptized in the name of the Father, the Son and the Holy Ghost, so now at his death he was blessed by the symbol of Trinity, this time expressed not in words but by their military equivalent. The firing takes place after the solemn words: "Earth to earth, ashes to ashes and dust to dust."

CHAPTER XIX

the origin of sporting terms and pastimes

MAN has had his hobbies from earliest times and even Adam is said to have dug in his garden as a pastime. They do not merely extend far back into history; they reach into human nature and may serve as an indication of character. To know what a person is really like, one has only to observe what he is doing when he has nothing to do.

Civilization has been rightly defined as what people do with their leisure time. A nation's or individual's hobbies reveal their culture, education and refinement — or their lack. They range from bull-baiting, cock-fighting and horse-racing to reading, mountain-climbing and chasing after (non-existing) leprechauns.

In his "Conquest of Happiness" Bertrand Russell described the ability to fill leisure hours intelligently as the very best product of civilization. Unfortunately, however, progress has led to the development of more and more machines providing more and more people with more and more leisure time in which to be bored.

As games and sports have always been part of life, they have enriched our language in numerous ways. From the cockpit arose not only "showing the white feather" but also "crestfallen". To "throw in the sponge" comes straight from the boxing ring. Similarly, "beating about the bush" and "running riot" are original hunting terms.

Of all hobbies one of the most fascinating and entertaining is the pursuit of their origin.

CHESS

Today chess is considered a game for the most peaceful of men. Actually, monastic orders introduced it to break the monotony of their life. However, it was invented in India in the 7th century A.D. as a game of war: to illustrate and rehearse army movements. It is thus not surprising that in modern times the playing of chess was a valuable part of the training of Russian soldiers.

Even the name of the game retains its martial beginnings. The word is derived from the Indian *Chaturanga*, meaning "consisting of four divisions". These referred to the four kinds of troops that made up the traditional Indian army; infantry, cavalry, chariots and elephants. Added to them, as a matter of course, was the Supreme Commander in the person of the King and his Minister.

The names of the pieces, as they are known now, hardly remind us of the field of battle. This is not the result of intentional camouflage of the soldiers but due to the development of language and the moves of chess through many lands.

Persia adopted the game from India, and when the Arabs conquered Iran, they made chess part of their life and carried it wherever they went. That is how, with the spread of Islam, chess also extended as far West as Spain, as far North as Turkestan, as far East as the Malayan Islands, and as far South as Zanzibar. It did not take long to penetrate from the Moslem countries into those of Christian Europe.

Italians, Frenchmen and Englishmen adopted many of the original terms for the pieces. Whenever they knew what the words really meant, they simply translated them into their own tongue. But if the meaning was obscure to them, they retained the foreign words, which might still baffle the uninitiated.

The piece of smallest size and value, the pawn, without our realizing it perhaps, represents the infantry. It is the medieval French word for the foot-soldier, derived from the Hindu description of an attendant. Rooks, on the other hand, literally recall the ancient Persian armed chariots.

It was the Italian people who determined to change the battlefield into a model state. For that purpose they did not even desist from changing sex — at least on the chessboard. The Minister was made by them the Queen of today. Then, perhaps remembering how thick-skinned politicians must be, they converted the original Oriental elephant into an Elder of State, not inappropriately in ecclesiastical Italy, represented by a Bishop.

Of all terms of the chessboard, *checkmate* — the declaration of final victory — is the most interesting. It has become part of our everyday speech, expressing the thwarting of effort and the foiling or outwitting of others.

Checkmate is the traditional exclamation by which a player announces he has put his opponent's King into such a position that it cannot escape capture. The word could not be more explicit, if it is realized that it retains (though in Anglicized form) the original Arab victory cry "The King Is Dead", *check* being the corrupted Arab title for a king — *Shah* — and *mate* the Arab's description of all that is "dead" *(mat)*.

There are other, and much earlier, claims about the invention of chess. Some give the credit to the ancient Egyptians, and base this on an interpretation of early wall paintings from the time of one of the Pharaohs called Ramses.

Others believe that, as in so many other things, the Chinese first enriched the world with this game of skill, which they designed to help their soldiers pass the time in their winter quarters in the country of Shen, from the name of which the word chess, so it is said, is derived.

King Solomon, perhaps because of his proverbial wisdom, is asserted to have been the first chess player, just as Aristotle, Greek luminary in the field of philosophy, has been called the father of chess.

DICE

One of the root causes of man's gambling is his innate love of taking a chance. The modern poker-machine is the latest robot to serve an urge that has possessed man from the beginning of history. Even the Bible tells of the drawing of lots to determine human fate.

People gamble not merely to acquire money but as an escape. They need stimulus and nothing spurs on man more than an opportunity of getting something for nothing.

Modern society, with its streamlined life and mechanization, has created boredom in unprecedented measure. People gamble to relieve their tensions, trying to give some taste to a dull existence of everyday routine. Gambling is the artificial adventure for those unable to find the real adventure of life.

Dice-throwing is one of the most ancient of games. It was even enjoyed by our savage ancestors. In effect, apart from a few refinements, it has changed little for more than 5000 years. The earliest dice were in the simple form of knucklebones and pebbles.

The antiquity of the game is documented by countless finds all over the world in graves, on inscriptions and in historical records. Cheating at dice is almost as old as the game itself. Ancient loaded dice have been found more than once.

Homer relates how in a quarrel over dice the young Patroclus killed a friend. Antique vases, excavated in modern times, show pictures of fighters in the Trojan war bent over gaming boards, eagerly watching the fall of dice. Frequently, the imperial palace of the Roman emperors had a dicing room.

Paintings on ancient Roman tombs depicted the dead enjoying the game, which suggests that dice-throwing was considered worthwhile even in after-life. The six-sided cube became an oft-recurring motif on graves, symbolizing the uncertainty of human existence.

Sacred Indian lore made special mention of dice and in an early Indian administration a "Superintendent of Dicing" was appointed.

German tribes adopted the game from their civilized Roman neighbours and became so addicted to it that, as Tacitus records, they were sometimes prepared to lose even their freedom for the sake of continuing a game. They would then sell themselves into slavery to the Romans.

The earliest dice were of two kinds and accordingly marked — those that meant good fortune and those that brought ill luck. Ancient Egyptians stamped their dice with small circles, each representing a unit.

One of the most popular Greek games, especially among women, was played with five knucklebones. These were simultaneously thrown into the air. The player tried to catch all of them with the back of one hand. If any dropped he had to make an attempt to pick them up with the same hand, without dislodging those already caught.

Soon the four sides of the knucklebone were marked by four faces, so that there was no possibility of confusing them. The first face was convex, the second concave, the third almost flat, and the fourth a profile. Eventually, other materials replaced the rather gruesome bone and primitive pebble. The substitutes were of stone, wood, ivory, bronze, lead and sometimes amber.

Dice were invented, it is claimed, during the siege of Troy when the heroes played the game in their tents in between battles. The historian Herodotus, however, credits the Lydians with the invention. During a famine, he asserts, they had supplied their people with dice. As they had not enough food to eat daily, men and women were given dice to throw every other day. In the excitement of gambling they forgot about their hunger; one day they ate and the other they played.

Yet, in reality, originally the game of dice was not just a kind of amusement or a subtle means to fight hunger. It was believed that dice revealed the will of the gods! The way they fell showed their favour or disapproval, predicted success or failure. African tribes used to throw dice on the eve of battle for those reasons. Their fall indicated whether they would be victorious or defeated.

PLAYING-CARDS

The Devil himself has been credited with the invention of playing-cards. However, that assertion and all it implies is rather unappreciative of the good cards have done, apart from their obvious evil. They have provided man with relaxation and, as psychologists have pointed out, even more so, helped him to canalize his aggressive instincts into innocent channels.

It is a fictitious claim that we owe playing-cards to itinerant gypsies and that they first devised them for their fortune-telling. The fact that a French craftsman was commissioned in 1392 to paint a set of cards for Charles the Mad led to a third suggestion — that cards originated as a kind of occupational therapy. They had been invented to soothe the king's nerves — whenever he had a bout of insanity.

Actually, playing-cards stem from China where they first

appeared more than 1000 years ago. A claim that they had been invented during the reign of 12th century Emperor Seun-Ho to keep his concubines amused is probably nothing but malicious gossip.

The Chinese used circular cards made from various kinds of wood or plant-fibre. Simple in design, they were painted in rich colours. From the East, cards eventually reached Europe through the Arabs.

Some of the oldest specimens in existence came from Venice. They, too, were painted but still lacked numerals and special names. At first, the European-type of cards pictured a whole galaxy of emblems and figures. These included the sun, moon and a star; the Emperor and Empress; the Wheel of Fortune; Justice; "the Lovers", and "the Hanging Man". They also showed the Fool, the Mountebank and the Devil.

Only then did people start to number the cards and divide them into suits. These distinguished cups (representing faith), swords (justice), money (charity) and clubs (fortitude). The painting of cards became a special craft and their supply a monopoly and — for the state — a special source of revenue by taxation.

From Italy and Spain card-playing spread to France where it created an industry. Though there is no record of the date on which cards were introduced into Britain, they certainly were known there by 1480. A Royal decree, issued 15 years later. prohibited card-playing by servants and apprentices, except during the Christmas holidays. Yet even the Puritans could not suppress the love of the game. King James I was an addict. He had two courtiers in constant attendance, one to hold his cards and the other to suggest which one to throw.

Cards were now elaborately decorated and illuminated with gold and silver. With the passing of time and the increased popularity of the game, the original simple collection of cards had become numerous and complicated. But eventually the pack was again reduced and limited to the present number, 52, apart from the joker.

Various countries adopted their own names and figures. Spain and Portugal retained the original Italian cups, swords, money and batons. Germany and other Northern European nations preferred to have hearts, bells, leaves and acorns. From France, England chose hearts, diamonds, spades and clubs.

Practical considerations were responsible for a further development. Painted cards were rather expensive and not easy to shuffle and people began to have them stencilled and, finally, printed. They were bought not in ready-made packs but in sheets, with several cards printed on each of them to be cut out by the player.

In the excitement of the game, some players were at a disadvantage. Those sitting on the "wrong" side could not at once recognize the card's value when it was thrown on the table. An ingenious Frenchman thought out a remedy. Instead of picturing a whole-length figure, he introduced the double-headed one, equally recognizable from either side.

THE FOUR SUITS

Six hundred years ago the early card makers of Paris inaugurated the four suits familiar today. These were said to represent the four main classes that made up French society at that time.

Hearts depicted ecclesiastical powers, the very heart of the community — the bishops and the clergy. Though, another interpretation sees in them the Knights' shield of nobility.

The military class was symbolized by the points of spears, which came to be called *spades* in Britain.

The *club* has its roots in the picture of a clover leaf. Obviously this was chosen as the emblem of farmers and peasants. Yet its symbolism goes much deeper than at first appears.

People who are lucky are still spoken of as being "in clover". Generally, this phrase has been explained as referring to cattle feeding on clover — the best fodder. However, ancient mystical belief was that clover was especially potent for bringing luck. The clover's three leaves were the sign of trinity. It had been assumed that this was a great power for good long before the advent of Christianity. Like a charm, the trinity gave protection and assured good luck. Thus the three-leaf clover could hardly fail to bring good fortune.

The Roman historian Pliny recorded how the trefoil was looked upon by his countrymen as a powerful antidote against the poison of serpents and scorpions because of its trinitarian magic. Brews made with the plant were used to combat sickness as well as to give a woman's face greater attraction and special freshness.

That is how in the pack of cards the clover in the form of the club became a symbol of good luck, apart from representing that class of society which was closely associated with the clover of the field.

The simple shape of the *diamond* was chosen to represent the rest of the citizens, the middle-class. This was mostly made up of merchants and tiles of diamond-shape are said to have been used to pave their exchange.

THE ACE

The simple "spot" both on dice and cards is known as the *ace*. But in spite of its apparent simplicity, its genealogy is quite considerable and its ancestry rather dubious.

An ancient tradition has it that the Celts invented the ace which they called *as*, because in their tongue this word described the first of all things, the source of being, the origin.

More plausible is the explanation that the ace came from the Romans. In their Latin they referred to it as the *unit*, the "one" — *unus*. Greeks corrupted this numeral into *onos* and Germans adapted it into *Ass*, which eventually deteriorated into *ace*.

Most likely is a third suggestion — that ace originated from the Roman coin called the *as*, which also served as a unit of weight.

A French writer was convinced that the ace of cards and on dice was so called because it pointed directly to an ass — a fool.

LOVE IN TENNIS

Many people have been puzzled by the fact that "no score" in tennis is announced as *love*. This practice goes back at least to the year 1742. Seeking an explanation of the expression some have thought that anyone failing to score must be playing the game for love.

However, it is much more likely that "love" in tennis may have had its roots in France, just as the game (and its name) originated in that country. Tennis is derived from the French word *tenez*, meaning "take it" or "play".

Nil, or nothing, is zero, the figure whose shape resembles an egg. The French, always subtle and quick on the uptake, adopted their (word for) egg, *l'oeuf,* to announce "no score". Crossing the Channel, the *l'oeuf* was adapted to British tongues by being rendered *love.*

THE CROSSWORD PUZZLE

The crossword puzzle is of comparatively recent origin and to solve the mystery of its first appearance is therefore not so difficult. The credit belongs to America. The puzzle was invented by Arthur Winn and published for the first time in the "New York World" on December 21st, 1913.

Actually, it was a development of the old word-square. This consisted of a set of words of the identical number of letters which had to be found and so arranged in a square that they read the same horizontally and vertically.

The new and ingenious kind of puzzle in the Supplement of the Sunday edition of the New York World was welcomed so enthusiastically that it was retained as a weekly feature. Eleven years later the first book of crossword puzzles appeared on the market. Its impact was tremendous. Almost overnight a craze for the new brain-teaser swept America and then spread throughout the world. Newspapers everywhere adopted the crossword puzzle as a standard feature.

Britain succumbed to it in 1925 and soon developed her own style, pattern and definitions. Crosswords now exist in almost every language except those, like Chinese, which do not lend themselves to this kind of up and down manipulation of words.

It was only in 1930 that crossword was included in dictionaries as a legitimate word. It was a deserved recognition of what had become an institution. After all, it was those very puzzles that had boosted the sale of dictionaries in unprecedented measure.

THE QUIZ

Quiz is a modern word. It has the distinction of being the only one added to dictionaries as the direct result of a bet. More surprising is the fact that when the word was first formed, it was meant to mean exactly — nothing.

Quiz, as a word, was born in Ireland about 1780. Its parents were the manager of a Dublin theatre (a Mr. Daly) and some of his friends.

One night they discussed the gullibility of people. Daly asserted that "the mob" could be made to believe and accept well nigh anything. His friends maintained that people were not as stupid as all that. But Daly was adamant and said he was prepared to prove his point. He claimed he would make the masses adopt a new word — a meaningless chain of letters — just overnight. He was ready to take a bet on this.

His friends felt quite safe in agreeing to the wager.

All night Daly and his friends rushed through the streets of Dublin with pails of paint and brushes.

Next morning, Dubliners, wherever they went, found — on houses, pavements and fences — four mysterious letters: Q U I Z.

Everyone *asked* what they meant. Later, the quiz spread from Dublin all over the world. Introduced to prove man's foolishness, it is now used to demonstrate the extent of his knowledge, which is yet another paradox of human life.

Some people have seen in the quiz an abbreviation of the word inquisition, i.e. questioning.

BLUE FOR THE FIRST PRIZE

The Blue Ribbon is the most ancient distinguishing mark of merit. The sky was the highest man could see and it was blue; therefore its colour was chosen as a symbol of distinction.

Ribbons are the traditional badge of an Order of Knighthood. That is why those honoured by the Order of the Garter, the most noble and famous decoration awarded by the British Crown and established by King Edward III in 1348, wear the broad dark blue ribbon.

Eventually, the blue ribbon was used to express outstanding achievements in many other spheres of life as well. The expression "blue ribbon of the turf" to describe the famous English race, the Derby, is said to have been coined by Benjamin Disraeli.

One of his friends, Lord George Bentinck, was complaining to him that a horse he had sold had subsequently won the Derby. Since Disraeli seemed unsympathetic Bentinck accused him of not even knowing what the Derby was. Prime Minister Disraeli promptly replied: "Indeed I do. It is 'the blue ribbon of the turf'."

The same tradition is responsible for the award of a blue ribbon to the liner fastest in crossing the Atlantic Ocean and the first prize in shows.

THE SMOKING OF CIGARETTES

The Holy Land, it is claimed, was not only the source of the three world religions of monotheistic faith, but the place where man enjoyed his first cigarette.

This occurred in Acre in 1832 and in a strange combination of circumstances. During the Turko-Egyptian war and the siege of Acre, Egyptian forces occupied the city. It had been invested by the British, who were aiding the Turks.

During a bombardment of the fortress a cannon ball made a direct hit on a store of hookahs and totally destroyed it. Known in their more primitive form as hubble-bubbles, hookahs are the Oriental kind of pipe, in which the smoke is drawn through water by means of a flexible tube.

The loss was soon felt by the Egyptian soldiers. One of them, dying to have a smoke, improvised a new way of enjoying tobacco. Picking up discarded containers of gunpowder (known as "Dutch tubes"), he used them as wrappers around tobacco and smoked this new device — the first cigarette. The experiment succeeded. Once again, necessity had been the mother of invention.

Some 20 years later, British soldiers serving in the Crimea smoked the "little cigars" and took the vogue to England.

Inventions, however, have a peculiar way of their own and "famous firsts" are often proved to be not so original after all. This certainly applies to the Oriental claim of the first cigarette.

It is now known that thousands of years earlier natives in the West Indies and Mexico smoked cigarettes. They used thin palm bark or maize husks as the wrapper. It was part of the old Maya culture to blow tobacco smoke towards the sun and the four points of the compass. The Aztecs used reeds filled with tobacco for this purpose.

Sixteenth-century Spanish explorers first discovered this ancient habit in the New World. They adopted it and through them it spread over all the Mediterranean countries, as far as Asia Minor — the future Turkey. At that early stage, Spaniards started experimenting with all types of wrappers, including paper, which became popular in the 17th century.

Perhaps — giving the Egyptians the benefit of the doubt — the habit of smoking cigarettes was lost to be rediscovered that fateful morning in the fortress of Acre.

CHAPTER XX

on the stage

A CRITIC once wrote of a poor play that "It opened at 8.40 sharp and closed at 10.40 dull". The theatre can truly excite and bore, exalt and debase. Tragedies have agitated the human soul, and comedies, at their best, have provoked "thoughtful laughter". The theatre is as old as man himself. Play-acting has been a human instinct from earliest days. But in the beginning, the theatre was not meant to entertain. It was a matter of life and death. Among primitive tribes and in the early civilizations, the theatre was not a pastime but part of life and religion.

The word *theatre* comes from the Greek and means "a place for looking". Originally, plays were performed not to be heard but to be seen. A *drama*, therefore, is literally something "acted" in the way of a mime.

Drama's 3000 years of history tell about man himself, his tears and laughter, his fears and loves, the strange quirks life can play and its many paradoxes.

THE THEATRE

Long before the actual birth of the theatre, people performed. They did so, however, not to amuse themselves, or others, but to survive.

The theatre originated in one of the most primitive forms of religious worship — sympathetic magic. This holds that if you properly act something, you can make it really happen. If you want to ensnare a beast, or see your fields and cattle prosper, or kill a man, you can achieve those aims by "remote control". You merely have to enact the scene and, by magic, fiction will be translated into fact.

Hunting tribes, for example, lacking meat, would enact a hunting scene, with some men representing the game and others the successful party of huntsmen. Fertility rites were man's earliest "theatre". Dances then performed were thought to promote, magically, the falling of rain and consequently the growth of vegetation and the increase of cattle. Primitive man was convinced that on such play-acting depended his prosperity and adversity.

A theatre resembled a sacred shrine, and the actors were the priests whose dramatic performance magically directed nature and the gods to do their bidding. Thus early "productions" were not restricted to a limited circle of art lovers but concerned all people. They were a communal event, second to none in importance.

The noise the "actor" made whilst moving rhythmically (with stepping feet and swaying body) in his mimic dances, eventually led to tribal chants, the chorus, and ultimately to poetry. It is, therefore, not an accident that the measure of a verse is the "foot" and that there is a close affinity between the ballet and the ballad. Dramatic performances gave not just aesthetic pleasure but, much more so, roused religious passion and sensuous excitement.

THE TRAGEDY

The theatre, as it is now known, grew out of a popular celebration held in Athens 2500 years ago. It took place once a year in honour of Dionysus, the god of nature and wine. This, in turn, was an adaptation of an even more ancient Egyptian festival whose theme was the death and rebirth of nature.

Thousands of people, from all over Greece, flocked to Athens to participate in this event. The festival was meant to celebrate and propitiate procreative powers and all its ritual centred on fertility. The people then joined in the singing of obscene songs and a greatly enlarged replica of the phallus was carried around in processions.

The educated class soon rebelled against the low level of those celebrations and all they implied in orgies and licentious living in praise of a god. They demanded restraint, decency and a ritual altogether more fitting for the occasion. As a result lyric choruses were introduced. They were sung by a choir of 50 men and boys and the stage was set for the future theatre.

The tragedy, as the first dramatic form to come into existence, developed from that earliest choral lyric performed at the festival of Dionysus. <i>Tragedy</i> literally means a "goat-song". The origin of this peculiar term for a play of a serious nature with a disastrous or fatal ending is obscure and has given rise to many and varied interpretations.

It has been pointed out that the men and boys in the choir were disguised as Satyrs and dressed in goat skins. Hence their song and performance were referred to as a "goat-song".

A second opinion is that the odd name derived from the fact that the original, religious festival included as one of its main features the sacrifice of a goat to Dionysus and that the chorus was sung over the goat's dead body.

Finally, it has been suggested that the tragedy, as a goat-song, received its name because of the prize offered at the annual "art festival" of classical Greece. This trophy was not in the form of a shield, a cup or a wreath but of a <i>tragos</i> — a goat! The winner had the privilege of offering it as a sacrifice to Dionysus. Its slaying was the climax of the play. Therefore it is not so far-fetched that any theatre performance that ends with the death of the hero is linked with that ancient goat sacrifice and still called a tragedy.

What a world of difference there is between this early goat-song of the tragedy and our own "acting the goat".

THE PIT AND THE STALLS

In the 17th century, the ground floor of the theatre was known as "the pit". From it, and under the open sky, the audience watched the play standing up. Later, they were seated on wooded benches without backboards against which to lean. There was still no roof to shelter the spectators from inclement weather. They must have been so absorbed in the play that they just did not care for or notice their own discomfort.

This alone is evidence of the popularity of many of those early stage productions. The name pit has another significance. The first performances of dramatic art in England took place in arenas previously used for cock-fights. Obviously, the pit is a survival of *cock-pits,* the place in which birds were *pitted* against each other. London's first theatre, built in 1618, where Shakespeare's plays were performed, stood on the site of a famous cockpit in Drury Lane.

Centuries passed, architecture developed, and the theatre changed into a refined centre of culture. Auditoriums were no longer remembered as former arenas, and playgoers demanded comfort.

Theatre managers obliged. As the seats nearest the stage were favoured most, they were also the dearest. Only well-to-do people could afford to book them. To cater for these patrons' taste and at the same time give value for money, front seats were most luxuriously equipped. Appropriately, the former pit was now called by the fashionable French word *fauteuils,* meaning "armchairs". Soon the French term was Anglicized and became stalls.

Yet as if to remind the unsuspecting, comfortably placed spectator of what went before, the "stall" still recalls, at least etymologically, the former cockpit. The word stall is derived from an old-English term which meant "standing room". Thus, to speak of a stall-seat is really a contradiction in terms. You sit down on something that denotes "standing room" only! This is yet another symbol of the make-belief world that is the theatre, so full of paradox, where the play's the thing!

CHAPTER XXI

In the way of speaking

SOONER OR LATER practically everyone uses two ways of speaking his mother tongue. One is more or less grammatically formal and the other is slang.

Colloquially speaking, people like to "call a spade a spade" and good slang "hits the nail on the head". It conveys one's meaning succinctly, vigorously and to the point. Certainly, slang words and phrases have to struggle for their existence but the apt ones survive. Eventually they become accepted and a respectable part of the vocabulary. Popular expressions above all prove that a language lives. Nothing can take their place. Napoleon was astonished what power words have over man and modern dictators, following him, have made use of that knowledge.

Words and phrases offer a mine of information. What is "fair dinkum" to the Australian might be "O.K." to Americans, though to find "the real McCoy" is at times very difficult.

THE REAL McCOY

It is very rare that the person responsible for a phrase himself explained its origin. But, according to one version, this is the case regarding "the real McCoy".

He was a famous boxer, Charles ("Kid") McCoy, a one-time world welter weight champion, who died in 1940. For many years he was unbeatable in his class and so his name became a legend. The real McCoy came to mean the real thing, the genuine article! It was the finest praise anyone or anything could receive. People came to speak of the real McCoy in every sphere of life, when-

ever they wished to describe the best of its kind or someone who
excelled in his class, profession or sport.

Yet even so it did not assure happiness for the real McCoy,
once so celebrated and adored by the American people. He accidentally killed his sweetheart and was sentenced to serve a prison
term at St. Quentin. While there, he rescued a pilot whose plane
had crashed near a road-gang of prisoners and as a reward and
recalling the ex-boxer's former happier days, the warden presented him with a pair of boxing gloves and a punching bag to use
when not employed in prison duties.

While serving his sentence (he received his parole in 1932),
he had many friendly talks with Warden Duffy. On one occasion
McCoy gave his own version of how his name came to be perpetuated in American speaking. Duffy relates the story in his
book, "88 Men and Two Women".

Duffy says McCoy told him that while having a drink with a
lady friend in a saloon, a man accosted the woman. Trying to
brush off the intruder without much fuss, McCoy asked him to go,
adding as a warning which needed no further explanation "I'm
Kid McCoy!". But the man persisted in pestering the lady, not
believing that McCoy was the American champion fighter. He remarked with scorn "Yeah? Well, I'm George Washington!"
McCoy said he struck the man once and quite lightly. The man
collapsed and when, ten minutes later, he regained his senses, he
rubbed his eyes and called out "Jeez, it *was* the *real* McCoy!".

And so, according to Kid, it was this incident that gave birth
to the now commonly used phrase of approbation.

It is sad to know that the life of the real McCoy, whose name
had come to stand for the finest and best, ended tragically. After
his release from St. Quentin, he worked for the Ford Motor Company in Detroit. In 1940, whilst looking forward to his 10th marriage, he died from an overdose of sleeping tablets.

Nevertheless, in spite of McCoy's own testimony, there are
other intriguing claims and definitions of the phrase's origin.

The Irish were not slow to recognize in his name one of their
own kind and took the phrase as a general tribute to Irishmen's
honesty and excellence.

Their people were famous as fighters. No one could match
them. A ballad of the 1870s tells of an Irish woman who had

beaten her husband mercilessly – just to prove that she was "a real McCoy".

There is also the claim that the phrase relates to the days of prohibition in the U.S.A., when bootleggers prospered. Some took advantage of the fact that, even should they defraud their thirsty customers, these could not claim any compensation or take their dishonest supplier to a court of law. Therefore the greater proportion of illegal liquor sold them as the real thing was heavily diluted with all kinds of substitutes.

One bootlegger named McCoy, however, refused to cheat his clients and supplied only the best-quality, undiluted imported whisky. His name became a trade mark and a recommendation and his product was referred to as "the real McCoy". The phrase soon caught on and survived prohibition and bootlegging days to become a general term of praise.

FAIR DINKUM

The Australian saying "fair dinkum" describes something as really genuine. Yet research shows it goes back to English colloquial speech where, in provincial dialect, it meant "fair play".

Intriguing, though not so factual, is an explanation that links the origin of the term with Australia's gold digging days and an early influx of foreigners.

Australians in those times, even as now, always liked to drink and to gamble, especially after a day's hard work in search of gold.

On the gold fields around Ballarat they persuaded their newcomer friends from abroad to join them in their pastime. These "diggers" from overseas soon realized that a mind befuddled by strong liquor was no good for keen gambling and that to keep sober, at least until the game was over, meant also to keep one's money, or even add to it. So they refrained from drinking till afterward.

The locals, faced with heavy losses, were not slow in finding out what was happening. They demanded "fair play", which, to them, implied "fair drinking" as well. That is why eventually, to show their good intentions, the foreign diggers assured their Australian partners that there would be "fair drinking" all round: not only after, but before, the game.

Somehow (so the story goes) by their accent they made their promise sound like "fair dinkum". The "Aussies", highly amused at their mispronunciation, took a liking to it and adopted it themselves. So, fair dinkum, a foreign contribution to the Australian language, came to be known as a dinkum Australian word.

"O.K."

Winston Churchill was convinced that the short words are the best. O.K. is now the universal slang to say that "it's alright". No one will mistake the meaning of these two capital letters. Yet views differ on how they first came into existence as a vivid term of approval and approbation.

This shortest and internationally adopted expression supplies one of the longest lists of possible explanations. Illiteracy, political slander, a clever election campaign, bureaucratic efficiency, a Red Indian chief and the French, they all, in turn, have been credited as the originators of the O.K..

America's Presidents are no mere figure heads. Frequently, they have been known as the policy makers of their country, directing the course of their nation's history. Yet none of them has had the distinction of having been a word maker as well, except Andrew Jackson, the seventh President of the United States. He has been called the father of the O.K..

This claim, however, was not made by his admirers but by those who sought to discredit him during the Presidential campaign in 1838, as a completely illiterate man and not qualified to lead the nation.

His enemies spread the rumour that Jackson, then a General and one of the candidates, so lacked even the rudiments of ordinary education that he used the abbreviation of O.K. for "All Correct", as he, so untutored and ignorant, thought that the words were spelled *"Orl Kerrect"*!

It is quite possible that Jackson was fond of calling things that were correct O.K.. But if he really did so, it was not because of any lack of education or faulty spelling. It is said that he derived it from the Choctaw Indian word *okeh*, which they used to emphasize the validity of a statement or the hope that what they said would come true, in much the same way as we use Amen.

Other authorities hold that O.K. came into being in a different American Presidential election campaign. It was invented, they say, as a slogan, not to malign an opponent, but to boost a candidate.

A catchy phrase if cleverly chosen is worth thousands of votes where mere policy speeches go unheeded. Disraeli rightly stated that "With words we govern men".

In 1840 Martin van Buren was standing for a second term as President of the United States. Though he was generally known as "The Little Magician", his chances of success were doubtful. His followers therefore tried every possible means to get him votes. What they needed most was a good slogan.

Van Buren was born in the township of *Old Kinderhook* in the State of New York. By combining the initials of its otherwise rather cumbersome name, supporters referred to him as O.K.. Soon those two letters became a rallying call. In New York his party organized even an "O.K. Club", further to popularize the cause and – quite unintentionally – the new "word".

As it happened, the "Old Fox of O.K.", as he was known, was not re-elected, but the two letters survived van Buren's defeat, to become a favourite colloquialism among all English-speaking people.

To add further to the confusion, another view states that O.K. stems from the Red Indians after all, although it is not one of their actual words. It represented the initials of *Old Keokuk*, the name of one of their famous chiefs, who, believing that time was money, saved it by signing treaties with his initials instead of his full name.

So O.K. came to stand among the Indians as an affirmation of things said or done: the final approval. Unfortunately, none of the documents is preserved to verify or disprove the claim.

Other explanations of the O.K. are interesting, yet most unlikely. One attributes the expression to an old French term. The other suggests that, in reality, the O.K. is altogether an error. Originally, the letters were not O.K. at all but O.R., which stood for "*Order Recorded*", a once customary endorsement of documents.

Certainly, there is ample choice of possible explanations for the O.K. but we are left to wonder which is truly O.K..

CHAPTER XXII

the BEGINNINGS OF WRITING

PEOPLE have always wondered how writing first came into existence. From earliest times myth and legend have tried to give an answer.

Egyptians believed that only a god could have revealed the art of writing and they called their script *hieroglyphics,* meaning "sacred carvings". They worshipped Toth as the giver of script and, for this reason, always presented this bird-headed deity as holding a reed brush and ink palette in his hands.

The Chinese attributed the invention of the alphabet to the four-eyed, dragon-faced god T'sang Chien and said he took the pattern of his symbols from nature — the footprints of birds, the marks on the back of a turtle, and so on.

According to Hindu myth, the god Brahma created the letters. He wished to write down his teachings on leaves of gold. But as there was no alphabet in existence, he had to invent it. He did so mostly by copying some of the peculiar tracings formed by the seams in the human skull.

The known facts about writing are, of course, less exciting, though still fascinating.

Clearly, a *manuscript* literally means "written by hand", though nowadays it is mostly typed. However, many other terms and implements of writing do not disclose their background and story so easily. To understand their past, enlightens their present.

A *pen,* in any shape, recalls the original quill. The word is derived from a Latin root, meaning "feather". Any *text* is words "woven" together to display some pattern of thought.

THE ALPHABET

All alphabets — and there are more than 200 of them — derived from one original alphabet. This came, as so many other benefits of Western civilization, from the Orient. Just as the Ten Commandments were revealed on the Sinai Peninsula, so — as discoveries of inscriptions in our century have suggested — one of the earliest alphabets, if not the very first one, was conceived in that very region as well! There is no doubt that the desert land between Egypt and Babylonia, between the home of hieroglyphics and cuneiform, gave mankind its alphabet. The approximate date of its birth is the second half of the 2nd millennium B.C..

The alphabet's very name reflects its Semitic parents, *Aleph* and *Beth* being the first two letters of the Hebrew alphabet. It was adopted through the Phoenicians by the Greeks, who spread it throughout Europe.

All letters developed from pictures. The prototype of our present-day writing are drawings of some common object, such as a fence, a camel, a hand, a head, a fish or a spear. In Oriental languages the letters are still called by their names, whose initial sounds represent the letters of the alphabet in most tongues to this day.

"A" originally depicted the head of an ox (*Aleph* in Hebrew); "B" was the simplified drawing of a house (*Beth* in Hebrew); "G" derived from a camel (*Gamal* in Hebrew); in the "M" we can still recognize water, shown by one of its waves (*Ma'yim* in Hebrew), and in the "O" the shape of an eye. The "T", most obviously, is a cross.

The number of the letters in the alphabet differs slightly from nation to nation. Whilst the English alphabet, for instance, counts 26 letters, that of the Russians has 36, of the Spanish 27 and of the Hebrew language 22 characters.

The reason for this fluctuation is easy to discover. The general rule of the alphabet is "one sound — one letter". People vary not only in the language they speak but in the kind of sounds they are able to produce. Arabs are even more guttural than the Germans. The Greek tongue could not make any use of our "C" and "V", whilst the letter "J" was "unpalatable" to the Romans.

The sounds represented in the earliest alphabet completely lacked any vowels. Originally, this consisted of consonants only, which complicated interpretation. The most simple text would thus baffle the reader, who had to decide for himself where a vowel was intended and which one was needed.

Take, for example, one of our best-known nursery rhymes. Written in the ancient manner it would appear thus —

MR HD LTTL LMB

Even if it were suggested what this line of consonants represented, it would still take some considerable time to read into it that —

MaRy HaD a LiTTLe LaMB.

But this is exactly how, in earliest times and for almost 2000 years, people wrote. A simple three-letter word, for instance, made up of the consonants BRD thus presented a choice of many meanings. It could be read as —

BeaRD, BaRD, BiRD, BReaD, BReeD, BRoaD or BRooD

— to mention the most obvious possibilities.

It is not surprising, therefore, that this lack of vowels became a frequent source of misunderstanding and error, as actually "reading" was merely "guessing". When, finally, vowel signs were introduced they were simple in form — Morse-like dots and dashes.

Other obvious features of present-day script are equally the result of thousands of years of evolution. Originally, only capital letters were known; small or lower case letters were not developed until the Middle Ages. At first, all writing moved from right to left, as Hebrew and Arabic still do to this day. To unravel the above nursery rhyme would thus be an even greater problem:—

BML LTTL DH RM

Another later development was punctuation, which for centuries was non-existent. A further difficulty of early writing was that all words were strung together without spaces, in order not to waste precious writing material like papyrus and parchment. Applying the original way of writing, from right to left and without vowels and spacing, the verse would have been this short line of consonants —

BMLLTTLDHRM

No wonder that the reading of documents was confined to a small circle of experts!

It was one of the great innovations in the history of civilization when, for the first time, an unknown genius comprised the idea "literally" to pause between words and to separate them not only on his tongue but on whatever then took the place of paper.

The alphabet is one of the most revolutionary inventions made by man in his cultural development. It came into existence not suddenly but, as has been shown, as the result of continuous growth and many stages of trial and error. We owe our letters to the brilliant minds of men whose names and identities we shall never know.

"TO MIND ONE'S P's AND Q's"

The curious phrase "to mind one's P's and Q's" — meaning to be careful in one's words and behaviour — evolved from the shape of the letters themselves.

However, the letters as capitals provide no clue to the original reason for the saying. But once p and q are written or printed as small letters their similar appearance must strike the eye. Without special care, children learning the alphabet or inexperienced typesetters might easily confuse these characters. Young pupils and printers' apprentices were thus specially reminded not to mix but "to mind their p's and q's".

But the most obvious answer need not always be the real one, and particularly so in this case. After all, the same danger of confusing similar shapes of letters applied to other parts of the alphabet as well. Further investigation confirms this assumption and offers two totally different interpretations of the phrase. These have nothing to do with either the art of calligraphy or of type-setting but belong to the social side of human life.

One explanation leads straight into ale houses of former times. Innkeepers then used to keep a score of what customers drank by chalking up on a board (or the wall) a record in pints and quarts, which they indicated by P's and Q's.

A careful drinker, anxious not to be overcharged, would remind the publican to be exact when chalking up the score — in other words, to mind his P's and Q's.

On the other hand, and this is no less likely, it could have been the innkeeper who, concerned that people should not drink above their (monetary) capacity, warned them, especially when they were well advanced in their rounds, to mind (the number of) Pints and Quarts, lest, when the final account was rendered, they were unable to pay.

More far-fetched, but still possible, is another origin of the phrase, which links it with French court etiquette of the 17th century. During the reign of Louis XIV men used to wear huge wigs. When greeting members of a higher class, especially royalty, they bowed low. This needed much practice. Men might stumble over their feet, or worse still, in the course of the bow their wig might become disarranged or even fall off altogether.

Dancing masters cautioned their pupils always to "mind their feet and wigs". In French this was *pieds* (feet) and *queues* (wigs). When the English adopted the French fashion and caution, being of a practical mind and perhaps not too sure of the right accent, they shortened the French "feet" and "wig" to their mere initials. That is why we now speak of minding one's P's and Q's.

THE QUESTION MARK

The question mark has a fascinating past. In Latin a query was indicated by the word *questio*, meaning "question", which was placed at the end of a sentence. However, this took up valuable space on the page.

An unknown economist in the art of writing, whom we might also consider an early pioneer of shorthand, had the idea to abbreviate QUESTIO to QO. But this was not satisfactory, since it could be mistaken for the ending of a word. Writers began to place the Q on top of the O.

It did not take long for the Q to deteriorate into a squiggle and the O to contract into a dot. Our present question mark had finally arrived.

PAPER

Trying to trace the origin of paper, we are led back thousands of years to two centres of ancient civilization, far removed from each other.

The word "paper" comes from Egypt's papyrus, that tall straight reed once covering acres of marsh to a height of 19 ft. In wild thicket and later in cultivated fields, Egyptian workers used to cut the papyrus stems individually for their "factories".

Papyrus was then the raw material for many things. Its base was eaten as a delicacy. Its rind made loin-cloths for the lower classes and its inner pith was used for sails, boats, baskets, ropes and sandals; but above all it served as the source of writing material.

The choice of the old Egyptian word papyrus for this plant was not without purpose either. *Papyrus* meant "The Royal". It proclaimed the reed as a royal property and the manufacture of "paper" as a strictly guarded State monopoly.

For centuries papyrus was the only substance in the world from which "paper" was made. The Egyptians wrote on it as long ago as the year 3000 B.C.. From there it reached the Greco-Roman world, where it was used for more than 1000 years.

Yet it had disadvantages. One of them was that supply of papyrus was limited to regions where the plant could be grown or be exported in sufficient quantity. Furthermore, it yellowed with time and was rather brittle.

That is why it was replaced by parchment, made of animal skins. This name came from the city of Pergamum in Asia Minor, where parchment became a substitute for papyrus in the 2nd century B.C., when King Ptolemy stopped its export from Egypt.

Parchment then surpassed the unobtainable paper in many ways. It was much tougher, lasted longer and could take twice the amount of writing, as both sides could be used. But it was still expensive and only the rich could afford it. Nevertheless, it conquered the world and, for the next 1100 years, was most favoured by Europe's scribes, monks and scholars.

However all that time, though unknown to the West, a much cheaper writing material was available in the Far East — real paper, invented in ancient China.

For once we are lucky to know even the name of the man said to have made it, his profession and the year. T'sai Lun manufactured the world's first paper in 105 A.D. after many experiments with varieties of bark, fibres and waste. The astonishing fact is that T'sai Lun's own profession had nothing to do with learning. He belonged to the Imperial Palace and his appointment was that of Chief Eunuch to the Emperor Ho Ti.

For hundreds of years the use of paper was restricted to the Far East alone. In the 8th century Chinese prisoners revealed the art of paper-making to their Arab captors. These, in turn, introduced it into Europe where — in 1340 — the first paper mill was established in the town of Fabriano in Italy.

The ancient "royal" name of the Egyptian papyrus was then welded to the "modern" Chinese 'material, and the paper took over the name of its earliest predecessor. Thus the East and the West combined in bringing enlightenment to the whole world. Literary knowledge was no longer restricted to a small coterie of scholars but available to all the people.

It was the new kind of paper that made possible the invention of printing in 1450.

FOOLSCAP

An old watermark and a corrupted Italian term have both been cited as the origin of "foolscap" paper, which now measures 13½ inches by 17 inches. The earliest known specimen dates from 1540. For many years, until the 17th century, the head of a jester with cap and bells was used in Britain as the watermark of paper of this special size. Most probably people began to refer to the paper as that of the fool's cap.

Opinions differ on how the watermark was introduced. The suggestion that a German resident in Britain started it is least probable. His name was Herr Spielmann (later Sir John Spilman). He was jeweller to Queen Elizabeth's court and established a paper mill at Dartford in 1580. It was the second in England.

Anxious to mark his product, he made use of his name. A *Spielmann* in German is a person who acts or plays. Why could it not

be a man who played the fool, he reasoned. It must be remembered that, between the 13th and 17th centuries, jesters were a
privileged class, employed by courtiers and the nobility. Their
emblem was a cap and bells. Spielmann decided to choose this
sign as trademark for his paper.

Another unlikely explanation links the introduction of the
fool's cap as a watermark with history. The story is told that when
King Charles I found his coffers empty, he explored every means
of raising funds, including the granting of privileges to certain
people prepared to pay a high premium.

The monopoly of making paper was thus sold. At the time it
bore the royal arms as its exclusive watermark. With the defeat of
the Royalists, Oliver Cromwell and the Rump Parliament were
determined to express their break with the past in every possible
way. They ordered the removal of the royal sign wherever they
found it, even from note-paper, but especially from the large-
sized pages of the Parliamentary Journal, where it was used as a
watermark.

It is said that to ridicule the former king and add further in-
dignity to his memory, Cromwell substituted a fool's cap for the
royal arms. However, with the prorogation of the Rump Parliament this mark of contempt was again removed. Yet, ever since,
paper of the Journal's size has been referred to as foolscap.

Others believe that the description of paper as foolscap is
based on a misunderstanding, that it is a corruption of the Italian
foglia capa, meaning a "first-sized sheet", a chief or large page.
Like the English word foliage, the Italian *foglia* is derived from
the leaf of a tree, used as an early writing material and still remembered as such when we speak of the leaves of a book.

Eventually, Britain replaced the watermark of the fool's cap
with the figure of Britannia or that of a lion rampant, supporting
the cap of liberty or a pole. But the original fool's cap survives,
if not as a watermark, as a term for the paper it once distinguished.

INK

An ancient Greek word for a branding iron is the base of the
modern word *ink*. Literally this means "burnt in" and refers to the
custom of sealing by heat both wounds — cauterizing them — and

colours — fixing them more durably. The Greek *enkauston* and Latin *incaustum* became the names reserved for the (Tyrian) purple fluid with which Greek and Roman emperors signed official documents.

The earliest use of ink dates back to Egypt and the 4th millennium B.C.. Then it was not a liquid but a dry substance, made chiefly from soot scraped from cooking pots or, in the form of carbon, from charcoal. This ink was kept in small cakes and was made liquid by mixing it with either water or gum.

Independently, the Chinese began to use carbon ink about 2000 B.C.. According to tradition the inventor was T'ien Chu. In both China and Japan pine soot and lamp black served as a base.

The Old Testament mentions the use of ink only once. Baruch, Jeremiah's secretary, relates how he recorded what the prophet dictated to him: "He pronounced all these words unto me with his mouth, and I wrote them with ink in the book."

Carbon ink of that early type could easily be washed off. Additives of vinegar and wormwood were thought to make it more durable and to repel mice. But drawbacks soon became apparent. Once mixed, the ink thickened in no time and clogged the pen. With the introduction of parchment as a writing material, the carbon-liquid proved even less satisfactory. Something more fluid and more permanent was needed.

Scribes realized that ink with a mineral mixture had the advantage of penetrating the material, although sometimes it also gradually destroyed it. This resulted in the introduction of an iron-gall liquid. It was known to the Hebrews as early as the 6th century B.C. and is still retained in principle.

Even coloured inks were produced in most remote times. However, except for red, they were applied only to drawing. The Egyptians made their red ink from cinnabar and used it for several purposes. It indicated the final sum in their accounts, and marked the beginning of paragraphs in their writings. Not least, they wrote the names of evil creatures in red, for this was the colour of hostile powers.

BLOTTING PAPER

Blotting paper was discovered by accident. It was the result of a workman's forgetfulness. He was in charge of the mixing vats at a paper mill in Berkshire, England. One day he forgot to put in sizing, one of the essential ingredients in the making of paper, and the finished product was useless.

There was a large quantity of it and the factory proprietor, a thrifty man, was reluctant to throw it away. If it was not saleable as paper, he thought, at least he would make use of it himself for rough notes. However, he found that that was not possible either. The ink spread all over the sheets and was completely absorbed.

Suddenly he got the idea that this peculiar fault might be the beginning of a novel line with a considerable market.

For hundreds of years people had used sand to dry ink. This was a long and cumbersome process. Now the factory owner advertised the spoilt goods as "blotting paper". In no time he disposed of the complete stock. A thriving new industry had been born.

Originally, most blotting paper was produced in a pink or red colour because of a wish to utilize matter which otherwise would have been of hardly any value. Red was a fast colour and difficult to bleach. In paper-making red rags certainly were not a paying proposition. But for blotting paper, any colour would do and red was as satisfactory as the purest white. Thus the law of economics determined the original colour of blotting paper as well.

CHAPTER XXIII

counting and accounting

MAN has always felt the need to take the measure of things and anything that could assist him to do so he gladly employed. That is why he first of all used parts of his body, such as the feet, for a measure, and the fingers for counting. The power of a horse and the weight of a stone were other aids. The sun, moon and stars helped him as ready reckoners of the passing of time.

Coins are unrivalled story tellers and an important source of historical data. Payment by money replaced the more primitive method of barter, a term that not accidentally also meant cheating.

The earliest currency did not consist of coins but of objects, such as knives, just as Roman soldiers were paid in salt, essential for life and still ingrained in our present-day "salary". The original type of money was not counted but weighed, which explains the English *pound*, at first describing a "load" of 7,680 well-dried grains of wheat.

It is often said that "money is the root of all evil". This is a misquotation from the New Testament, which says that it is the love of money that is the source of wickedness, and not money itself. Boldly Mark Twain amended this passage by stating that not love but lack of money was the root of all evil. Though it is good to remember that sometimes you can pay too much for money.

"ONCE IN A BLUE MOON"

When we speak of "once in a blue moon" we mean "very rarely indeed". Obviously, a blue moon is not an everyday occurrence.

The moon has been blamed — rightly or wrongly — for many things. She has given us lunatics and the tides. We speak of the moon as being yellow as cheese, though in reality its proper colour is probably a dark, brownish-black. The "blue moon" is an optical illusion. It has never existed in reality.

All light of the moon is reflected sunshine, and the colour in which it appears to the eye changes according to the atmosphere surrounding the earth through which the rays have to pass. That is why the moon may look bright yellow, whitish, orange or, very rarely, blue.

Any change in the atmosphere, which is caused by particles of dust or other matter being absorbed in it, immediately influences the colour of the rays of light reflected by the moon from the sun.

That is why in 1883, for example, the world saw a blue moon. The moon had done nothing. But on earth, the Indonesian island of Krakatoa had been blown almost into halves, and enormous clouds of volcanic dust and water vapour had been thrown into the atmosphere and were circling the earth for many weeks.

This dust and other matter changed the light rays reaching the earth from the moon, and made people believe that the moon was blue. Things are not always what they seem to be.

THE FORTNIGHT

If telegraphy had been invented at the time, we could have assumed that the word fortnight originated in the minds of thrifty people who, knowing that every word was counted and charged, were anxious to save money by making one word of two. Fortnight is the combination of two old English words, fourteen nights.

It is surprising that Americans, who are usually keen on economizing and streamlining matters, up to recent times had not adopted fortnight but used in its stead the more cumbersome "two weeks".

The fortnight's antiquity is indicated by the fact that its reference is to nights. That our calendar also originally took more note of lunar changes than of solar circumstances is apparent in several other terms in daily use.

The word month — literally — has the (word) moon inside it

and was used to describe the moon's phases. In Oriental countries every new month still coincides with the appearance of the new moon.

Similarly, the starting of the celebration of Christmas on its eve relates to the early domination of night over day. This was first expressed and emphasized by the biblical story of Creation in which it is said "there was evening and there was morning — one day". The day began at night!

A BAKER'S DOZEN

Present-day business methods subject us to all kinds of temptations to buy certain goods. Most common is the promise of a free gift for the purchaser of an article thus advertised.

It might be assumed that it was also a wish to foster trade that caused bakers to give any customer buying 12 loaves of bread a 13th loaf free of charge. However, the baker's dozen is not the result of ancient trade-promotion. It is a survival of an early type of price-control.

Bread was the staple diet of the people who purchased it in the form of either cut pieces or whole loaves. Anticipating modern strict regulations, loaves not only were counted but had to be of a certain weight. Heavy penalties threatened any baker selling short weight.

As bread loses weight after it has become dry and shrunk, the baker wisely started adding an extra loaf or piece of bread to every dozen sold. This was called the in-bread and what the baker thus lost on the swings, he got back on the round-about. The gift of some extra dough in the proportion of one to twelve saved him from the loss of more precious "dough".

There is a suspicion that self-interest of another kind might have accounted for the baker's dozen. People were afraid of evil forces, ever ready to spoil their luck unless they were given "protection money". To propitiate them, the baker, anxious to prosper in his trade, may have added the extra loaf. This gave rise to the saying "Twelve for the baker and one for the Devil".

"BY RULE OF THUMB"

When we use the phrase "by rule of thumb", we mean to say that we apply a very rough and ready method and certainly not an accurate and scientifically dependable procedure. There are several conjectures on the origin of the expression.

In the early days, the thumb, like the foot, was an always-available instrument of measure. The last joint of the thumb was taken as approximately equal to an inch. (It became a widely established custom, reminiscent of the baker's dozen, to allow "a thumb" as an extra to every yard when measuring cloth.) And precisely because this was a very rough calculation, the rule of thumb came to signify that.

Another possible explanation leads back to Southern France, to Bordeaux, and 1814. French contractors were then paid in Spanish dollars. To calculate their worth in francs, their own money, they often made notes on the thumb nail. The military gentlemen were highly amused by this method. They were convinced that it was all pretence, and that it was impossible by such "rule of thumb" accurately to assess the correct exchange of francs for dollars.

A third interpretation relates to the brewing of beer and has its birthplace in Yorkshire, England. To ascertain whether the infusion of malt had reached the right degree of fermentation, it was necessary to check the temperature of the mixture. As no scientific instruments were available for the purpose, the thumb was dipped in the liquid. Thus by rule of the thumb, it was known more or less, whether or not the brew was ready.

THE PIGGY BANK

A favourite medium for savings, among children and adults, is the piggy bank. Modern potteries often turn it out in the shape of a pig with a slot in its back.

Though piggy banks have contributed much to man's savings, in one way they have also added to his confusion. Why, people wanted to know, was the "coin holder", of all things, thus called and even shaped?

Pigs have been known for many things, but certainly never and nowhere for being thrifty or concerned with the future, saving up for a rainy day.

Dogs bury bones. Camels are said to store away water. But as for pigs, even the proverb says that you will never make a purse out of a sow's ear, and Holy Scripture reminds us of the futility of throwing pearls to swine.

Indeed, there is no true relationship between a piggy bank and a pig. All similarities are merely coincidental. The fault is not that of the swine. It is all a human error. Actually, there is no pork of any kind in a piggy bank — only clay.

During the Middle Ages metal was rarely used in the manufacture of common household utensils; it was too expensive. More economical and pliable was a type of clay then commonly known as *pygg*. This was so popular for dishes, pots and jars that eventually people referred to all earthenware as pygg.

Frugal housewives then, as now, put what they could save into a pot or jar, which then was made of pygg. And that is how, by a natural process of evolution, that container, serving the purpose of the family treasury, came to be known as the pyggy bank.

In time, however, the origin of the term was forgotten. In 19th century England potters, being excellent craftsmen but not good etymologists, did not realize the true meaning of pyggy — that ancient clay. Therefore, when customers ordered a pyggy bank, they produced erroneously a pig-shaped money-box.

Mistakes always prosper. In no time the piggy bank caught people's imagination. Subconsciously they might have remembered the fertility of swine, hoping that their money would multiply likewise.

THE STROKE BETWEEN SHILLINGS AND PENCE

The stroke placed between shillings and pence arose through a case of mistaken identity.

Up to the 19th century, people who wanted to register any amount of shillings and pence indicated them by the letter S (for shillings) and D (for denarius, the principal silver coin of the Romans, out of which developed the penny).

At the time, the shape of the letter S was much longer than it is today, looking more like the modern small f, without its crossstroke. People writing in a hurry often failed to give the long S its proper curve. When this archaic S was replaced by its modern equivalent, its original purpose and meaning were forgotten when figures were used. It was then believed that the transfigured S was nothing but a line, employed to separate shillings and pence.

THE RIM ON COINS

Ever since the invention of money, there have been forgers. Our modern counterfeiters have had their unworthy predecessors even at times when paper-money was non-existent and its precautionary water-marking could not be employed. Savage penalties like cutting off the hand of the offender, which was common for centuries after early Saxon times, did not deter them.

The earliest coins were hand-made and, although of marked weights of gold, silver or bronze, could differ in shape. This allowed forgers to clip the rims of the coins and steal the metal thus gained. The practice was so widespread and troublesome in the reign of Henry V of England that it was classified as treason and made punishable by death.

In 1695 a special window tax had to be introduced in England to cover the nation's enormous expenses for replacing clipped and defaced coins. (This tax was levied on all houses which had six or more windows and was not repealed until 1851.)

But the mere threat of punishment proved insufficient. It did not stop unscrupulous persons from continuing to shear around the edges of gold and silver coins. Further precautionary measures were called for to make their iniquitous practice more difficult, if not impossible. That is how an ingenious mind conceived the idea of "decorating" all coins with a graining around their edges known as milling. The rim around coins, therefore, was introduced first not as an ornament. So to speak, it was a case of "milling vs. clipping". Any coin lacking the grained rim was no longer acceptable as currency.

Obviously, some of the more persistent forgers must have tried — after clipping the coin — to provide the reduced disc with their own home-made edge.

Discovering this new ruse, Oliver Cromwell decreed that, instead of milling the edge, this should be inscribed with suitable mottoes. First these legends piously referred to God and faith. Eventually they became very explicit. In some cases they read: "THE PENALTY FOR CLIPPING THIS COIN IS DEATH".

However, at the time of Charles II, the inscription became less threatening, saying briefly: "AN ORNAMENT AND A SAFE-GUARD".

Modern coinage is not valuable enough as metal to tempt clippers. And yet the milled edge is kept as a tradition. Perhaps this might still serve as a safeguard, though of a different kind. It may help people to grasp the coin more firmly and thus enable them to hold it longer in their hands before, inevitably, it will roll away.

"& CO" ON CHEQUES

To "cross a cheque" by writing the words "& Co" between two lines is a remnant of earlier banking days.

To make sure that the cheque did not go astray or would not be cashed by a person not entitled to the money, it was specifically addressed to the payee's bank — its name being written conspicuously between two lines.

It sometimes happened that the drawer, when making out the cheque, did not know the name of the payee's bank. He therefore left it to the payee to fill this in himself, but courteously and precautiously prepared the way by drawing the two lines and filling in the last of the entry — which, since it related to the times when all banks were private — was presumed to be "and Co.". The payee thus had merely to complete the draft and all was in order.

THE PAWNBROKER'S THREE BRASS BALLS

As in all money matters an element of uncertainty is attached even to the pawnbroker's sign of the three brass balls. It is generally acknowledged that his trade-mark originated as the emblem of Italian nobility, the Medici family who came from Lombardy. They introduced money lending into England, arriving there, it has been suggested, as financial agents of the early Popes, to collect their dues. They are known to have financed the kings of England to the time of Edward III.

To indicate their place of business, they displayed the three balls, their family crest, outside the house.

As money lending on pledges proved itself a lucrative trade, it did not remain for long a monopoly of the Medicis. Soon other merchants entered the field, wisely copying the sign which by then in people's minds had become identified with this type of financial transaction. Ever since, the three brass balls have served as a pawnbroker's trade-mark.

Yet it is still a matter of doubt how in the first place the Medicis came to adopt their crest. One explanation is that the name Medici is derived from the art of medicine and that the early and prominent members of the family were physicians for whom a pill was a trade-mark. In medieval times it was customary to gild pills to make them more acceptable to rich customers.

Even those who deny an early association of the Medicis with medicine, maintain that the obvious pun, the mere similarity of sound, had led the family to adopt the three enlarged pills in their coat of arms.

Another theory relates the three balls not to the healing of the sick but to the defeat of an enemy. Averardo de Medici, who served as a commander with Charlemagne, was famous for an encounter with a giant, Mugello, whom he slew in combat. After the battle he carried with him as a trophy the giant's club, weighted with three iron balls. To commemorate the victory Medici adopted the three balls as his arms.

A further tradition is completely divorced from the Medicis and links the pawnbroker's symbol with the emblem of St. Nicholas of Bari and three purses of gold he is said to have left three poor, pious sisters, to help them find husbands.

To nickname a pawnbroker "uncle" is neither a family matter nor does it reflect any special familiarity. Actually, it introduces a note of corruption into this otherwise honest trade, though only in the way of speaking. This type of uncle is merely a mispronunciation. The word is derived from the Latin *uncus,* which described the "hook" once commonly used by pawnbrokers to store and remove the pledges.

BLACKMAIL

Blackmail has a very sad history indeed. It has come down from most respectable circles, eventually to become mixed up with illegal extortion. It started in Scotland hundreds of years ago and involved hard-working but poverty-stricken farmers.

Most of the land there was then owned by the English. They charged high rents to the Scots who farmed the soil. This "tribute" paid to the absentee landlord was known as *mail*, at one time a Scottish term for rent and taxes.

One of the conditions stipulated was that all payment should be made in silver. This was referred to as *white* mail.

But life was hard and the farmers often could not raise the money for the mail. The English landlords then agreed to take produce in lieu of silver. The goods became known as *black* mail but they were quite legal and no opprobrium was at first attached to the term.

However, dishonest creditors began to take advantage of the farmers' distress. They demanded goods far in excess in value of the money owed and they backed their demands with threats. The term black mail deteriorated into meaning payments extorted from persons by intimidation.

Another explanation also associates the origin of the present-day use of the term with the Scots, however, dating it back to the boundary warfare between England and Scotland. According to this interpretation, "blackmail" was the protection money paid, in the form of produce, by the border farmers to freebooters. These promised, in return, to guard them against plunder by rapacious chiefs on either side of the frontier.

CHAPTER XXIV

the measurement of time

MUCH OF MODERN society is possessed by the notion that "time is money". Punctuality is praised as a virtue and split-second timing has become an essential in research, industry and almost every type of scientific and technological endeavour.

Life is ruled by the clock and regulated by schedules. Failure to be punctual may lose a man a job, a courting male his date and a business executive his travel connections.

Early man certainly had no trains or planes to catch; he did not have to clock in at work or to attend a shareholders' meeting, scheduled to commence "on the dot". Nevertheless, he, too, had his kind of appointments to keep, especially in the service of his tribe and his gods. How did he know then when to arrive and to worship his deity at just the right moment?

The calculations and dates of the calendar serve many aspects of human endeavour. The calendar reflects various obligations of man, as well as his organizational talent. It fixes events and is a reminder that life does not stand still.

And yet the calendar, which seems so definite, fixed and of most ancient date, is full of errors, inexactitudes and incongruities. It is divided into two periods — the years preceding and those following the birth of Jesus. We indicate them accordingly by the common abbreviations of B.C. (*Before Christ*) and A.D. (*Anno Domini*, meaning "in the year of the Lord"). But somehow the year "0" got lost: the year 1 A.D. immediately follows the year 1 B.C., whilst the actual year of Christ's birth is missing. Above all, it is now generally assumed that Christ was born four years "Before Christ"!

That January 1st is the beginning of each year is taken for granted. Yet until 1752 not January 1st but March 25th was New Year's Day!

Originally, a month was a moonth—the time it took the moon to revolve around the earth, approximately 29 days. Thousands of years ago, a method of measuring time by the sun was adopted. The term month, however, was retained, although a misnomer.

We are a Christian country and pride ourselves on our enlightened mind. But in the naming of the months and days, we still reflect beliefs in astrology and pagan gods. It has been said that a calendar is always up-to-date. However, turning its pages backward, we shall find the exact opposite.

Life would be dull if one day were like another. Then truly the calendar, with its changing dates, would merely impress the passing of time on us and make us melancholy.

That is why it is essential that we not only add years to our life but life to our years. As if aware of this need, the calendar has provided annually recurring Red Letter Days. They interrupt the monotonous flow of time and give people a chance to let themselves go.

Each of these special dates has its own story. Their origin goes back into the distant past and is the result of man's battle with nature and his own complexes, fears and desires.

Some of the days and months of the year have become linked with certain mysterious notions and telling phrases. Not only are they part of our chronology, they are full of romance, the fanciful beginnings of which it is good to know.

THE CALENDAR

At first the term calendar did not relate to anything written down (there were originally no lists of dates), but to a herald's announcement!

Actually, the *calendar* is derived from the Latin, meaning "to call out". The beginning of each month was proclaimed by the head-priest or another appointed official.

No one knew beforehand when exactly the new month would

start. It had to coincide with the appearance of the new moon and only when this had been duly observed could the official declaration be made. That is how at first the *calend* merely referred to the first day of each month.

The development of commerce and financial transactions led to the writing down of these significant dates which by then, through the ever-growing knowledge of the movements of the sun, the moon and the stars, could be determined far in advance.

Merchants and money-lenders thus began to keep their own calendar — tables listing the initial dates of each month which enabled them to know when accounts had to be settled and interests became due. Out of these early account-books of the Romans grew the now indispensable tabulation of the passing of time, whether fixed on the wall, put on the desk or carried, in the form of a diary, in our pockets.

THE NUMBERING OF YEARS

Even the most primitive races needed some sort of calendar. To them it was almost a matter of life and death. It was essential for them to know the proper time for sowing and reaping; when to seek shelter from heat or cold, from wet seasons and dry and from the inundations of rivers. Hunters and fishermen depended on the annual migrations of animals and fish. Not least, early man was conscious of his total dependence on the will of the gods, whom he had to serve at the proper moment. Therefore the timely celebration of feasts was to him a vital part of his religion.

Observation taught man that the seasons coincided with certain positions of heavenly bodies and other celestial phenomena. That is why astronomy assumed such an important place in the life of the earliest races and became the fountainhead of all calendars. Indeed, the daily and annual movements of the sun, the moon and the stars offered themselves from the very start as a basis for the division of time. We can only wonder at the remarkable accuracy of early astronomical perception.

From the rotation of the earth on its axis came the divisions of day and night. The period of the revolution of the moon around the earth suggested the month. The time it took the earth to rotate around the sun created the year.

At first, years were not counted continuously but related to some outstanding event, such as a flood, an earthquake or a conquest. People said "it was so many years since they happened".

Then the calendar used the accession of rulers as the reference point, as the Bible shows. Each year was dated from the beginning of the reign of the monarch that ruled at the time. So we read in early records that an event took place, "in the year X of the reign of King Y".

With the further progress of civilization, continuous numbering of the years was introduced. Its starting point differed from nation to nation and largely depended on the people's outlook on life.

ORDINARY TIME

The Hebrews dated their calendar back to the creation of the world. This, they calculated, had taken place 3760 years and three months B.C.. To this day they follow this early (fictitious) scheme.

The sports-minded Greeks reckoned their time from the first Olympic Games in 776 B.C.. The Romans chose the foundation of Rome in 753 B.C. as the start of their chronology. Julius Caesar revised it in 46 B.C. and brought it "up-to-date". As this "Julian calendar" was in use when Christianity arose, the Church followed it and continued to do so for five centuries. The calendar of the modern Christian era, which counts the years from the date of the Incarnation of Christ, was adopted only in 530 A.D.. Its introduction was due to a learned monk in Rome, named Dionysius Exiguus. He based the starting point of the new epoch on the tradition that Jesus was born "in the 28th year of the reign of Augustus".

The new style of numbering the years took hold very slowly. In England, the Christian era was inaugurated more than a hundred years later at the Synod of Whitby in 664 A.D..

THE MONTHS

The choice of the moon for the division of time was not accidental. This principal luminary of the night was worshipped by almost all primitive races. They considered it was a mysterious being which, unceasingly and regularly, had to pass through the stages of birth, full maturity, decay and death. The moon's revolutions around the earth were used as a measure of time for thousands of years. The day of the new moon, always anxiously looked out for, was celebrated as a holy day, the start of the new month.

The names of the months are derived from the Latin, as we owe each one of them to the ancient Romans. They started the year, not as we do now at the height of summer or the depth of winter, but in (their) spring. It was a natural choice, as the time of sowing. But being a bellicose people, they also used this month to prepare for their military campaigns.

Not surprisingly, therefore, they named this month in honour of the god Mars. Originally, he had been linked with the fertility of the soil but later had become the god of war and death as well. Thus it was just the right time to protect their fields and homes from all foes — both physical and spiritual. That is why the year began with the worship of *Mars,* whom we still honour in MARCH.

APRIL carries on the cycle of nature. From the Latin word meaning "to open", it marked the season when the Roman country-side began to blossom and the buds *open*ed up.

In the following month, our MAY, all plants were growing and, therefore, the choice of its name fell on *Maia,* the goddess of increase, to whom sacrifices were offered on its first day. Another interpretation claims that the month received its name in honour of the *Majores,* the Senate in the original constitution of Rome.

JUNE honours *Juno,* the queen of heaven and personification of womanhood, who was considered the guardian of marriage. According to another school of thought, June was named after the *Juniores,* the lesser branch of the Roman legislature. A third theory is that the name derives from *Junius* Brutus, one of Julius Caesar's murderers.

The following two months no longer commemorate gods or seasons. They honour famous historical figures.

JULY is the birth-month of *Julius* Caesar, in whose honour Mark Antony is said to have named it in the year of his assassination.

As *Augustus,* Caesar's nephew, followed him on the throne, so he does in the sequence of months. He himself gave AUGUST his name, as he had then celebrated some of his greatest triumphs and put an end to civil war.

Somehow the Romans must have lost interest in their gods and emperors after the sixth month of the year, as following it they just numbered them prosaically: SEPTEMBER (the *seventh*), OCTOBER (the *eighth*), NOVEMBER (the *ninth*) and DE-CEMBER (the *tenth*).

The original Roman calendar consisted of ten months only — from March to December. There was an uncounted gap in the winter between the years. Tradition relates that it was Numa Pompilius, the second king of Rome, who in 713 B.C. added the missing two months.

JANUARY was so called in honour of *Janus*, the Roman god of the beginning of things and the patron of births. Logically, the beginning of the year was moved to this month. But, negligently, it was omitted to adjust the names of the numbered months, which no longer fitted. That is why we still call our 9th month "the seventh" (September), the 10th "the eighth" (October), the 11th "the ninth" (November) and the 12th "the tenth" (December). No one has had the courage or wisdom to put things right.

Janus also was the deity of doors and gates. His two-faced head looked both forward and backward and, so fitting at the start of a new year, could be said simultaneously to gaze at the past and to look into the future.

A Roman festival of atonement, held with special rites of purification on FEBRUARY 15th, gave this month its name. It is derived from the Latin word meaning "to cleanse" — *februare*. Women who had proved barren were then beaten with the thongs cut from the hides of two goats, sacrificed on the occasion. It was thought that this drastic treatment would purify the women and make them fertile.

THE DAYS OF THE WEEK

While the years and months are the result of the observation of natural phenomena, the week owes its origin to early astrological and superstitious beliefs. There was nothing in the order of nature that suggested it but merely man's vivid imagination, his limited knowledge and his assumption that his fate depended on the stars.

The figure 7 has always been considered holy and magical. It stood for completeness and was thought to bring luck. The seven-day week undoubtedly goes back to ancient Babylonian astrology which linked each day with one of the seven known planets.

This scheme of dividing time into units of seven days was then adopted by the Hebrews. They did so probably during their Babylonian exile in the 6th century B.C. and purified it — temporarily — from its astrological associations.

They, in turn, brought it to Egypt. There, it is claimed, priests were the first actually to name the seven days after the planets. They assumed that the heavenly body which was in charge of the first hour of a particular day controlled the day as a whole. Thus they obtained the following list of "regents" and days: Saturn, Sun, Moon, Mars, Mercury, Jupiter and Venus.

From Egypt the week found its way to the Romans, to whom it had been unknown in pre-Christian days. From them it spread all over Europe and then to England.

But in a strange kind of selection "up North" only some of the Roman names were retained. Others were replaced by their Nordic equivalent. Thus throughout every week we recall, in a peculiar mixture, pagan deities both of Roman and Teutonic lineage.

SATURDAY was *Saturn's* day. It was the planet associated with the Roman god of that name who had taken the place of the Greek god of Time. Saturn is said to have devoured all his children except three. It was imagined for a long time that people born under his star were unlucky, as they had entered the world under an evil omen.

It is perhaps more than a strange coincidence that many Sabbatical prohibitions are paralleled by regulations concerning the Roman festival of Saturn. During it law courts had to be closed, no public business could be transacted, schools went on holiday, no war could begin and even criminals could not be punished.

SUNDAY obviously is the day of the *sun*, which controls all its events. It was only in the 4th century that the Church declared it a holy day, in commemoration of the Resurrection of Christ and replacing the observance of the Jewish Sabbath.

The *moon's* day became MONDAY.

Then, suddenly and for no known reason, the English changed

their system and, for the remaining four days of the week, made use not of Roman but Norse mythology.

TUESDAY was so called in honour of the Scandinavian god of war — *Tiw*. Formerly, he had been a daring Norse hero who had lost his hand in a fight.

WEDNESDAY recalls the god *Woden,* which is the Anglo-Saxon for the better-known Odin. He was the god of storms who welcomed brave warriers to Valhalla and treated them there to the delights they had most desired on earth.

His dominion extended to the realms of wisdom, poetry and agriculture. The latter accounts for the widespread belief for many centuries, that Wednesday was specially favourable for sowing the crops.

THURSDAY belongs to *Thor,* god of thunder and Woden's son. Strong, brutal and greedy, these very qualities endeared him to the people. He was famous for his hammer, which typified lightning and thunder, his belt of strength and his iron glove with the aid of which he threw the hammer.

FRIDAY is *Frigga*'s day. She was Woden's wife and chief goddess and patroness of love, marriage and fertility. Originally a moon goddess, she travelled in a chariot, drawn by two cats.

Thus every week without realizing it we continue to honour the planet Saturn and worship the sun and the moon and pay homage to war, storm, brute force and love.

RED LETTER DAYS

We speak of a Red Letter Day when we wish to stress or recollect some special, joyous occasion.

This colourful description of a momentous day seems always to be associated with some completely worldly matter. Yet the origin of the Red Letter Day is just the opposite. It belonged to the Church and its most sacred and solemn occasions.

It goes back to the time when Saints' Days and Holy Days appeared in the calendar in red print. This distinguished them from all other days and, at the same time, indicated that special services for them were contained in the Book of Common Prayer. The rest of the year was shown on the calendar in ordinary, plain black type.

The colour was not chosen just because it was conspicuous. Red had always had a sacred association, especially in the minds of the pious. They were reminded by it of the blood shed by the martyrs.

APRIL FOOLS' DAY

Everyone loves a laugh. Yet to do so at other people's expense is rightly considered uncivil and wrong. But the calendar has made provision to suspend this generally accepted rule once every year. On April 1st until noon we are permitted to make fools of others. April Fools' Day is one of man's unique institutions — a holiday for laughter. Explanations of its origin and real purpose are many.

Some people date the day back to Noah and think it was all his fault. They reason that, having spent much time in the Ark, he was anxiously waiting for the Flood to subside. When mistakenly he thought that at long last this had happened, he opened the window and sent out the dove. But it was on a fool's errand. Unable to find any land, the bird returned to the boat. It had been a most futile mission.

This trip took place on a Hebrew date which is said to correspond to April 1st. Ever since, this day has been appointed as All Fools' Day, the "all" being a corruption of the ancient *auld*, meaning "old". It is a reminder of the unfortunate circumstances of Old Noah's time and perpetuates the memory of man's deliverance from the Flood.

Those who forget the event and all it implies are punished by sending them on an ineffectual errand, just as Noah had done with the dove. This is intended to jerk their memory and teach them a lesson so that never again will they ignore "April 1st" and its message of the second chance given to man, and his duty not to forfeit it.

One of the most significant occasions in ancient times was the celebration of the vernal equinox. Then, with laughter and joy, men welcomed the coming of spring. Happy that the winter was over and exuberant at the rebirth of nature, they indulged in all kinds of frivolity and fun-making.

This festival fell on (or about) April 1st and people thus concluded that All Fools' Day owed its existence to those early pagan celebrations. Indians, too, at the coming of spring held their Feast of Huli during which they took great pleasure in sending people on fools' errands.

Others have claimed that the day is closely linked with the Roman Saturnalia, when the population in like manner loved fooling about and making fun of each other.

Again, there is a suggestion that April Fools' Day has nothing to do with man's rejoicing at the arrival of spring but commemorates special incidents in the passion of Christ, which also took place about that time.

Christ's foes, determined to torment and mock Him, enjoyed sending Him backward and forward. Medieval mystery plays duly dramatized those tragic events. They showed how Jesus was asked to go from one person to another, from Annas to Caiaphas, from Caiaphas to Pilate, from Pilate to Herod, and then again back, from Herod to Pilate.

Some authorities believe it was through these religious, medieval productions that the custom arose of ridiculing people by sending them without rhyme or reason — just as had happened to Christ — from place to place. Thus All Fools' Day was not intended to be a source of merriment. On the contrary, it was a solemn reminder of the ridicule heaped on Christ at that season.

The Scots call an April fool a cuckoo. In France he is known as an April fish — *un poisson d'Avril*. At that time of the year, it is felt he acts like the young fish when they appear in French rivers. Lacking experience, they are easily caught. In colloquial English we would refer to them as suckers.

Yet another theory is that April Fools' Day originated from the practice of letting insane people be at large on April 1st. Crude generations did this to amuse the crowds who asked the unfortunates to perform acts which obviously could not be done.

All these interpretations are colourful but perhaps unconvincing. Most probably, All Fools' Day goes back not to Noah's Ark or Christ's passion, but to 16th century France and was the result of a peculiar combination of circumstances. These included man's ancient delight in celebrating the New Year, the change of calendar then introduced, some people's forgetfulness and others' rather perverted sense of humour.

The old Romans took pleasure on New Year's Day in visiting friends and taking them gifts. Throughout the Middle Ages, New Year fell on March 25th. But the fact that this date frequently coincided with Passion Week, or even Good Friday itself, caused the actual merriment to be postponed to April 1st.

But in 1564 the French adopted the reformed Gregorian Calendar and consequently moved New Year's Day back to January 1st. Many people at first could not get used to the change and forgot all about the new New Year. Taking advantage of their confusion, jokers paid them mock visits on April 1st. The pranksters, being seriously received and welcomed, did not fail to make fools of the host.

Eventually even the dullest took due notice that times had changed, and April 1st was "out". Yet the custom of making fools of people on that day persisted. It was kept on even after its origin was no longer remembered. After all, it appealed to man's sense of fun.

The conservative English adopted the new calendar and, with it, All Fools' Day only in the 18th century.

No matter by whom and when April Fools' Day was first introduced, it has a strong social and psychological significance.

In societies which are still at a comparatively low level there is often an obsession to force all its members into one single mould. Still today, as a relic from times when the herd-instinct ruled supreme, people sheepishly love uniformity and try to exclude anyone who differs or excels.

It is humiliating to be laughed at. Whoever makes a fool of us unconsciously wants us to efface ourselves and hide in the anonymity of the crowd. In his study, "Laughter", Henri Bergson claimed as laughter's main function an attempt to intimidate the individual and thereby make him conform.

But laughter serves another purpose as well. Next to society's love of conformity there is the individual's wish for superiority. By making other people ridiculous, man experiences a feeling of power. The practical joker thus enjoys his egoism and, sending friends on a fool's errand, looks upon them as puppets whose strings he pulls.

However, All Fools' Day serves most of all, perhaps, as a

wonderful means of relieving tension and for one day at least every year gives man a chance to forget his worries.

MAY DAY

In many countries May Day celebrations today are political demonstrations. It has been called the Festival of Labour. Its origin, however, has nothing to do with socialism, class warfare or a holiday for the working man. The day goes back to most ancient and primitive times and the worship of nature.

May Day was the time when things began to grow again and man did everything he could to show his joy and his gratitude to the gods. He was deeply concerned also that the fertility of nature, on which his own life depended, should be assured. To that end he not only employed every type of magic but was even prepared to bring as a sacrifice those he treasured most.

The old Phoenicians thus threw their own children into the fiery mouths of idols. It was their priceless offering to the god of vegetation. They fed Moloch with their cherished children to buy his goodwill so that their fields would prosper and their cattle multiply.

It was a horrible practice, fiercely decried in the Bible as "an abomination of the heathen". But who would imagine that the bonfires lit at many places on May Day are a relic of this murderous, ancient rite, propitiating the god-head!

Other less cruel races, equally possessed by the wish to assist nature in renewing herself, also used magic. They believed that by masquerading in flowers and leaves they helped the bare earth to clothe itself again with verdure, and that by playing the death and burial of winter they expelled that gloomy season.

These primitive rites account for our own floral decorations on May Day and for its revelry and dances. Their original purpose was not to entertain the people or to adorn the homes. It was a dramatic device to force the pace of nature.

The beribboned May pole is nothing but the early representation of the phallic symbol. And the dance around it recalls primitive man's worship of the forces of reproduction.

Everything thus done on May Day goes back to man's fervent wish and anxious care to bestow fertility on his crops, his cattle and — his women!

The immediate ancestor of our May Day, however, is the Ancient Romans' Festival of Flowers — the Floralia.

BOXING DAY

Although December 26th is St. Stephen's Day, honouring the first Christian martyr, British countries — and they alone — call the first weekday after Christmas, Boxing Day.

The name has nothing to do with pugilists or prize-fighting. It relates to the ancient custom of presenting a gift *in a box* to a person who was owed a debt of gratitude.

Although the box has long been discarded, it is still customary to give a Christmas box — a well-deserved and expected gift.

The custom originated with the Romans and their feast of Saturn, during which they gave each other presents as an expression of the merry spirit of the celebration of the winter solstice. It was this association of the practice with paganism that led the Church to denounce it and call on the faithful to discard it. Their appeal fell on deaf ears.

Unable to destroy heathen ways of giving, the religious authorities re-interpreted them. The original link with pagan revelry was suppressed (and then forgotten) and replaced by a new and sacred tradition.

People should still give to others of what they had, not for sensuous enjoyment but for the sake of the soul. The Church provided special boxes to receive the gifts, thus enabling Masses to be said for the donors.

Masses were now celebrated for almost every contingency of life. For instance, when a ship was about to leave, priests put on her a box which they dedicated to a saint under whose protection she would sail. Everyone on her was expected to make some contribution. The box was not opened until the ship's return. Its contents were given to a priest to say Mass for the men, so that their misdeeds during the voyage might be forgiven.

That was the earliest kind of *Christ's Mass*. The receptacle into which voluntary offerings in payment of its celebration were placed came to be known as Christ's Mass Box.

There were further developments of the now Christianized pagan custom. The box became the symbol of church charity. It was in every house of worship and was opened on Christmas after the morning service. Money in it was called "the dole of the Christmas box" or "box money". It was distributed by the parish priest next day, which appropriately assumed the name of Boxing Day.

Then the wheel turned the full circle and the religious custom to aid the poor and destitute again became secularized. At Christmas, apprentices began to go among their masters' customers with a box in which they expected them to place a small gratuity.

Boxes are no longer carried. Nor is it only apprentices who expect this recognition of services rendered, as every housewife knows.

A far-fetched interpretation of the Christmas box sees in it a survival, etymologically as much as practically, of the Oriental *baksheesh*. During the Crusades, this theory alleges, Knights brought back from the East both the word and the tipping practice.

THE CLOCK

The alternation of day and night offered the earliest means of keeping time. But just to say "We'll meet when it's dark (or light)" was insufficient. In search of something to assist him in being more specific, man looked up into the sky and duly noted the movement of the sun. He observed that it travelled westward as the day advanced.

Man's first clock thus was God-made — the sun. The day was divided according to its position — whether it was high or low in the sky, in the East or the West, rising or setting. That is how man began to speak of dawn, morning, noon and evening. Actually, *Orient* still means (the) *rising* (sun) and in many languages the word for *evening* is derived from a term denoting the *West*.

Man soon felt the need to become more exact and to divide the time of day into much smaller and more definite units. From the sky, he turned his eyes to the ground and discovered the shadow. He watched it with fear and trembling as some kind of mysterious being which followed on his heels as long as the sun shone.

He also observed that the shadow's length and direction changed continuously throughout the day. When the sun was high, the shadow was short; when the sun was low, the shadow was long. During the first half of the day, when the sun was in the East, the shadow pointed to the West, and vice versa.

Most likely, the Babylonians first took note of these significant facts and began to use the moving shadow in telling the time much more accurately than had ever been done before by merely watching the sun.

That led to their invention — in the second millennium B.C. — of the first man-made clock, the sun-dial. It was one of the simplest instruments ever devised, consisting of a stick, stuck vertically in the ground. As the sun advanced, the stake's shadow told the time.

Dial comes from the Latin word for day. That is how the shadow-clock, as an instrument telling the time of *day* by means of the *sun*, came to be called a *sun-dial*.

The movement of the stake's shadow described a curve. It did not take man long to realize that, for practical purposes, this curve could be divided into various parts. To identify these, the obvious thing to do was to allot them numbers. Each section was called an *hour*, which is a Greek word meaning "the time of day". Thus we owe our hours to man's earliest clock and the Greek people.

Another important question still had to be settled — the number of segments most suitable for the division of time. Immediately, the figure 12 had suggested itself to the Babylonians for both religious and practical reasons; to them, it was a mystical number. Also, they found it most convenient to use it as it could be divided evenly by 2, 3, 4 or 6. That is how the twelve-hour day started.

Sundials were very useful. Yet they had obvious disadvantages. They worked only when the sun was shining but in the dark or on a cloudy day the hours vanished. Furthermore, the speed of the travelling shadow was most irregular and hence the length of the hours varied. Some hours were short and others long, according to the season of the year and the sundial's geographical location.

What man needed was a time-piece to make him independent of the sun and assure the division of time into regular hours. The Egyptians led the way in achieving that aim. They did so by inventing the water-clock. In its simplest form, it consisted of a pot with a hole in the bottom. As it always took the same time to empty the vessel, people could easily tell the hour of day and night by merely watching the water's level in the bowl.

From Egypt, the new clock spread all over the Mediterranean world. In the course of time man learned to improve its design. A floater was put on the water, now gathered in a vessel beneath, and linked to a gear which moved a pointer that turned in a circle. Behind this "hand" was placed a dial marked off all around and at regular intervals with the old sundial's figures from 1 to 12. The face of the modern clock had made its appearance.

Yet water-clocks, just like their predecessor, the sundial, still suffered from a disadvantage: they depended on the elements of nature. In a cold climate they were apt to freeze in winter and, once again, time stood still!

Further progress was made in the search for a more reliable time-recorder by the invention of the hour glass about the year 250 B.C.. This replaced water by pure, dry sand. The quantity passing through a narrow neck between two bulbs determined the time.

Opinions differ as to where, and for which purpose, the sand-clock was first devised. Some say that it originated on sailing ships. Others assert that the Roman army first introduced it to measure "watches" in the night. A monk at Chatres, skilled in glass-blowing, is credited with having created its final shape in the 8th century A.D..

The sand-clock was retained for thousands of years and served man in diverse ways. It timed his tournaments in the Middle Ages, helped housewives in boiling their eggs and congregations in restricting the time of their parson's sermon. They placed an hour glass conspicuously on the pulpit.

But again, even sand had its drawbacks. Its enemy was damp weather, in which it either got stuck or flowed so slowly that time began to drag.

Where water and sand failed, the burning of a light (or, as among the Chinese, of incense) succeeded. Thus, a burning candle was used as yet another way of measuring time. The candle became shorter at a steady rate. All that was necessary was to mark the taper, before it was lit, according to the passing of hours. It was a simple and effective (yet more expensive) way of telling the time.

Thus through the early history of man the sundial, water-clock, hour glass and burning candle either displaced or supplemented each other. However, all of them were crude devices of poor accuracy which gave only a very rough estimate of the passage of time. There was still much room for improvement. Yet it was not until the Middle Ages that further advance was made and the first mechanical clock designed.

This applied the principle of the water-clock, but instead of using water to move the hand it employed weights. The invention of the pendulum, the escapement and the spring completed the development of the clock which had extended over almost 5000 years.

THE NAMING OF THE CLOCK

We owe the name of the clock to religious practice.

Experience has shown that the progress of mechanization alienates man ever more from his God. But not so in the case of the clock. It is now believed that the earliest mechanized time-keepers were invented specifically to help people in saying their prayers.

Once, prayers belonged to everyday life and were a regular habit. It was not left to the individual to worship whenever the spirit moved him which, after all, might never be. A ritual had to take place at the appropriate hour and a service had to be held at the right moment. That applied especially to those who had dedicated their lives to God — monks and nuns.

How could they know that the hour had come for devotion, particularly after nightfall? A clock that struck the hour was the answer. Thus the chiming of bells became part of the first mechanical clocks. The discipline of monastic orders and not necessities of civil life brought the modern striking-clock into being. Actually, the earliest models indicated the time not visually, but audibly, by means of bells.

The French word for bell is *cloche*. That is how, from the regulated and properly chimed hours of worship, and through the French tongue, we received the name for our clock.

THE WATCH

Not faith in God but suspicion of men was responsible for the naming of the watch. This was first used in 1588 to describe a timepiece sufficiently small to be carried in the pocket.

To prevent crime and catch criminals, guards were appointed. It was their duty to patrol the streets and keep *watch*. These early policemen followed their "beat" rather haphazardly, both as to where they went and the time they took. After all, they could not know the exact hour of the day or night.

Then the invention of the drive-spring revolutionized not only the working but the size of the clock. No longer weighted, it could now be carried. Its new small dimensions had changed it into a portable time-piece. The first still rather clumsy, iron-cased pocket clocks began to appear everywhere. They were just what the guards needed to keep a definite schedule in their watching. Soon they prided themselves on owning the new device.

People naturally took due notice and it did not take them long to associate, in every sense of the *word*, their *watch*men with the portable clocks they carried. Eventually, the small pocket clocks became completely identified with the men of the watch!

CHAPTER XXV

ReLIGION and Its symbols

MANY RELIGIOUS customs have become part of our everyday life and we follow them automatically, not stopping to inquire about their purpose and meaning.

Our mothers may have taught us in childhood to join hands at prayer. People kneel in worship. The sound of church bells has long been synonymous with the call to Christian service. The halo seems to belong from the beginning to Christian saints and only to them.

But why, how and where did these and other religious traditions start? Opinions differ and have caused much dissension.

As if to echo the great controversies aroused in the name of religion, even the very word has been subject to arguments and disagreements. Its linguistic root, of course, is Latin. But there is no conformity on the word's meaning.

Some link *religion* with the ancient description of taboo, a bond and restraint of a non-material kind. *Relegere* meant "to treat with care" and represented the opposite of neglect. In that sense, religion would suggest awe and fear, respect for the sacred and the punctilious performance of rites.

Others felt that the verb *lego* was responsible for the word. This signified "to pick" or "gather together", and as *relego*, "to read again". So explained, religion would refer to the close observation of omens and portents which, by being put together and read again, assisted man in his search for their right interpretation.

A further suggestion saw in the word a combination of *re* (back) and *ligare* (to bind) and consequently found in religion something that bound man up with his gods, the forging of a link between the terrestrial and celestial.

An inquiry into the beginning of religious customs reveals yet another bond. It shows how almost all of them, in some way or other, are shared among most varied faiths and are tied up with ancient, and sometimes primitive, beliefs.

THE "DOG-COLLAR"

The clergyman's badge of office — his collar worn back to front — is of comparatively recent origin and far from being ecclesiastical. To wear it is really contrary to the early wishes of Church authorities, who were strongly opposed to a priest putting on any distinctive kind of dress. Indeed, Pope Celestinus, in 428 A.D., reprimanded those bishops who dared to wear a costume that distinguished them from other people. This was considered a denial of the original democratic and non-professional character of Christianity.

When, despite these views and directions, priests eventually appeared dressed differently from the laity, their clothes were not a new ecclesiastical type of uniform. On the contrary, they were a continuation of a pagan mode of attire! It did not originate in biblical teachings or traditions but in old Roman custom.

When in the 6th century fashions changed and people abandoned the traditional Roman kind of apparel, the clergy, conservative in all things, did not follow suit. They refused to adopt the "modern" garment and continued to use the now outmoded dress.

Whilst laymen got used to putting on the new short tunics, trousers and cloaks, priests persisted in wearing the Roman toga and long type of tunic, still surviving today in the surplice, cassock and frock. Indeed, Pope Gregory the Great, determined to obstruct any change, decried the new fashion as barbarian and decreed retention of the Roman garb by his priests.

It was only in the 9th century that Christian authorities tried to add to this Roman way of secular dress some likeness to the ancient priestly vestments, worn by the Aaronites in King Solomon's Temple.

The clerical collar itself is a development, or more accurately a relic, of that part of medieval "priestly" garb which was known as the Amice. This was a square of white linen worn in the 11th century by priests celebrating Mass. Tied both at back and front with a series of strings, it formed a triangular type of scarf. This was modified in Tudor times to become a white neck cloth with long tag ends which, eventually, were dropped.

The original purpose of this "dog-collar" had no religious association but was most utilitarian. It was a sort of scarf (worn already by Roman public orators) to protect the throat and neck of speakers against cold and a very practical way of preventing the rest of the garment from being stained by perspiration.

The cloth is attached to a white collar. This is merely the old white neck band which was worn by everybody from the 16th century onward until the introduction of our modern collar late last century.

JOINING OF HANDS AT PRAYER

From the earliest times, men have accompanied their spoken prayer with gestures and postures. Most common, and first in Hebrew and Christian worship, was the spreading of arms and hands towards heaven. Later on, this custom was reduced to the hands being folded or crossed on the breast, one wrist resting on the other.

The joining of hands, as we know it now, was then unknown. It is not mentioned anywhere in the Bible and did not appear in the Christian Church before the 9th century. Its origin is divorced from religion and far from peaceful. It leads back to men's early desire to subjugate each other and developed out of the shackling of hands of prisoners!

Though the handcuffs eventually disappeared, the joining of hands remained as a symbol of man's servitude and submission and his inability (or even lack of inclination) to grasp a weapon. Many examples are at hand to show how the custom — long before being accepted in Christian circles — had become a standard gesture. Indeed, it was used as the real or imaginary shackling among pagan people. Tacitus relates, for instance, how a German tribe, the Semnones, venerated a sacred wood "into which none penetrated without being bound as a sign of dependence and as a public homage to the power of the gods". Greeks and Romans adopted the identical gesture as a magic means to bind the Devil and other occult powers and thereby to compel their obedience. Feudal lords finally adopted the joining of hands for their vassals, who thus had to swear and indicate their loyalty.

It was from those various sources that Christianity took over the gesture representing shackled hands as a sign of man's total obedience to divine power. It has also been suggested that there was Indian influence at work, as Hindus for many centuries prior used to join hands at prayer. All other explanations are of a later date.

Prayer to be perfect demands complete relaxation, one's being at ease and at rest. To attain this mood, the body has to be comfortable and motionless. To keep thus the hands together avoided any fidgeting and assured a natural position of repose. Man with his hands joined sloughed off the turmoil of daily life and was able to look inward with all the force of his spirit.

It is a well known fact that our instincts, without us even realizing it, help us to attain certain goals. The pressing together of hands or the clenching of our fingers into a fist somehow generates in the body additional electric potentials and impulses. It may be that by joining hands forcefully or clasping the fingers we add considerably to the store of spiritual power as well and make prayers all the more potent and effective.

The study of comparative religion suggests yet another possible origin of the gesture. Idol-worshippers were accustomed to stretch out their arms and point with their fingers to the objects whose help they wished to invoke — toward the sea, the sun or the statue of one of their gods. Sometimes they even went so far as to touch and to stroke the idol. It is possible that as a reaction and protest against these pagan habits, Christians made sure of avoiding any pointing by joining their hands in the shape of what has later been interpreted as that of a church steeple.

A final psychological observation may be added. The mere fact that the early Christian custom to spread the arms far and wide has been replaced by the humble and inconspicuous gesture of joining the hands is indicative of the secularization of life. Once religion was a powerful force, proudly displayed with the passion of men who wished that their faith should embrace the world. Now it has become much less demonstrative, almost meek and mild, and its retiring posture seems almost apologetic.

KNEELING

Kneeling is a most ancient custom and well attested in Holy Scripture. King Solomon knelt when dedicating the Temple and Daniel went down on his knees in worship three times every day to give thanks to God. Jesus knelt in prayer on the Mount of Olives at the fateful hour preceding His arrest. To St. Paul kneeling and prayer were synonymous. In Hebrew the term for praise is rooted in the word "knee".

Kneeling is even more characteristic of Mohammedan worship. This is accompanied by much genuflecting, a fact responsible for the very name of the Moslem sanctuary: *Mosque* meaning a place of "kneeling".

The custom itself stems from the Orient and Greeks decried it as such. It expressed a man's total submission to a higher power. In essence, kneeling itself is a survival and a small part of the complete prostration of one's body on the ground, of a vanquished foe before his conqueror, a vassal in front of his lord and a subject before his king.

Originally this was not merely a symbolic gesture, but a humbling position in which a man was helpless and could not commit any aggression.

That religion adopted this posture was due to several reasons. God was the King of Kings, who demanded complete submission. In homage to Him and in self-abasement, man bent his knee and threw himself down. Like an offering, he presented himself to God. That is why St. Paul in his Letter to the Romans could say: "I beseech you that you present your bodies a living sacrifice, holy, acceptable unto God . . ."

But religions also realized the close relationship between outward attitude and inward feeling. Kneeling thus not only symbolized but fostered a mood of humility, so essential for prayer. It was further felt that man's whole being had to participate in it: not only his mind but his body as well.

THE ROSARY

According to traditional belief it was 12th century St. Dominic who instituted the devotion of the rosary. He was "admonished by the Blessed Virgin" to preach it "as a special remedy against heresy and sin". In fact, however, rosaries were in existence — even in Christianity — long before then. St. Dominic merely extended and popularized the custom which in reality originated in Asia and is very ancient.

Hindus and Buddhists made use of it centuries before Catholicism. The oldest reference to a rosary has been traced to India, where it was used by Hindu monks. When Marco Polo visited the king of Malabar, he was surprised to watch the monarch worshipping with a rosary of more than 100 precious stones.

Some authorities claim that the Crusaders brought the custom to Europe, having adopted it in the East from the Mohammedans. Nevertheless, examples of rosaries of one kind or another were known in Western Europe before then. Thus it is said that Lady Godiva of Coventry, who died before 1070, bequeathed to the monastery she established "a circlet of gems which she had threaded on a string, in order that by fingering them one by one, as she successively recited her prayers, she might not fall short of the exact number".

The rosary was a simple device to keep count of prayers — an aid to memory. Appropriately, it was referred to in Sanskrit as "the muttering chaplet" or "the remembrancer" and, early in Europe, as "calculi" and "numeralia".

Devotion demands complete concentration. For the mind to wander, even for a moment, because of having to think of other things, would interrupt man's communion with God. According to ancient tradition, frequent repetition of prayers and their multiplication added to their efficacy. In the early days of the Church it was a well-known practice to recite privately all of the 150 Psalms and to repeat the Lord's Prayer 50 times. Centuries later, Knights Templar who could not attend choir, had to say the Lord's Prayer 57 times and, on the death of any of their brethren, were required to recite it 100 times daily for a week.

The absence of prayer books made it most difficult to keep count of the many and varied petitions and Psalms the devout had to or wished to recite. To count and pray at the same time, even by using the fingers, was practically impossible. Mechanical help was needed. At first, most simple means were employed, such as discs of bone, fruit stones, berries, pebbles and knots in a cord.

When, for instance, in the 4th century, Paul the Hermit imposed on himself the task of repeating daily 300 prayers, he collected an equal number of pebbles and threw them away, singly, at the end of each prayer. Monks of the Greek Church used cords with 100 knots to count their numerous genuflections and signs of the cross.

A bead simply means a prayer. The word is derived from the Anglo-Saxon *bede,* also retained in the German *Gebet.* Hence people "said their beads". Lest they omitted any, they tied knots in a string — one knot for each prayer. Eventually, they began to call each knot a prayer, that is, a bead. But to identify part of a string with a petition to God seemed unworthy. The crude knots were therefore discarded and replaced with precious stones and sometimes even with little balls of gold. As these remained the symbol of prayer, they continued to be known as beads. The modern woman does not realize that her necklace of beads goes back to the worship of the Desert Fathers and recalls not precious ornamentation but fervent prayer, even in its literal sense.

There was another, psychological function of the rosary which is not always realized. People found it helpful to let their hands play with an object while their mind concentrated on an image or an idea. Somehow the activity, carried on almost unawares, intensified the thought-process. Hugo von Hofmansthal, who wrote several librettos for Richard Strauss, kept in his desk a small box of coloured glass balls. He was convinced that fingering them fired his imagination.

The beads of the rosary, then, helped the worshipper in his meditation. To let smooth round objects slide through his fingers released tension and soothed the mind. It increased his spiritual power and added to his creative spirit, in which the soul laid itself open to the divine.

To ascetics and mystics in quest of union with God, the counting of beads not only symbolized but promoted progress towards the supernatural realm. They believed that as each bead passed through the hand, they reached nearer to God. Thus, Indian Sikhs could pray: "Thou art the string, Thou art the beads of the rosary, Thou art its knots, Thou art its chief bead, Thou art God."

The word rosary means "a garland" or "a wreath of roses". The term itself probably did not appear till the 15th century. Its origin has been explained by simple facts, symbolism and a legend.

Early on, so it is said, the beads were carved out of rosewood, and it was the choice of this material that was responsible for the name. Others have suggested *rosaire,* French for bead, as the linguistic root. As there were so many beads strung together, people began to call the mechanical aid to prayer simply "the beads", using the Latinized form of the French word.

The rose was a symbol of beauty and perfection. Thus, early and medieval Christians chose it as the emblem for the Virgin Mary — the rose of womanhood. Since, according to tradition, she herself handed the first chain of beads to St. Dominic, this has been called ever since by one of her titles, the *rosa* mystica.

At some time its individual beads were marked with her emblem, the rose, and that is how, it is further claimed, the rosary really received its name.

An early legend, known all over Europe, relates its origin and description to a vision. In it the Virgin Mary was seen watching a young monk at prayer. While he was uttering repeated Hail Marys with deep emotion, the Virgin appeared to gather rosebuds from his lips, one for each salutation. These she wove into a garland, which she put on her head. It was the first "rosary".

The "complete rosary" of Catholicism, consisting of 150 beads, goes back to the ancient Desert Fathers and their recital of 150 Psalms of Hebrew Scripture. The purpose of the Mohammedan "string of prayer" is mainly to help Moslems in the uttering of Allah's 99 names because, according to their tradition, "whoever recites them (in their full number) shall enter into Paradise". Accordingly, an equal number of beads is counted, with an added terminal one called *Imam,* the Leader. The beads are of aloes or other odoriferous and precious wood, seeds or corals.

During the Middle Ages praying-strings frequently served especially for the repeated recital of the Lord's Prayer and thus came to be known also as Paternosters, the prayer's first two words in Latin, "Our Father".

Manufacturers of the praying-strings were called Paternosterers. They comprised a recognized craft-guild of considerable importance and their concentration in one London street is said to have given it its name — Paternoster Row. It is still in existence.

FISH ON FRIDAY

Paganism considered Friday the luckiest day of the week. It was ruled by the planet Venus, whose influence was thought to be most fortunate. Named in honour of Freya, goddess of Love, it was a day most propitious for marriage.

But in Christian lands Friday has always had a gloomy association, brought about by traditions of both the Old and the New Testaments. It was on a Friday that Adam and Eve were said to have eaten of the forbidden fruit, thus bringing sin into the world. And on a Friday they died. Jesus suffered and was crucified on a Friday. Hence, every Friday became a memorial of Good Friday, as every Sunday was a little Easter.

That is how it was thought to be unprofitable, even inviting disaster, to start a new task or journey on a Friday. For centuries sailors refused to leave port on that ominous day and even at the beginning of this century statistics showed that in France bus takings were lowest and train travellers fewest on Fridays.

The story is told that when the reluctance of seamen to sail on a Friday had reached such proportions that it interfered with naval operations, the British Admiralty decided to prove once and for all the fallacy of the belief. The keel of a new vessel was laid on a Friday, she was launched on a Friday, and she was named H.M.S. Friday. On her first voyage, beginning on a Friday, she was commanded by Captain James Friday. Everything had gone according to plan up to that moment. The ship sailed. Nothing has since been heard of her or her crew. That the identical story has found its place also in American lore speaks for itself.

It was in memory of the Crucifixion that Catholicism made Friday a fast day, which is explained as "an act of penitence and physical mortification imposed by the Church for the health of souls".

It is obligatory for all over the age of seven. Nevertheless, in certain circumstances, absolution may be obtained. However, there is no passage in the New Testament that commands a fast. In fact, St. Paul, in I Timothy IV, 3, alludes to the abstention from meats as a mark of apostasy and a sign of weak faith in that it attaches importance to such comparatively trifling matters. The Kingdom of God, he said, was not meat and drink, but righteousness, peace and joy in the Holy Spirit.

The idea of a fast has been understood differently by various faiths. Jews fast for 24 hours on their Day of Atonement, the only fast day expressly ordained in the Old Testament. During that period they do not eat, drink or smoke.

Moslems keep a whole month — Ramadan — as a fast. They are not even allowed to swallow their own spittle or enjoy the fragrance of perfume. However, they observe the fast only during daylight and partake of food during the night.

There are various reasons why Catholics consider a meatless day as a fast. Some of them are completely divorced from religious considerations.

It was a Jewish tradition to abstain from meat on days of sorrow and as a sign of penitence. Thus Daniel (X, 2.3) refrained from all pleasant food for three weeks: "I ate no . . . bread neither came flesh . . . in my mouth." Ever since the destruction of the second Temple in 70 A.D., pious men refused to eat meat at any time because they felt that, as there was no longer an altar on which animals could be offered to God, no man should enjoy their flesh. Abstention from meat was to them a symbol of grief and a constant reminder of the tragedy that had befallen their people.

It was not difficult for Christianity to adopt this tradition, reserving it for one day a week only and linking it with the tragic death of Christ instead of with the burning of the Temple.

There is a possibility that the custom of eating fish on a Friday and during Lent entered the Christian faith not from Jewish sources alone, but from the pagan world as well, and that it was entirely independent of ascetic motives or ideas. Greek philosophers believed that a vegetarian diet was helpful to their faculties and contributed to clarity of thought.

It might well be that eating fish on Friday also continued an old pagan practice. Fish was said to be sacred to Aphrodite, the foam-born goddess of beauty and fertility, who was also worshipped as the goddess of the sea. The Romans identified her with Venus, to whom they dedicated Friday. It was in her honour that fish was then eaten, most probably in the belief that it promoted fruitfulness.

To refrain from eating meat expressed grief and reverence to Christ. His passion and death were thus remembered one day every week, not merely in one's thoughts but in one's very way of life.

In ancient days it was believed that the eating of meat stimulated man's passions. Hence, a meatless diet made chastity easier. To conquer his fleshly lusts and enable him to concentrate on spiritual exercises, abstention from meat appeared as a most helpful means.

In much later years, political and economic reasons reinforced the peculiar kind of fast on Friday. These were purely mundane — to restrict the eating of meat and foster consumption of fish. This achieved several aims. A fish diet once a week was cheap and aided the poor without making them feel inferior. It helped to protect a valuable breed of cattle and controlled the meat price, keeping it at a moderate level.

On the other hand, it ensured an increase in the sale of fish, thus boosting the fishing trade, the building of boats and the number of men going to sea. All these factors, it was realized, combined to further the strength of the British navy.

It was with those thoughts in mind, and "not to put holiness in one kind of meat and drink more than another", that in 1548, the second year of the reign of King Edward VI, an Act of Parliament ordered abstention from meat on the fast day and that, similarly, during the Elizabethan era, a proclamation commanded the keeping of "fish days".

THE COMMUNION SERVICE

The Holy Communion service, with its bread and wine, began within the Synagogue. It is derived from the ancient Hebrew custom of offering special thanks to God at the beginning of every Sabbath and festival, which was always on their eve. The head of the family praised God at the festive table, before the actual meal. He did so over wine and bread, which symbolized the bounty of the vineyard and the field. All present partook of the bread he broke and the cup of wine he blessed.

According to the Synoptic Gospels Jesus's "Last Supper", His final meal on the night before the Crucifixion, took place on the eve of the Jewish Passover and was, therefore, the traditional Passover celebration. This was held in every home all over Jerusalem and the Holy Land. Its ritual included the blessing of wine and bread. But instead of ordinary loaves, unleavened bread (known as *Matsah*) was broken, in memory of the Israelites' affliction and their exodus from Egypt.

As a Jew, Jesus followed meticulously the ancient practice of breaking the bread and blessing the wine and then sharing both with His 12 disciples. But while doing so, the Gospel account relates, He referred mysteriously to the bread as His body and the wine as His blood.

Tremendous conflicts were joined over these words and their interpretation. Their very brevity and obscurity laid them open to various explanations. Critical scholars were reminded of pagan sacramental rites in which, by means of a joint participation of sacred food, the eaters were knit to the god and to one another. Did Jesus intend, it was asked, to introduce similarly a mystical and sacramental idea into the Jewish practice, linking it with His forthcoming sacrificial death?

Or, conscious of the forgetfulness of man, was He concerned about giving His disciples and those who followed them some way of remembering Him and of holding them together when He had gone? An association of thought could serve as the best reminder. The substance of bread would suggest to them His body and the red colour of wine would bring to mind His blood.

No matter what Jesus really meant when He uttered the words, the fact is that the Eucharist, which became a central act of Christian worship, is the perpetuation of Christ's last Passover supper and of the Jewish practice of thanking God by breaking bread and blessing wine, still carried on in every Jewish home.

Indeed, its Jewish tradition survives in the very name of Holy Communion, the Eucharist, meaning "to give thanks". The term itself is not found in the New Testament and stems from the Greek. That the thin wafer, used as the Host, must be unleavened equally recalls its Hebrew origin: the unleavened bread of the Jewish Passover feast.

COVERING OF HEAD IN SYNAGOGUE

For a man to cover his head in a synagogue and generally at prayer is now accepted as a Jewish religious custom. It is followed throughout the world, except by Reform congregations in the United States and Britain. Anyone entering a synagogue, Jew and Gentile alike, is expected to keep his hat on, or, if without one, to use a skull cap.

The fact that Christian Church dignitaries, including the Pope, wear the same type of skull cap, and that Moslem worshippers also cover their heads, shows not only the ubiquity of the custom but how it has spread from Judaism to its daughter religions.

In its origin, the covering of the head had no religious implication. The earliest Hebrews did not know the practice, and it is not mentioned anywhere in the Old Testament. The custom entered Judaism at a later date from the outside world and possibly, first of all, for health reasons.

People in the East suffered from the frequent and considerable changes of temperature and felt the need to protect the head. Long before the establishment of the first synagogues, the Hebrews prayed in the open. In the Temple of old, the altar on which the sacrifices were offered stood in a courtyard and those participating in the ceremonial were exposed to the sun. To cover the head, for that reason as well, became a wise precaution.

The original, practical purpose was soon forgotten. The custom became a gesture of humility and submission. Bareheadedness, on the other hand, was considered obscene and a demonstration of defiance. Thus, pious mourners put ashes on their heads. By that act they tried to proclaim visually their resignation to God's inscrutable will. Eventually, anyone standing before his God began to cover his head.

At first, only the priestly class were appointed to serve God. They did this on behalf of the people and mainly by the sacrificial cult. They were distinguished by their head-dress, the High Priest wearing a mitre, a cloth of fine linen, coiled around his head like a turban. But after the Romans had destroyed the Temple in 70 A.D., the offering of sacrifices became impossible. Consequently, the chief office of priesthood lost its justification and ceased to exist.

Prayer came to take the place of animal sacrifice, and the whole of the Jewish people took over the task of the ancient priesthood. At long last they were able to fulfil the biblical injunction that not just a selected class but all the Israelites should be "a kingdom of priests and a holy people". To indicate their assumption of priestly duties, they adopted the custom of covering the head, formerly reserved for the High Priest and the ministering clergy.

While Western man raises his hat as a courtesy, Eastern tradition demanded the opposite. When entering a home, you had to take off your shoes, but keep your head covered. A host, similarly, did not dare appear before his guests bareheaded, as that would be considered a breach of good manners. Eventually, the hat, or whatever took its place, acquired an almost sacred significance.

Western man swears by his Bible, the Arab by his headcover. By a natural process of assimilation, the Jews of the Orient adopted the custom of their environment, probably first in Babylonia, and covered their heads as a general symbol of deference and a simple act of civility.

But, if you covered your head to pay respect to your fellow man, was it not more essential to do so when standing before your God and addressing Him? That is how the custom became part of synagogue worship. When the Jews migrated to Western lands, they continued to cover their heads, carrying with them the Eastern style though, in their new homes with their different code of etiquette, its original purpose had lost its meaning. They were no longer aware of its roots and it was given new interpretations and considered as a hallowed tradition. It had become one of the most striking, yet least significant, features of Jewish worship!

CHURCH BELLS

Church bells were unknown to Christians for at least the first five centuries — and for obvious reasons. Christianity at first was declared illegal by pagan authorities and its worship was punished. The devout had to gather clandestinely, in the catacombs and at night.

When Christianity became a recognized faith, it was even then a blast of trumpets and not a peal of bells that summoned the faithful to worship. Bells came into general use in the church after the 8th century only.

Bells developed out of small pieces of concave metal. That is why the word bell is derived from the Latin term for a foot-pan or basin. The original purpose of all bells was to make a loud, but not necessarily musical, sound to drive off evil spirits. It was for this reason that they were first introduced everywhere and could be found in Hindu temples, the Hebrew sanctuary and Christian churches. Still in the year 1280 A.D. a theological work dealing with the Christian ritual records that "bells are rung in processions that demons may fear and flee. For when they hear the trumpets of the Church militant, that is the bells, they are afraid."

And this first and most important function of bells survived for centuries in many customs. The "passing bell", tolled at funerals, for instance, is known today as the herald of death and draws attention to the fact that a soul is "passing" from this world to the next and asks for our prayers on its behalf. Originally, however, its sound was meant to drive away evil spirits hovering around the dying man, ready to pounce on his soul.

Bells, likewise, were struck at times of sickness and natural disaster. Both were ascribed to the presence of fiends which only loud noise could scare away. That is why a blessing of church bells, suggested by Egbert, the Archbishop of York in the 8th century and included in his Pontifical, read: "Wherever this bell sounds, let the power of enemies retreat, so also the shadow of phantoms, the assault of whirlwinds, the stroke of lightning, the harm of thunders . . . and every spirit of the storm winds." In modern times, French Church authorities have had the bells rung to ward off the effect of lightning, and in 1852 the Bishop of Malta ordered the tolling of bells to "lay a gale of wind".

Roger Bacon, often quoted as the inventor of gun-powder, recorded the prevalent belief of the demon-chasing quality of the sound of bells, saying that "the great ringing of bells in popular cities charmed away thunder and also dissipated pestilential air". Being however of a scientific bend of mind. he tried to rationalize the ancient superstition. He claimed that it was not really the sound of the bells but the concussion of air, caused by their tolling, which purified the atmosphere, driving away pestilence and turbulence.

It was firmly believed that the bigger the bell and the louder its sound, the farther the spirits were compelled to flee. Thus ever bigger church bells were used to guard God's sanctuaries and to keep them unsullied and at peace.

The tolling of bells as a call to prayer is a comparatively late development. Many other functions of bells have been added down the centuries. They make up a colourful list and have been subject to fascinating and sometimes even amusing interpretations.

In pre-Reformation days "church-going bells" were rung, not to make people leave their homes right away but as an invitation to a preparatory prayer there that would put them in the right frame of mind for divine service. Later on, bells were sounded not so much as a call for spiritual preparation but as a reminder that people should get ready and dress for service, due to commence only an hour later.

On the other hand, it was also a custom at one time to ring bells at the conclusion of the sermon or end of the service. This has been variously explained. Some said that it was a procedure introduced to announce to those who had stayed away from worship that another sermon was to be preached, or service to be held, that same night which gave them a chance to make up for their lost opportunity. But then it was also interpreted as of special (and non-spiritual) benefit to the clergy, who were said to like a hot Sunday dinner. It was to warn their cooks that the priest was about to leave church and that they had to hurry to be ready with the meal. Hence this particular tolling came to be known as "the pudding bell".

In Westmorland bells were chimed during the service, immediately after the recitation of the Creed. This was done so that dissenters should know that now they could join the congregation in worship — without any qualms of conscience.

At St. Michael's in York, bells were rung every morning at 6 o'clock. This was the result of an early incident, when people wandering in the nearby forest got lost and spent a terrifying night in the wood. They discovered their whereabouts only next morning, when they heard the chiming of the bells of St. Michael's. Out of gratitude and to help any future lost travellers, they endowed a fund which provided for the tolling of bells as a "homing beacon" at the same hour each day.

THE HALO

The halo is pagan, practical, and completely un-Christian in origin.

Centuries before Christ, natives used to ornament their heads with a circle of feathers. They did so to symbolize their relationship with the sun-god: their own "halo" of feathers representing the circle of light that distinguished the shining divinity in the sky. Indeed, people came to believe that by adopting such a "nimbus" men turned into a kind of sun themselves and into a divine being.

The circle of light eventually lost its obvious link with the sun and became symbolic of any god and not only of that identified with the solar body. Soon it expressed the essence of divine power generally.

That is how, in painting and sculpture, Greek and Roman deities were represented with a halo and in Indian art Buddha, too, was shown with the celestial aura of light surrounding his head.

The development did not end there. When Roman emperors began to imagine themselves as divine beings, they often appeared in public with a crown, which was meant to imitate the orb of light of the sun. It was a foregone conclusion that artists, when creating the emperor's image, likewise would surmount his head with the celestial ornamentation.

The practice of placing a shield behind the head of a victorious emperor on his triumphal procession was a further contributory cause in the creation of the halo. In the minds of the people it became a distinguishing mark of power and glory.

And yet, perhaps more than anything else, utilitarian considerations were responsible for the general introduction of that peculiar kind of disc. Statues were kept not in museums but in the open. Therefore they were subject to deterioration through various causes. To protect them from the droppings of birds, the rain and the snow, a circular plate — either of wood or brass — was fixed upon their heads!

Thus pagan worship of the sun and artistic concern for the preservation of objects of art combined in the creation of the halo. It is a fact that the early Christian Church, well aware of the original pagan association, at first carefully avoided the use of the halo altogether. And when finally — and only in the 6th century — ecclesiastical authorities adopted it, they did so, first of all, not in its interpretation as a spiritual symbol but merely for its usefulness as a kind of umbrella.

In the Middle Ages the round halo was used only for angels and saints. When attached to Christ, it had to bear in addition a cross or the monogram of *Alpha* and *Omega*. Modern Catholic regulation permits a halo only for persons who have been canonized or beatified, or whose worship has otherwise been authorized by the Church.

Just as the halo's sacred significance is of a late date, so even its very name, now descriptive of celestial glory, once was most earthbound. Literally the halo was born on the threshing floor of the old Greeks!

Many centuries before Christ, they used, as was only to be expected, very primitive methods in threshing their grain. They heaped the sheaves of corn they had gathered on hard but level ground, over which they drove round and round a team of oxen. Their numerous circuits eventually created a round track, and it was this which the Greeks called a "halo"! In the 16th century astronomers resurrected the word, applying it to the luminous orb around celestial bodies. And it was hence, quite appropriately, that theologians adopted it for the crowning of the heads of their saints!

Such is the most unexpected and fantastic story of the halo. In its simple shape it combines traditions of Greek farming, the Roman deification of megalomaniac rulers, medieval astronomy and an early protective measure against dirt and inclement weather.

THE CROSS

There is a language of symbols. More eloquent than words, they can rouse the human spirit and revolutionize life and society. That is why modern political movements have used such symbols as the clenched fist, crooked cross and bundle of rods.

Thousands of years earlier, each of the three world religions, Judaism, Christianity and Islam, knew of the symbol's dynamic power. They realized that a picture could talk louder than words and its impact outlast them. Therefore they chose the Star, the Cross and the Crescent to represent their beliefs, spread their faith and conquer the hearts and minds of men wherever they might be and no matter what their station.

The cross is one of the world's oldest and most universal symbols. Many centuries *before* the Christian era it was a common pagan emblem and it has been found as such, carved in stone, in remote ages.

The reason for its choice was that it was one of the simplest figures to draw, and expressive in its message. Its arms pointed upward, downward, and sideways. Therefore the cross became a sign of all-embracing space. The East was represented by its top, the North by its right limb, the South by its left branch and the West by its lower portion.

The arms of the cross came to represent the rays of the sun as well. The ancient Assyrians used it as a symbol of the sky and its god Anu, and from earliest times it symbolized solar power. Consequently, it became the sign of fire and of the suffering of existence, where eventually everything is burnt up. Indeed, it is quite likely that the arms of the cross developed out of the two kindling sticks with which primitive man produced fire.

The cross stood for the world axis — the bridge that linked heaven and earth; the ladder with which man could reach out towards God. It became the symbol of the joining of opposites, the linking of the left and the right.

Then, the cross was regarded also as showing the division of the world into four quarters whence rain came and the winds blew. Accordingly, it indicated the four cardinal points from which droughts and floods could bestow blessings or curses on man.

The similarity of the cross to a simple sword associated it also with a weapon wielded to kill all that was evil.

By pointing to the sources of warmth, storm and rain, the cross became a visible symbol of fertility. It assumed this role even more so as a wooden cross, easily constructed from two simple

branches, and was seen as the emblem of all that grew and prospered. It was the tree of life. Stuck into the earth in fertile soil,
an apparently dead and withered twig would start sprouting, as
is still experienced today in the case of the "living fences" on the
islands of the South Pacific. No wonder, therefore, that such
miraculous change from a dead branch into a living tree seemed
to represent the power of life over death. That is how, first of
all, the cross became a symbol of resurrection.

Legend relates that after Adam's death his son Seth planted
on his tomb a branch, taken from the tree of life of Paradise. The
slip grew into a tree. From it Moses obtained his magic rod and
Solomon essential timber for his shrine. Finally, so it is said,
Jesus's executioners cut from the tree the beams for the cross
on which they crucified Him at Calvary.

All the many and varied early meanings of the simple sign of
the cross gave it, in the minds of men, magical power. From a
belief that it indicated the sources of warmth, winds and rain,
people started believing that it actually controlled those vital
elements in the life of man and nature. Thus, eventually, a cross
was used as a magic wand with which to exorcise or ward off
evil spirits which harried man.

Numerous crosses were excavated at Troy. Thousands of years
ago the emblem was used there not as a decorative sign but as
a magical defence against the entry of Devils into the city and
its individual homes.

The sign of a "looped cross" was found equally frequently on
ancient Egyptian artifacts. Indeed, in this shape, that of a T with
a circle on its top, it became part of early hieroglyphic writing.

How this came about has been variously explained. Most probably, the sign represented the keys used for the canal locks which
regulated the flow of water. The key's picture was carved on the
canal walls because, so the Egyptians imagined, its presence
would magically control the volume of water and thus avoid
both floods and droughts. Then the symbolic key assumed the
importance of the very key of life which surmounted by a handle
— the loop — was used by the gods to awaken the dead to an
existence above.

Others recognized in the early occurrence of the cross on
Egyptian soil pictures of the phallus, the loincloth worn by men,

or a jar standing upon an altar. The message of these many inter-pretations is clear and identical. The cross was the symbol of the vital germ and key of life.

Methods of execution have differed from country to country and changed throughout history. Crucifixion was practised by Greeks and Romans. It was tainted with shame and reserved for the worst of offenders, especially those who were foreigners, and for slaves. The criminal was either nailed or bound on a wooden post, surmounted by a cross bar, and left there till he died.

When Jesus was condemned to death, it was this type of ignominious penalty which the Romans, as the occupying power of the Holy Land, chose for him. That is how the cross gained a new meaning throughout the world. It became the venerated symbol of Christ's resurrection and man's salvation.

However, few people realize that this cross, though now the most widespread symbol of the Christian religion, is certainly not the most ancient one. Christians adopted it as such only many years after Christ's death. Indeed, the crucifix, the cross with the body of Jesus nailed to it, was adopted as a religious emblem only in the 7th century after His death.

Most people think now of one type of cross only. Yet the Heraldic Encyclopaedia lists 385 different kinds. These vary in the direction of their limbs, form and extension. Best-known are:

★ The GREEK TAU CROSS — resembling the letter T.

★ The EQUILATERAL CROSS — also referred to as the "Greek Cross", of which each limb is of identical length, a vertical line being bisected by a horizontal one of equal dimension.

★ The LATIN CROSS — in which the lower branch is longer than the three others.

★ The LOOPED CROSS — which, like the Egyptian hiero-glyphic, is a T with a circle on its top and is also known as the "Handled Cross".

★ ST. ANDREW'S CROSS — in the form of a capital letter X, so called because St. Andrew, patron saint of Scotland, was martyred on a cross of that shape.

★ The MALTESE CROSS — formed of four triangles joined at their apex.

★ The SWASTIKA — or "Crooked Cross" — common in India,

representing the solar wheel turning darkness into light
and night into day.

THE FISH

The sign of the fish was the original Christian symbol. It preceded that of the cross by many years.

The first Christians, ostracized and persecuted by the Romans,
needed a badge for recognizing each other and proclaiming
their faith in Christ, the Redeemer of man. Their creed was then
still banned and to spread its message was considered high
treason. Where there was no time for words, a simple sign,
quickly drawn and easily identified, spoke for itself.

The choice of the fish was thus, first of all, the result of political
circumstances. It could be traced in no time. It immediately
caught the eye and its message could be understood at once.

From the earliest days of Christianity there was a close association, literally and figuratively, between the new faith and
sea creatures.

Christ's first disciples were fishermen and it was natural that
they should be described as fishers of men, spreading their nets
to gather in followers from the surging ocean of a pagan world.

The story of the miracle of the fish, how a few nourished
thousands of hungry men, was well known. Thus the fish was
expressive of a faith that worked wonders.

Finally, the fish was not only a picture but a word with a mystical meaning. In its Greek form, the language in which the New
Testament originally was written, it contained a summary of
Christian faith in the form of an acrostic. The Greek word for
fish, *ichthus,* spelt out the initial letters of the new revolutionary
creed, speaking (in its English rendition) of *Jesus Christ, the Son
of God, the Saviour of man.*

Thus the fish, both in its image and name, became the perfect
symbol of a new religion that challenged the world.

THE STAR OF DAVID

The Star of David is the Jewish emblem. It appears on synagogues in every country, forms the centre-piece of the Israeli
flag and surmounts the graves of fallen Jewish soldiers of all

nations. In Israel the "Red Cross" is represented by the "Red Star of David".

In the beginning, the six-pointed star (like the cross) was a pagan emblem. Undoubtedly its first use was magical. Primitive man employed it as a guard against dangers and hazards, to ward off or to control evil forces. Its first appearance belongs to the 7th century B.C..

From antiquity to even most modern times, people went on believing in its magical power. In the Middle Ages alchemists saw in the star a combination of their familiar triangular symbols of fire ($\triangle$) and water ($\triangledown$), which, thus fused ($\maltese$), were considered all-powerful.

Others saw in the symbol the footprint of the demon of the night. Its replica served alike to conjure up its evil spirit and to keep it at bay. Still today some people wear the star as a charm.

Jews adopted the symbol and made it their own for different reasons. They used it as a sign of the coming Messiah who, descending out of the Heavens, would redeem mankind. Did not the Bible itself (in the Book of Numbers) foretell the time when a star would come forth and bring freedom and salvation? And as it was always believed that the Messiah would come out of the House of David, people spoke of the "Star of David".

Actually, however, the literal meaning of the Hebrew term for the symbol refers not to a star at all but to a shield. It was this original meaning which led people to assume — erroneously — that King David himself, in his fight against Goliath, used a shield of the very shape which is now perpetuated as Jewry's symbol. Its construction was well-suited to protect both arms and head. The fact is, of course, that David did not use a shield but approached his adversary with only five smooth pebbles and a sling.

Another explanation dates the star's place among Jews back to the 6th century B.C., when Judaism fought a decisive spiritual battle against the dualist philosophy of Persian Zoroastrianism, which was then sweeping the world. This taught that not one God but two powers ruled the universe. They were Light and Darkness. Each one had its own symbol — a triangle with the apex pointing upward or downward. Man had to choose which one to serve. To proclaim the indivisible unity of God, who was

the creator of Light *and* Darkness, Jews combined the two
Persian signs into one indissoluble symbol — the Star of David.

Yet it may be that not a spiritual battle but an actual war was
responsible for the association of the hexagram, the technical
term for the star, with the Jewish people.

In the 2nd pre-Christian century, Greek forces confronted the
small Hebrew army. Uniforms were then unknown and the shield,
covering the soldier, prevented his being recognized as friend
or foe. Some kind of identification was needed.

It was natural that the shield should be marked on the outside
with a distinctive sign. If rightly chosen, this could serve as a
forceful symbol which, in addition to revealing the soldiers'
allegiance, was able to intimidate his adversary. Like a challenge, it could proclaim, in concise and dramatic form, the cause
for which the soldiers fought.

In the minds of the Jewish people there was no greater hero
than King David who, centuries earlier, had led the Israelites to
victory in their battles. Surely, his memory could save them once
again. To fight under his sign would assure victory.

Several problems presented themselves. The symbol was addressed not to the Jews, but to their foes who, in the heat of
battle, had to grasp its meaning quickly. The space of a shield
was limited. Conciseness was essential. How could David's name
be shortened in a way that contained both a definite message and
a memorable sign?

Each difficulty was overcome in turn. As Hebrew was unknown
to the enemy, his own language, Greek, was chosen. David's name
began and ended with the identical letter — *Delta* — which consisted of a triangle. Instead of the king's full name, a combination
of the two *Deltas* was used. To save further space, they were not
placed next to each other but interlocked. The result was the
Star of David which, embossed on the shields of the fighters, soon
came to be recognized as the Jews' symbol and has remained
such ever since.

In later years, other, more spiritual meanings were added to
the sign. Its symmetrical form was explained as a symbolic expression of the identity of the two worlds, the natural and supernatural. The star's six points were seen as representative of God's
universality; of the range of His powers to North, South, East,

West, Below and Above. The intertwined equilateral triangles were believed to join mystically the beginning of the world with present-day existence, the six points being the six days of the Creation.

The simple sign of the Star of David thus links ancient magical superstitions with memories of a spiritual battle, and recollections of a fight for survival with thoughts of the One God whose power extends to the ends of the earth.

THE CRESCENT MOON

Islam's symbol today is the Crescent Moon. It represents the moon in a state of increase and, therefore, points to a faith's growth from small beginnings until one day, so Mohammedans believe, it will fill the world "all round".

This sign of the youngest of world religions is not indigenously Mohammedan. Like the cross and the star, it goes back to most ancient and certainly pagan days.

People had always been puzzled and awed by what they saw in the sky. The waxing and waning of the moon indicated to primitive man the presence of a miraculous power that dwelt in the crescent — a germ of fertility.

Like the moon's sickle, its replica, whether drawn on cloth or shaped in metal, was thought to ensure an increase of all that man sought after most — first of his own fertility and that of his fields and cattle, and then of his wealth and power.

The figure of the crescent thus became not only a symbol of growth and prosperity, but also a magical means of attaining it. That is why ancient Egyptians and early Greeks decorated their gods with the emblem and Athenians of illustrious birth wore a crescent of ivory and silver. It was for the same reason that Romans chose it as their Empire's symbol, hoping that, magically, it would foster her might.

It is said that an event in 339 B.C. gave the Crescent Moon an additional significance in Asia Minor and hence in the Middle East. Philip, father of Alexander the Great, experienced great difficulty in his attempt to conquer Byzantium, the future Constantinople. Besieging the city, his forces were unable to scale its walls and he decided to enter the fortress through tunnels. At first all went well. But then, a crescent moon suddenly appeared and revealed to the Byzantian defenders men building tunnels. Byzantium was saved!

In gratitude for their deliverance, thanks to the new moon, the citizens adopted the crescent as their badge.

Another story links the choice of the symbol with Othman, the Sultan. He is said to have seen in a vision a crescent moon whose horns grew ever wider until they extended from the East to the Far West. He chose the crescent for his standard, believing that under its sign his rule, likewise, would spread to the ends of the earth.

When the Turks rose to power over the Byzantians, they took over the emblem of the convex figure of the waxing moon. And because the Turks adopted Mohammedanism, people soon forgot the original national meaning of the Crescent Moon and mistook it as the religious symbol of the faith of Islam.

THE CHRISTMAS TREE

Few people realize that many Christian customs have their root not in Christianity but in paganism. The fact that Christmas is observed on December 25th (though generally so only since the 4th century) is revealing. Probably this is not the birthday of Christ at all which, according to some early Christians, fell on May 20th. December 25th was chosen by the Church to counteract the Saturnalia, the pagan festival celebrated with revelry at this season of the winter solstice in honour of Saturn, god of vegetation and husbandry.

Each of the beautiful customs of Christmas has its own background. It is interesting to learn their story and to see how the genius of the human mind has been able, through the centuries, to give them a different and sacred meaning.

The Christmas tree is German and its adoption in English lands was due merely to the fact that Queen Victoria married a German prince. In Germany the tree cannot be traced beyond the 17th century. Its origin, however, goes back into the far-distant past — long before the birth of Christ.

It is a fact that the Christmas tree stems from primitive pagan customs. Its main features, green foliage and candles, were associated with the winter solstice when nature seemed dead, and green branches and trees were used in a magical rite to ensure the return of vegetation and the victory of light over darkness.

Later, the tree was seen as the direct descendant of the world tree of Norse mythology whose branches and roots joined together heaven, earth and hell. The tree became the symbol of enduring and renewed life and the green of its leaves the emblem of immortality.

Egyptians used palm branches with 12 shoots as a sacred expression of the completion of the year and of the triumph of life over death.

At the time of their Saturnalia the Romans decorated homes and temples with foliage on which they hung images of their gods! It was a season of good will toward all. Schools were closed. No battles could be fought. Punishment could not be inflicted on anyone and distinctions of rank and class were put aside. It was the carnival of antiquity when all joined in a mad pursuit of pleasure.

The Jews celebrated, at this very season, the Feast of Lights and for eight consecutive days kindled flames on an eight-branched candlestick in their homes.

Christianity knew of all these traditions. The Fathers of the Church realized the impossibility of abolishing them root and branch. Thus they wisely retained the ancient institution of the green tree and the burning lights but gave them a completely new interpretation. In justification, they quoted the prophet Isaiah who had spoken of the "righteous branch" and foreseen the day when "the glory of Lebanon shall come unto you: the fir tree, the pine tree, and the box tree, to beautify the place of My Sanctuary".

How the first modern Christmas tree came into being is told in numerous legends.

A Scandinavian story tells of the violent deaths of two lovers and a consequent occult occurrence. At the spot where the murder took place, a beautiful "service tree" grew out of the blood-soaked soil. On it, flaming lights miraculously appeared annually. These could be seen from far away and nothing could put them out.

Germans explain the introduction of the Christmas tree by an incident said to have taken place when Christianity was first brought to their country. When St. Boniface arrived from England to convert the pagans, he was determined to root out all that was heathen. In the city of Geismar he cut down a sacred oak. The felling, which took place on Christmas eve, angered many people and, to pacify them, St. Boniface gave the city a fir tree as a symbol of the new faith he preached.

Another German tale links the first Christmas tree with Martin Luther, the great Protestant reformer. The story says that one Christmas eve Luther was returning home through the snow. He was deeply moved by the beauty of the sky with its thousands of glittering stars. Later he wanted to describe the spectacle to his wife and children, but words seemed inadequate. Suddenly, he had an idea. He went into the garden and cut down a small fir tree. He put it in the nursery and lighted its branches with many candles so that it presented a lovely picture of God's glory as it had been revealed to him in the heavens on that cold winter night.

Thus at Christmas time the tree's lights illuminate every German home, and the evergreen of its branches symbolizes the deathlessness of the spirit. At the depth of the European winter, with its shortening days and their darkness and cold, Christmas tells of the rebirth of warmth and light, of the re-creation of nature and the eternal spring of hope. The gifts which hang from the branches of the Christmas tree provide a personal joy to young and old.

From Germany, the custom spread over the world, either through migrants (who made their new home in the United States) or sailors and merchants. It took root in Britain very slowly. Its earliest mention there among the British people themselves was amid Royalty. In 1821, at a children's party at Queen Caroline's Court, one of the members of her household introduced the tree to court circles.

However, the British hesitated to adopt what Charles Dickens described as "the new German toy" until the year 1841. Then, the Prince Consort, to surprise the young Prince of Wales and in nostalgic remembrance of his German home, had a Christmas tree put in Windsor Castle. This royal example was widely reported and thereby gained popularity for the tree in English lands.

THE CHRISTMAS CARD

The Christmas card was invented by Sir Henry Cole in 1843. He was a well-known London figure and was responsible for many innovations in British life. These ranged from the inception of a postal system to the construction of the Albert Hall, from the arrangement of the Great Exhibition in 1851 to the inauguration of the Victoria and Albert Museum.

Most of all, Cole wanted to improve public taste. He had an art shop in Old Bond Street which sold all kinds of objects meant to beautify life.

He tried to give aesthetic treatment to almost everything. Nothing was too small or too trifling to deserve his attention. He believed that, apart from being useful, everyday things should also be beautiful. That is how his fertile mind conceived the idea of the first Christmas card which he felt would add further lustre to this sacred day. Three independent factors may have prompted Cole in this endeavour.

There was the example of the Valentine card which had been in existence for almost a century.

Already, too, an 18th century Frenchman had adopted a simple method of conveying his Christmas wishes — verses printed on cards.

Finally, Cole must have been aware of a custom that had been introduced in English schools. Near the end of the winter term — around Christmas time — the boys were asked to produce "Christmas Pieces". Their purpose was twofold: to send seasonal greetings to the parents but at the same time to indicate to the teachers the pupils' progress in the art of writing.

The "pieces" were large sheets on which the pupils wrote copperplate Christmas wishes and they were decorated with coloured borders and headings.

Cole's conception of the first Christmas card was a drawing which would lend colour to greetings and wishes which had become too stereotyped. He commissioned a well-known artist, J. C. Horsley, R.A., to design the picture for the card, specimens of which are still preserved.

This adopted the common medieval artistic form of a triptych which actually consists of a set of three illustrations. The central piece depicts a jolly party of adults and children with plenty of food and drink — a fact that aroused severe criticism by the Temperance Movement in Cole's own time. Underneath the picture was expressed the seasonal greeting, wishing "a merry Christmas and a happy New Year to you". Each of the two side panels is a representation of good works — the clothing of the naked and the feeding of the hungry.

Cole, as well versed in the art of publicity as in that of beauty, did his utmost to popularize the new card, not for personal gain but for the improvement of public taste and the embellishment of the Christmas celebrations. However, his idea did not catch on until 20 years later. In the 1860s big business adopted the card and stationery firms produced thousands of Christmas cards. Cole's initial failure changed into a tremendous success.

In three decades British printers supplied 163,000 varieties of Christmas cards. These are now collected in 700 volumes, weighing almost seven tons.

In acknowledgment of his many services to the nation Cole was knighted and as Sir Henry, dying only in 1882, he must have still enjoyed the eventual success of his idea.

THE CHRISTMAS STOCKING

A coincidence of date, a legend and a painting are together responsible for the Christmas stocking, which at first had no real connection with the actual holy day.

The legend concerns St. Nicholas or Santa Claus. He was renowned for doing good, especially in secret. One day, according to this story, he heard of three lovely sisters who lived in a small house on the outskirts of a city. They were desperately poor and rumours even suggested that their poverty had tempted them to sell themselves into a life of shame.

St. Nicholas was deeply concerned. One night he went to the girls' home and, unnoticed, threw three pieces of gold into it through the smoke hole (chimneys were unknown). But the coins, instead of dropping on to the hearth, as St. Nicholas had intended, fell into the sisters' stockings which they had hung up near the fire to dry. The girls were overjoyed when they found the gold next morning.

Once the tale became widely known, other people, hopeful of similar pleasant surprises, began to hang up stockings.

The fact that December 25th was dedicated to the memory of St. Nicholas linked his life, his charity and the stocking with the celebration of the birth of Christ.

The beauty of this legendary explanation is not destroyed if it is also remembered that for many centuries it was customary to put one's savings into a stocking. Actually, before this, shoes had served the purpose. However, they were replaced by stockings the elasticity of which made them more suitable.

The famous painting by Clement C. Moore, "Visit from St. Nicholas", did most, perhaps, to popularize the custom of the Christmas stocking.

GOOD FRIDAY

The anniversary of Christ's Crucifixion, Good Friday, used to be kept as a day of fast, abstinence and penance. Its liturgical colour was black, no bells were rung and the Church organ was kept silent.

Numerous customs developed to express the tragic circumstances of the day. In Durham (England), for instance, blacksmiths would refuse to shoe a horse on Good Friday, as hammer and nails were associated with the Crucifixion. In Yorkshire, people walked barefoot to church, lest the nails in their shoes left a mark in the ground. The idea that hateful iron should not touch the soil and perhaps pollute it on that sad day was widespread in Britain. In the Scottish Highlands peasants would not plough their fields and generally throughout the country no graves were dug. Burials had to wait until Easter Saturday.

All these practices are easily understood because of the nails used to fix Christ on the cross. But people have often asked why such a tragic festival should be known as *Good* Friday. Several reasons may account for this apparent misnomer.

It is possible that the appellative was chosen simply to distinguish the day from all the other Fridays throughout the year.

Another explanation is based on the Christian dogma that Jesus's Crucifixion became the direct cause of human salvation. It was His sacrificial death on the cross that atoned for man's original sin. To stress the great good that thus has come out of evil, may well be why that day of gloom became known as Good Friday.

On the other hand, the term may merely be a corruption of *God's* Friday.

The Anglo-Saxons used to call it Long Friday, an allusion to the length of the church services, and in the Greek Church it is known as the Holy or Great Friday. The Germans refer to it as *Kar*freitag, stressing its *sorrowful* connotation.

HOT CROSS BUNS

Easter has been called "the feast of feasts". It celebrates the Resurrection of Christ, and many beautiful traditions are now associated with the festival and the Holy Week, of which it is the climax. Most of them are merely re-interpreted pagan customs, just as in the word Easter itself survives Eostre, the ancient pagan goddess of light.

The hot cross bun, eaten at Easter, is a pagan survival of bread once offered to idols! At the annual festival of the spring, the ancient Saxons ate such buns in honour of Eostre. Long before that, Egyptians, Chinese and Greeks baked and ate the same sort of cake in honour of their gods.

The word "bun" is derived from the archaic description of a sacred ox or *boun*. This used to be sacrificed at the time of the spring equinox and a symbol of its horns was stamped upon the celebratory cakes. Eventually, this mark became a cross and the early religious symbol took on a practical purpose as well. It made it easy to divide the cake into four equal parts, to be shared by the worshippers.

Such cross-marked cakes ante-date Christianity by many centuries. Some of them were found in the excavations at Herculaneum.

Ancient worship of the moon also contributed to the peculiar kind of indentations. The bun itself represented the full moon and the cross symbolized its four quarters.

The Fathers of the early Christian Church realized that it was almost impossible to wipe out ingrained pagan customs. Instead, they adopted and absorbed them. The ox-horn marks were re-interpreted as the sign of the cross.

New developments and explanations were added. The buns were kneaded from the very dough used for the baking of the consecrated Host and, therefore, it was said, to indicate the sacred association, they were marked with a cross. Priests distributed them to the communicants attending early Mass. This enabled the worshippers to break their fast even before getting home, an early anticipation of our *breakfast.*

New superstitions began to replace the old. The buns were credited with being charms against evil and as such people fixed at least one or two of them in their homes after Good Friday. Fishermen always carried an Easter bun in their boats, during the festival season and long afterwards, to protect them against shipwreck.

THE EASTER EGG

The Easter egg now caters for the tastes of the young and not so young. Who would think of it as a sacred symbol with a message of deep spirituality and creativity? For that is its real and only purpose and meaning.

The Easter egg is the emblem of renewed life after death and of resurrection. To all appearances an egg is lifeless matter. And yet out of it can come a new creature. Just as the chick is entombed, as it were, in the egg and brought to life in due course, so out of the grave will rise the dead to a new existence. That is why, from earliest times in all kinds of cultures, the egg assumed cosmic significance and has been a symbol of fertility and immortality.

The Greeks and Romans buried eggs, real or dummy, in their tombs. Scenes on Athenian vases show how baskets of eggs were left on graves. Maoris used to put an egg in the hand of a dead person before burial. Still today Jews present mourners on their return from the funeral of a relative with a dish of eggs as their first meal.

In the Northern Hemisphere Easter coincided with spring, the season of the renewal of nature. Out of the dead earth, so it seemed, sprang new life. It was the moment of creation and re-creation. Even as early as pagan times the egg symbolized the re-birth of nature at the time of the solar New Year. The shape of the egg was emblematic of the shape of the earth.

Christianity took this ancient sign of rejoicing at rebirth and applied it to the Resurrection of Jesus. The ritual of Pope Paul V included a prayer, in which the faithful acknowledge this very purpose of the Easter egg: "Eating it in thankfulness to Thee, on account of the Resurrection of our Lord."

Also, the fact that all through the fast of Lent eggs were forbidden made them all the more welcome on Easter day.

The tradition of painting the Easter egg in bright colours may have its origin in a legend that tells that Simon of Cyrene, who carried Christ's cross, was an egg merchant. When he returned from Calvary to his basket of produce, which he had left by the roadside, he found all the eggs miraculously coloured and adorned.

THE EASTER BUNNY

For obvious reasons the rabbit has always been considered a symbol of fertility and of the abundance of life. No wonder, therefore, that the animal became closely linked with the festival that spoke of birth and rebirth and the thoughts of which centred on dying and the belief in resurrection. The popularity of rabbits with children helped in spreading the tradition of the lucky Easter bunny.

"AMEN"

Amen is the most widely known and frequently used of all religious words. Jews, Christians and Moslems have made it a significant part of their worship. It concludes hymns, prayers, creeds and the recital of the first Sura of the Mohammedan Bible, the Koran. Marking their ends, it is like a seal, affirming what has been said or sung before, promised or threatened.

The word Amen is found 13 times in the Hebrew Bible and, strangely, occurs there first in the case of a jealous husband suspecting his wife of adultery.

An ancient ritual test demanded of her to drink "bitter waters". While she was doing so, a priest pronounced a curse to the effect that should she be guilty her belly would swell and her thigh sag. Whereupon the woman, still protesting her innocence, had to affirm the curse by uttering Amen twice.

The New Testament mentions Amen 119 times. Whenever Jesus wished to emphasize the significance and solemnity of what He said, He prefaced His words with an Amen.

Amen is a Hebrew word. Though commonly explained to mean "so be it", and hence to express simultaneously assent, agreement and a supplication, it is derived from a root that signifies "truth". Therefore anyone saying Amen confirms all that has gone before in speech or song as being true, trustworthy and reliable.

But some think that even the Hebrew Bible is not the original source of this affirmation and that the Amen actually goes back to *Amun,* the name of an Egyptian deity of highest rank, indeed their "king of gods", who at one time was worshipped all through the Middle East. His name meant "the hidden one".

So Amen might have originated in polytheistic faith, when Egyptian pagan believers (just as Greeks and Romans did later on, as we still recall in our own "By Jove") invoked their god in the form of an oath, saying "By Amun". Perhaps it was from those early Egyptian sources that the Hebrews adopted the Amen. Wisely, however, they gave it a new interpretation by linking it with all that was "true" and "established". Naturally both the Church and the Mosque, as children of Israel, continued the use of the Amen which, nevertheless, carries concealed, within itself the ancient Egyptian god.

Such a simple and common word as the Amen "affirms" the mystery and paradox that make up human life. We endorse our faith in spiritual divinity by a word that once described a pagan deity.

index